RESEARCHING AND WRITING

AN INTERDISCIPLINARY APPROACH

CHRISTINE A. HULT
UTAH STATE UNIVERSITY

Wadsworth Publishing Company
Belmont, California
A Division of Wadsworth, Inc.

English Editor: John Strohmeier

Production Editor: Robin Lockwood, Bookman Productions

Designer: The Quarasan Group, Inc.

Copy Editor: Suzanne Lipsett

Cover: The Quarasan Group, Inc.

Signing Representative: Stephanie Surfus

Print Buyer: Ruth Cole

Printed in the United States of America

1 2 3 4 5 6 7 8 9 10—90 89 88 87 86

ISBN 0-534-06150-8

Library of Congress Cataloging-in-Publication Data

Hult, Christine A.

  Researching and writing.

  Bibliography: p.

  Includes index.

  1. Report writing. 2. Research. 3. Library resources.
I. Title.

LB2369.H84 1986   808'.02   85-27439

ISBN 0-534-06150-8

Preface

Researching and Writing is an interdisciplinary research text that introduces students to research processes used in the sciences and technology, the social sciences, humanities, and business. Students who read this book will gain experience in posing and solving problems common to an academic discipline, learning both primary research strategies and library research strategies. A comprehensive list of library resources is included to provide students with access to the important tools used by researchers. Also included, as examples, are model student reports and research papers from various disciplines to show students how their peers have solved research problems similar to their own. The exercises are designed to guide students through research processes and to teach the important supporting skills of summarizing, synthesizing, and critiquing source materials. Complete listings of citations show students how to document their sources within each discipline. In addition, this textbook stresses principles of research presentation and documentation common to all disciplines.

Too often, students begin their academic careers with an inadequate overview of the nature of college research. Rather, they are introduced to various disciplines piecemeal, even though their potential success ultimately rests on their ability to interpret and employ research methods commonly used in each discipline. Thus, students are frequently confused about the larger issue of research—its nature and use in the humanities and sciences. Furthermore, they are confused about the relationships among academic disciplines. As a result, they are often unsure as to which major to choose or which course of study to pursue. In undergraduate courses, particularly English courses conceived as introductions to college writing, reading and thinking, *Researching and Writing* will help undergraduates at the start of their academic careers see important relationships among disciplines.

Many of the research guides now used fail to provide the broad introduction to research that students need. Traditional research texts are often focused very narrowly on the library "term paper." They discuss formal considerations at length, from the form of notecards and bibliography cards to the form of a completed term paper. But they do not explore the entire research process, which is an integral part of any successful research project. *Researching and Writing* is a research text that explains and fosters intellectual inquiry, compares research in the humanities with that in the sciences, and provides logical practice in research methodology.

Researching and Writing is divided into two main sections. Part One, "Research Methods and Resources," contains five chapters of general information about research methods and resources in the academic disciplines. In this part, students are first introduced to college research in general, and then to primary research methods, library resources (both general and discipline-specific), and library research methods. Next, students receive explicit instruction in the planning, writing, and presentation of research papers in any field. Part Two, "Model Research Projects," offers specific guidance in writing research papers for science and technology, social science, humanities, and business. Exercises in Part Two are designed to help students conduct their own research projects in a systematic and organized fashion.

Teachers will find *Researching and Writing* flexible enough to use as a primary textbook in a research/writing course or as a supplementary textbook and reference guide in a writing course that covers research. In most courses, students would first read and work several exercises from Part One as a general introduction to college research. Then, depending upon the time constraints of the course, teachers would allow students to select one chapter in Part Two as their research chapter (for example, a business major might choose to write a business report and an engineering major might choose to write a scientific or technical review paper). Alternatively, teachers of an entire course devoted to research writing could assign two or three short research papers based on the research projects outlined in Part Two. Whatever the actual assignments, students will find the information in Part Two invaluable in subsequent courses requiring research paper projects. *Researching and Writing* is both a comprehensive guide to research processes and an easy-to-use, complete reference tool designed to be used throughout students' academic careers and into their professional lives.

As with all research, my own work on this book has been a challenging process of discovery. I am grateful to the many researchers and theorists in the field of composition and rhetoric upon whose work this book is built. Though I have cited in notes only those authors whose ideas directly contributed to my own, many others contributed their ideas indirectly through journals, conferences, and textbooks. Teachers I have studied under and worked with, students who have patiently tried my ideas, and friends and family who have supported me along the way have all helped in the genesis of this book. Finally, I am grateful to the editors and production team at Wadsworth for their personal, professional attention, and to the reviewers of my manuscript: Bill Bridges, New Mexico State University; Ronald R. Butters, Duke University; Duncan A. Carter, Boston University; Toby Fulwiler, University of Vermont; A. Leslie Harris, Georgia State University; Gene H. Krupa, University of Iowa; Eileen M. Meagher, University of Tennessee at Chattanooga; Ken Risdon, University of Minnesota, Duluth; John J. Ruszkiewicz, The University of Texas at Austin; Elaine Travenick, North Seattle Community College; and Peter Young, Library of Congress.

Contents

PART TWO *Model Research Projects*   133

PART ONE

Research Methods and Resources

CHAPTER 1

College Research

■ INTRODUCTION

As a college student, regardless of your major, you are probably taking courses in the sciences, such as geology or chemistry, in the social sciences, such as sociology or political science, and in the humanities, such as philosophy or English literature. You may also be taking "applied" courses in home economics, agriculture, or business. Each of these academic disciplines seeks understanding and knowledge in traditional ways; each shares with all other academic disciplines basic research processes. In this book, we will explore the nature of college work in an effort to understand both the general processes of research and the particular research tools used in the disciplines. Exploring these important relationships among disciplines will help you to interpret and use the research methods and established ways of proceeding employed by researchers.

■ RESEARCH IN THE DISCIPLINES

What is research? Broadly defined, it is systematic inquiry designed to further our knowledge and understanding of a subject. Using this definition, nearly everything you do in college is "research." You seek to discover information about people, objects, and nature; to revise the information you discover in light of new information that comes to your attention; and to interpret your experience and communicate that interpretation to others. This is how learning proceeds both for all of us as individuals and for human beings together as we search for knowledge and understanding of our world.

People are interpretive animals. In our interaction with the world, we seek to represent internally to ourselves what we have experienced externally. We generally assume that the universe is an orderly, reasonable, meaningful place, and that, if we but look, we will be able to discern that order. However, we are confronted with problematical experiences in the world. At such times, since we are inquiring animals, we seek to discover the cause or a reasonable explanation for that problematical experience— that is, we "research" the subject to discover its meaning. In the accompanying cartoon, the character is confronted with a problematical experience. As he relaxes under the shady tree, he is rudely awakened from his reverie.

B.C.   **by johnny hart**

Reprinted by permission of Johnny Hart and News Group Chicago, Inc.

In searching his own internal representation of the world, the character finds a "solution" to the problem. The humor of the cartoon is the result of its parody of Archimedes, who shouted "Eureka" when he discovered a new principle of physics, and of Newton, who deduced the principle of gravity from a falling apple. Furthermore, we recognize the circular reasoning the character has used in solving the problem. Because we are familiar with the orderly procedures people use to solve problems, procedures that this character has not used, we understand that his response is ludicrous.

This same issue, concerning the falling apple, could be researched by a scientist, perhaps a physicist, who might ask the following questions: "Why does the apple fall? How fast does it fall? How long will it take to reach the ground?" Such questions involve broad issues about the nature of the physical universe and the "laws" that govern it. The physicist observes natural phenomena within reasonable limits and then develops a systematic body of principles to account for or predict other similar events in the universe. For example, physicists have deduced the following principle: "Any object at a distance from the earth will be acted upon by gravity, which is the force of mutual attraction among all bodies, proportional to the product of the masses of the bodies divided by the square of the distance between them."

A social scientist, perhaps an economist, researching the falling-apple issue might focus on the need for a reliable food source in a society, asking such questions as "How do people provide for their basic need for food? What laws of supply and demand operate on the production and distribution of food?" An economist also seeks to define the broad issues of how people in society structure their economic relationships. The economist develops a systematic body of ideas to be used in accounting for other similar economic systems or events. Thus, in response to the falling-apple issue, the economist might make the following statement: "The increasingly prevalent view by consumers that food is a public good and that all citizens should be assured of an adequate and nutritious food supply, plus the fear of prolonged food shortages together have led to a growing demand for change in the agricultural economic policy of this nation."

A humanist—perhaps an historian—researching this issue would attempt to explain and explore the human experience of the character in the cartoon by asking such questions as "What is the significance of the event to this character and to others of his historical period? How does this event relate to other similar events?" The historian would account for, reconstruct, and narrate all the events related to this character's so-called discovery that apples cure hunger, relating the discovery to other more general cultural events. Then, the historian might postulate the following explanation: "The invention of agriculture was a significant historical event, often called the Neolithic Revolution. Occurring between 8000 and 3000 B.C., the Neolithic Revolution involved a change from the gathering society (in which humans gathered wild grasses) to the agricultural society (in which humans prepared the soil and sowed seeds for harvesting)."

In the examples above, it is clear that researchers in different disciplines ask different questions about the same subject. What distinguishes them is the perspective that the researcher in each field takes.

■ THE IMPORTANCE OF RESEARCH

Researching—that is, exploring a problem systematically—is a crucial skill for an educated person. In college, you will gain habits of mind that will serve you in every endeavor. Learning to research will promote careful, critical, systematic thinking. Learning to write will promote the effective communication of the ideas and insights gained in the research. Researching and research writing necessarily go together, with each building upon and promoting the other.

Researching is different in kind from much of the work you did in high school and even from much of what you are probably doing in your introductory college courses. When you are first introduced to a new subject, you spend a great deal of time memorizing facts. However, once you move beyond that initial phase, you will spend much of your time both in and out of the classroom discussing and examining the bases for current beliefs and claims in an academic discipline, claims that may seem problematical or questionable. This type of intellectual activity occurs in *addition to* and goes beyond the simple recall of material. College teachers are not concerned with simply imparting information; their main objective is to present and examine the basis on which the information or claim rests.

Students and teachers together search out the justification for an accepted belief or claim. This search is research, because only such inquiry, not rote memorization, advances knowledge and understanding in an academic discipline.

For example, suppose your roommate says to you, "Everybody knows that Socialists are Communists." As with all claims, you would have to maintain reservations regarding this statement until you had reasons for believing it. To search out or research those reasons, you might begin by systematically exploring the basis or grounds for the claim. The "everybody knows" part of the statement implies that your roommate considers the claim to be common knowledge. But is it? Your roommate would need a pretty large research sample to justify the claim that "everybody knows. . . ." At the outset, then, you could reasonably discount the claim as unwarranted simply because it is overgeneralized.

What about the basis for equating Socialists with Communists? Perhaps your roommate is basing the equation on a knowledge of the Soviet Union, where communism is indeed a particular form of socialism. But perhaps your roommate is unaware that, as you find out from looking it up in the library, socialism is a social system that advocates community ownership of industry and capital, whereas communism advocates the control of the social system by a single self-perpetuating political party. It is possible to have Socialists, you discover, who do not advocate communism, but it is not possible to have Communists who are not Socialists. Consequently, the grounds upon which your roommate made the claim are tenuous. As a rational person, once you have investigated—that is, researched—the particular grounds, you would have to reject the claim.

Similarly, much of the work you will be doing in college, and much of the work researchers do, involves looking into a particular claim. A second kind of research involves the exploration of a problem or event to arrive at a claim or hypothesis. Whether you are investigating a claim or hypothesis made by someone else or exploring a problematical experience you have encountered yourself to arrive at your own hypothesis, the research process will be much the same.

EXERCISE

Briefly describe a research project that you did in the past. What exactly did it involve? How did you feel about the project's success? What did you learn from it?

The General Process of Research

Many accounts of the process of research have been written by scientists, artists, and philosophers. Researchers generally agree about the outlines of the process regardless of the discipline. The process often begins with a troubled feeling about something observed or experienced followed by a conscious probing for a solution to the problem, a time of subconscious activity, an intuition about the solution, and finally a systematic testing to verify the solution. It is possible to describe this process in a number of ways, but it may generally be divided into four stages: preparation, incubation, illumination, and verification.[1] I will discuss these stages in order, but it is not necessarily true that during a research project each stage will neatly follow the next. It is quite probable that the researcher will move freely back and forth among the stages and may even skip a stage for a time. In general, though, these four stages will be present in most research projects.

Preparation

The preparation stage of the research process involves the first awareness in researchers that a problem or a question exists that needs systematic inquiry. Researchers formulate the problem and begin to explore it. As they attempt to articulate the exact dimensions and parameters of a particular problem, they use language or symbols of their discipline that can be more easily manipulated than unarticulated thoughts or the data itself. By stating the problem in a number of ways, looking at it from various angles, trying to define its distinctive characteristics, and attempting possible solutions, researchers come to define for themselves the subtleties of the problem. Preparation is generally systematic, but it may also include the researchers' prior experiences and the intuitions they have developed over time.

Incubation

The incubation stage usually follows the preparation stage and includes a period of intense subconscious activity that is hard to describe or define. Because it is so indistinct, people tend to discount it as unimportant, but the experience of many researchers shows that it is crucial to allow the idea to "brew" and "simmer" in the subconscious if a creative solution is to be reached. Perhaps you have had the experience of trying and failing to recall the name of a film you recently saw. You tell your conversation partner, "Go ahead. It'll come to me." A few minutes later, when you are not consciously trying to recall the name but have gone on to other matters in your conversation, you announce *Blue Thunder*, out of the blue. This is an example of your subconscious mind continuing to work on a problem while your conscious mind has gone on to another activity.

We need to allow ourselves sufficient time for "incubating." If you have ever watched a chicken egg in an incubator, you will have a sense of how this works. The egg rests in warmth and quiet; you see no activity whatsoever, but you know that beneath that shell tremendous activity is going on. The first peck on the shell from the chick about to hatch comes as a surprise. This is analogous to the next stage of the process, illumination. You cannot really control the "incubation" of a problem, but you can prepare adequately and then give yourself enough time for subconscious activity.

Illumination

In the illumination stage, as with the hatching chick, there is an imaginative breakthrough. The idea begins to surface out of its concealing shell, perhaps a little at a time. Or the researcher leaps to a hypothesis, a possible solution to the problem, that seems intuitively to "fit." It is said that Isaac Newton discovered the law of universal gravitation as he watched an apple fall, and that Archimedes deduced his principle of floating bodies while in the bathtub. The illumination of a hypothesis can come suddenly or gradually, after laborious effort or after an ordinary event that triggers the researcher's thinking along new lines. We must remember, though, that the hypothesis comes only after the researcher has investigated the problem thoroughly. The egg must be prepared, fertilized, warmed, and cared for. The solution to a complex problem will come only after much conscious study and preparation in conjunction with subconscious intuition. Sometimes the solution will not be a breakthrough but rather a clearer understanding of the problem itself.

Verification

Once a researcher has arrived at a hypothesis, he or she must systematically test it to discern whether it adequately accounts for all occurrences. In some fields, this testing requirement will necessitate a formal laboratory research experiment; in others, only an informal check against the researcher's own experience will be necessary. In the sciences, the verification stage tends to be highly rigorous, involved, and lengthy. One should also be prepared at the verification stage to discover that the original hypothesis will not work. Though we are often reluctant to make mistakes, without a willingness to err we would never be led to make an original contribution. Research often progresses as a series of increasingly intelligent mistakes through which the researcher ultimately is led to a reasonable and workable solution. Sometimes hypothesis testing goes on for years and, for a particularly promising hypothesis, is performed by the research community in general. To be judged as sound, or verified, such a hypothesis must survive the critical scrutiny of the whole research community.

A Physician Uses the Research Process

In the following essay, Charles Nicolle, a physician and scientist of the early twentieth century, describes the research process he used to discover the mechanism that transmitted the disease typhus.[2] As you read the essay, pay particular attention to the research process Nicolle outlines.

The Mechanism of the Transmission of Typhus

Charles Nicolle

It is in this way that the mode of transmission of
exanthematic typhus was revealed to me. Like all those who
for many years frequented the Moslem hospital of Tunis, I
could daily observe typhus patients bedded next to
patients suffering from the most diverse complaints. Like
those before me, I was the daily and unhappy witness of the
strange fact that this lack of segregation, although
inexcusable in the case of so contagious a disease, was
nevertheless not followed by infection. Those next to the
bed of a typhus patient did not contract the disease,
while, almost daily, during epidemic outbreaks, I would
diagnose contagion in the *douars* (the Arab quarters of the
town), and amongst hospital staff dealing with the
reception of patients. Doctors and nurses became
contaminated in the country in Tunis, but never in the
hospital wards. One day, just like any other, immersed no
doubt in the puzzle of the process of contagion in typhus,
in any case not thinking of it consciously (of this I am
quite sure), I entered the doors of the hospital, when a
body at the bottom of the passage arrested my attention.

It was a customary spectacle to see poor natives,
suffering from typhus, delirious and febrile as they
were, gain the landing and collapse on the last steps. As
always I strode over the prostrate body. It was at this
very moment that the light struck me. When, a moment
later, I entered the hospital, I had solved the problem. I
knew beyond all possible doubt that this was it. This
prostrate body, and the door in front of which he had
fallen, had suddenly shown me the barrier by which typhus
had been arrested. For it to have been arrested, and,
contagious as it was in entire regions of the country and
in Tunis, for it to have remained harmless once the

patient had passed the Reception Office, the agent of infection must have been arrested at this point. Now, what passed through this point? The patient had already been stripped of his clothing and of his underwear; he had been shaved and washed. It was therefore something outside himself, something that he carried on himself, in his underwear, or on his skin, which caused the infection. This could be nothing but a louse. Indeed, it was a louse. The fact that I had ignored this point, that all those who had been observing typhus from the beginnings of history (for it belongs to the most ancient ages of humanity) had failed to notice the incontrovertible and immediately fruitful solution of the method of transmission, had suddenly been revealed to me. I feel somewhat embarrassed about thus putting myself into the picture. If I do so, nevertheless it is because I believe what happened to me is a very edifying and clear example, such as I have failed to find in the case of others. I developed my observation with less timidity. At the time it still had many shortcomings. These, too, appear instructive to me.

If this solution had come home to me with an intuition so sharp that it was almost foreign to me, or at least to my mind, my reason nevertheless told me that it required an experimental demonstration.

Typhus is too serious a disease for experiments on human subjects. Fortunately, however, I knew of the sensitivity of monkeys. Experiments were therefore possible. Had this not been the case I should have published my discoveries without delay, since it was of such immediate benefit to everybody. However, because I could support the discovery with a demonstration, I guarded my secret for some weeks even from those close to me, and made the necessary attempts to verify it. This work neither excited nor surprised me, and was brought to its conclusion within two months.

In the course of this very brief period I experienced what many other discoverers must undoubtedly have

experienced also, viz. strange sentiments of the
pointlessness of any demonstration, of complete
detachment of the mind and of wearisome boredom. The
evidence was so strong, that it was impossible for me to
take any interest in the experiments. Had it been of no
concern to anybody but myself, I well believe that I
should not have pursued this course. It was because of
vanity and self-love that I continued. Other thoughts
occupied me as well. I confess a failing. It did not arrest
my research work. The latter, as I have recounted, led
easily and without a single day's delay to the
confirmation of the truth, which I had known ever since
that revealing event, of which I have spoken.

Nicolle's struggle to discover a solution to the problem of typhus transmission illustrates a research process. Nicolle worked on the problem of typhus transmission both consciously and subconsciously; his "Eureka" experience came unexpectedly and forcefully. Nicolle was awarded the Nobel Prize for medicine in 1928 for his discovery and for the experiments that conclusively confirmed that typhus was indeed transmitted by parasites.

QUESTIONS FOR DISCUSSION

1. What stages of the research process outlined in this chapter are revealed in Nicolle's description?
2. What incongruity led Nicolle to research the question of typhus transmission?
3. What experience triggered the solution to the problem?
4. What procedures did Nicolle use to verify his hypothesis?

EXERCISES

1. The four research stages discussed in this chapter come from words we often associate with different contexts. For example, we use the term *preparation* in connection with preparing dinner or preparing for a test. First, briefly describe a situation (other than research) commonly associated with each term. Then, list any similarities between

the connotation of each word in your situation and the particular research stage:

    A. To prepare:

    B. To incubate:

    C. To illuminate:

    D. To verify:

2. Think of an activity with which you are familiar, such as a sport (football or tennis), a hobby (cooking or gardening), or an art (painting or dancing). In one paragraph, describe the process you use when participating in the activity and relate the process to the research stages discussed in this chapter (preparation, incubation, illumination, and verification).

■ THE INQUIRY PROCESS IN SCIENCE AND TECHNOLOGY

In the Western world, the sciences hold an authoritative position and are a dominant force in our lives. The sciences have been enormously successful at formulating and testing theories related to phenomena in the natural and physical world. These theories have been used to solve physical and biological problems in medicine, industry, and agriculture. Generally, the sciences have been divided into life sciences (such as biology and botany), physical sciences (such as physics and chemistry), and earth sciences (such as geology and geography). Scientific insights and methods have also been carried over to fields of applied science and technology, such as computer science and engineering.

The Importance of Observation in the Sciences

As discussed earlier in this chapter, the motivation or impetus for much research is an observed event or experience that challenges our existing ideas and promotes inquiry. In the context of existing theories, such an event is incongruous and thus sparks in the researcher's mind a question or problem to be investigated. The researcher must be prepared to recognize the inconsistency and see its importance. Therefore, he or she must be familiar with current theories and concepts about the natural and physical world. In general, the aim of scientific work is to improve the relationship between our ideas (theories and concepts about the world) and our actual experiences (observations of the world).

An example of a scientist using educated observation is described by René Taton in his book *Reason and Chance in Scientific Discovery.*[3] In 1928, Sir Alexander Fleming, an English biologist, was studying mutation in some colonies of staphylococci bacteria. He noticed that one of his cultures had been contaminated by a microorganism from the air outside. But instead of neglecting this seemingly inconsequential event, Fleming went on to observe the contaminated plate in detail and noticed a very surprising phenomenon: the colonies of bacteria that had been attacked by microscopic fungi had become transparent in a large region around the contamination. From this observation, Fleming hypothesized that the effect could be due to an antibacterial substance secreted by the foreign microorganism and then spread into the culture. Fortunately for us, Fleming decided to study the phenomenon at length to discover the properties of this secretion (which turned out to be a variety of the fungus penicillium, from which we now make the antibiotic, penicillin) on cultures of staphylococci bacteria. Fleming designed experiments that tested his hypothesis concerning the effects of penicillium on bacteria and, eight months later, he published his research findings in the *British Journal of Experimental Pathology*. Fleming's research is another example of the research process: first there was prepared observation, then a struggle with the problem and the formulation of a hypothesis, and finally the verification of that hypothesis using experiments.

The Importance of Formulating and Testing Hypotheses

On the basis of a scientist's prior knowledge and preparation, he or she formulates a hypothesis to account for the observed phenomenon that presents a problem. Arriving at a hypothesis takes much effort on the part of the researcher. Brainstorming for possible hypotheses is an important component of research. The researcher may have to test several possible hypotheses before deciding which one seems to account for the observed phenomenon. Fleming, for example, hypothesized that the clear circle he observed around the bacteria resulted from the contaminating microorganism in the culture. The sciences have developed systematic ways of testing a hypothesis once it is formulated. Fleming used such a procedure to verify his hypothesis: he demonstrated through scientific experiments that penicillium was effective against bacteria.

The following outline describes the systematic way scientists customarily proceed, often called the "scientific method":

1. The scientist formulates a question and develops a hypothesis that might possibly answer the question posed.
2. On the basis of the hypothesis, the scientist predicts what should be observed under specified conditions and circumstances.
3. The scientist makes the necessary observations, generally using carefully designed, controlled experiments.
4. The scientist either accepts or rejects the hypothesis depending upon whether or not the actual observations corresponded with the predicted observations.

Using the scientific method, a researcher is able to integrate new data into existing theories about the natural and physical world. In step 2 above, the researcher draws upon accepted scientific ideas and theories to predict an outcome for the experiment. Fleming, for example, predicted that his experiments would show the antibacterial action of penicillium when used on certain bacteria, and he confirmed his hypothesis through careful laboratory experiments.

Neither Fleming nor the scientific community of his day recognized the profound implications of his research for the field of medicine. Penicillium was a difficult-to-handle, impure, and unstable substance, which at the time made it seem impractical for widespread application. Subsequent discoveries and perfections of antibiotics, however, proved that penicillin would revolutionize modern medicine.

Ordinarily, the individual researcher uses currently held scientific theories and ideas to incorporate new data into the mainstream of current scientific belief. Research advances are the cumulative result of researchers working on various problems in various parts of the world; a synthesis of existing data is used to create new ideas and theories. Taton notes that many of the immense scientific discoveries of the twentieth century have been the collective work of teams of specialists from various schools working with more and more perfect technical resources.[4] Though the role of the individual researcher is important, he or she is but a cog in the wheel of the scientific community in general.

Critical Scientific Research

Though much of the research conducted by scientists is an attempt to incorporate new data into existing theories, another type of scientific research, critical scientific research, attempts to challenge currently held beliefs and theories in an effort to improve them. Critical scientific research investigates the adequacy, or the sufficiency, of theories about the natural and physical world. In this context, the question asked is, "How well do current theories actually explain the natural and physical world as we know and observe it?"

A particular field of science may operate for years under certain theoretical assumptions. For example, Newtonian physics, based on the theories of Sir Isaac Newton, dominated the scientific world for some time, and thousands of scientists conducted regular experiments based on Newton's theories. But because physicists encountered numerous phenomena that were incompatible with Newton's laws of physics, new theories became necessary. The physicist Albert Einstein challenged the agreed-upon Newtonian physics by presenting an alternative system that accounted for more of the observed data. Most physicists have now adopted Einstein's more comprehensive theories, or have gone on to develop and adopt new theories.

This process of challenging and replacing scientific theories is one way scientific fields advance their knowledge and understanding of the natural or physical world. So, scientific thought progresses both by regular scientific observation and experimentation using widely accepted theories and beliefs, and by critical scientific research that challenges those widely held theories and suggests new theories.

The Importance of Replicability and Scientific Debate

Scientists who have created and tested a hypothesis must then report their findings to other scientists, as Fleming did by publishing his experiments in the British journal. The goal of publishing one's findings is to have other scientists accept the hypothesis as true and correct. A report of the research must necessarily include a careful, accurate description of the problem, the hypothesis, and the method (experimental design) used to test the hypothesis, in addition to the researcher's experimental findings and conclusions.

Other scientists, then, test the validity and reliability of the findings by attempting to repeat the experiment described by the researcher. A carefully designed and executed scientific experiment should be accurately described in writing so that other scientists using a similar experimental process can replicate it. The community of scientists as a whole then critiques the new research, deciding collectively whether or not it is good, sound research. To do this, other scientists will test the experiment's validity (Did it measure what the researcher said it would measure?), its reliability (Can it be repeated or replicated with similar results by other scientists?), and its importance (How does this experiment fit into a larger theoretical framework and what does it mean for our currently held assumptions and beliefs?). The forums of science—the professional organizations and journals, universities, scientific societies, and research laboratories—combine to resolve scientific issues to the benefit of all scientists.

QUESTIONS FOR DISCUSSION

1. What is the general goal of inquiry in the sciences?
2. What often sparks a scientist's interest and motivates research?
3. How does observation contribute to scientific inquiry?
4. What is "critical scientific research"? How do its goals differ from those of science in general?
5. What is meant by replicability and why is it important in science?

■ THE INQUIRY PROCESS IN SOCIAL SCIENCE

Social sciences, such as psychology, anthropology, political science, sociology, economics, and education, have as their overall goal the systematic study of human behavior and human societies. The social sciences developed much later than the natural and physical sciences, and so are comparatively young disciplines. Since social sciences followed the enormously successful and influential natural and physical sciences, they understandably adopted much of the scientific method—its goals, procedures, and standards. The field of sociology, for example, has been called the *science* of social organization; psychology has been called the *science* of the mind. Many social scientists today study people using the scientific method: they develop hypotheses and design and conduct controlled experiments to test those hypotheses.

A notorious example of a controlled social science experiment was conducted by Stanley Milgram, a Yale psychologist, during the 1960s.[5] Milgram sought to determine to what extent ordinary individuals would obey the orders of an authority figure. Through his experiment, he wished to probe the psychological processes that allowed the Germans to carry out mass human exterminations during World War II. Using simulated shock experiments, which were admittedly controversial, Milgram showed that an alarming proportion of adults (65 percent of those tested) were willing to inflict severe and, as far as they knew, permanent damage upon strangers simply because they were instructed to do so by an authority figure, in this case the experimenter. The conclusions Milgram draws from this experiment are frightening:

> This is, perhaps, the most fundamental lesson of our study: ordinary people, simply doing their jobs, and without any particular hostility on their part, can become agents in a terrible destructive process. Moreover, even when the destructive effects of their work become patently clear, and they are asked to carry out actions incompatible with fundamental standards of morality, relatively few people have the resources needed to resist authority. A variety of inhibitions against disobeying authority come into play and successfully keep the person in his place.[6]

The research process used by Milgram closely follows that of other scientific research. His research began with a starting question: How could Hitler have succeeded in marshalling so much support from those who were called upon to carry out his inhuman orders? After sufficient preparation, Milgram set out to determine the extent to which ordinary individuals would obey immoral orders. The psychologists were surprised by their results, which showed a large percentage of normal people obeying immoral orders from an authority figure. From the results, Milgram was able to verify that, indeed, there was something in human nature that could explain the behavior of so many Germans during World War II. The people who followed orders to annihilate others were not brutal, sadistic monsters, he stated, but rather normal people who acted out of a sense of duty and obligation to their country and their leader.

The Importance of Observing Human Behavior

A great number of the experiments created by social scientists are designed to observe human behavior. Since the goal of any science is the systematic, objective study of phenomena, the social sciences had to observe those aspects of humans that were observable. The only objectively observable part of humanity is *behavior*. We cannot observe human emotions or consciousness directly, but we can observe the behavior that results from feelings and thoughts in human consciousness. The social sciences, consequently, have focused heavily on behavior and thus have been called the behavioral sciences. The Milgram experiment is an example of a behavioral-science experiment. Milgram observed how his subjects behaved in a carefully controlled experimental setting to arrive at his conclusions about why people act as they do.

The Importance of Understanding Human Consciousness

Many people, both within and outside the social sciences, have felt that this objectification of observable human behavior produces a false picture of human beings. The real "inside" of a person may be missed when only the behavior manifested on the "outside" is observed. Human beings are conscious beings; we have thoughts, feelings, and intuitions that are private and never seen by others. Some in the social sciences argue that since we cannot observe consciousness directly, it is not a proper subject for scientific study at all. Others take the position that it is not only appropriate to study human consciousness, but essential, because consciousness is what makes us uniquely human. Modern social scientists have developed methods of exploring human consciousness that are admittedly subjective but nevertheless reveal important information about how people think and feel. Such methods include case studies of individuals, clinical evaluation, psychoanalysis, and hypnosis.

Social scientists also study the interaction among people in societies. A social scientist attempting to discover social rules and conventions is somewhat analagous to a natural scientist attempting to discover laws of nature. The social rules and conventions adopted by a particular society are important for an understanding of human behavior within the society. For example, a Polynesian native accustomed to using shells as money would have a rude awakening in an American marketplace where, by convention, slips of paper are used to trade for goods and services. The slip of paper we accept as a dollar bill only has meaning for us within our particular set of social conventions. Much of the work done in social sciences attempts to describe and define the social "laws"—rules and conventions —by which people operate within societies.

An example of a social scientist whose work has been important in the twentieth century is the German psychologist Sigmund Freud, who sought to describe and predict the complex operation of the human subconscious mind. Freud also sought to apply his theories of individuals to the operation of humans in societies. In one of his last books, *Civilization and Its Discontents*, he expressed his views on the broad question of the human being's place in the world.[7] Freud posed the question, Why is it hard for humankind to be happy in civilization? Through his years of preparation and study, Freud was able to posit the hypothesis that human unhappiness is due to the inevitable conflict between the demands of instincts (aggression and ego gratification) and the restrictions of civilized society:

> If civilization imposes such great sacrifices not only on man's sexuality but on his aggressivity, we can understand better why it is hard for him to be happy in that civilization. In fact, primitive man was better off in knowing no restrictions of instinct. To counterbalance this, his prospects of enjoying this happiness for any length of time were very slender. Civilized man has exchanged a portion of his possibilities of happiness for a portion of security.[8]

Freud's sociological theories have been as influential as his psychological theories. Verification of this particular hypothesis—that instinct and society conflict—was achieved through Freud's extensive citation of examples taken from psychological case studies and from primitive and modern societies (including the Soviet Union and the United States). Through these examples, Freud showed that human instincts are in conflict with society's constraints.

As discussed at the opening of this section on the social sciences, researchers attempt to describe and predict human behavior and human relationships in society. Barzun and Graff, in their text *The Modern Researcher*, observe that "the works of social science that have made the strongest mark on the modern mind have been those that combined description with enumeration and imparted the results with imaginative power."[9] The work of Freud is a classic example of the way good social science research combines an understanding of individual human behavior and consciousness with an understanding of how people are organized and influenced by the societies in which they live and operate.

Objectivity Versus Subjectivity

In the sciences, researchers attempt to remove their own particular preferences, desires, and hopes from the experimental process as much as possible. Scientific researchers are looking for "objective" truth. However, because each researcher as observer necessarily brings background preparation, knowledge, and experience to the situation, it is seldom possible to remove the researcher from the research altogether. But what about the social sciences? Can they be as objective as the natural sciences in their search for knowledge and understanding? Many would charge that subjectivity and values are inescapable and necessary parts of social science research. The social scientist studies people, social systems, and social conventions. As a person, the researcher is necessarily a part of the system being studied. Perhaps this is not altogether a bad thing. A social scientist's own beliefs, attitudes, and values can contribute to his or her understanding of what is being observed. Or a social scientist can, to a certain degree, detach him- or herself from a situation and function as a relatively impartial observer. But the question of objectivity and subjectivity in the social sciences is not easily resolved, because it is not always possible to know exactly what subjective influences are affecting "objective" research. The issue of subjectivity versus objectivity is the cause of much ferment and continual debate within the social science fields as these young disciplines seek to define for themselves an appropriate method, whether it is modeled after the scientific method or something quite different.

QUESTIONS FOR DISCUSSION

1. What is the general goal of inquiry in the social sciences?
2. Why are social sciences often called "behavioral sciences"?
3. What is meant by the understanding of human consciousness?
4. What is the relationship between objectivity and subjectivity in the social sciences?

■ THE INQUIRY PROCESS IN THE HUMANITIES

The humanities, such as classical and modern languages and literature, history, and philosophy, have as an overall goal the exploration and explanation of the human experience. Some would include the fine arts (music, art, dance, and drama) in the humanities, but others view the arts as a separate category. (We will not discuss the performance of fine arts in this book, but we will touch on the interpretation of fine arts.) In most disciplines in the humanities, written texts are extremely important, particularly in history, philosophy, and literature. Historians attempt a systematic narration or documentation of past events related to a particular people, country, or period. Philosophers endeavor to examine coherent, logical systems of human ideas. Literary authors and artists attempt to capture for others their own lived, human experiences and their own understanding of the world. The humanities involve inquiry into human consciousness, values, ideas, and ideals, as they seek to describe how human experience shapes our understanding of the world.

Let's take an example to show how the sciences, social sciences, and humanities all contribute to an understanding of our world. The Mississippi River has played an important role in American history. A scientist —perhaps a biologist—would study the river's wildlife, fish, surrounding vegetation, and ecology in an attempt to objectively describe the river itself. A social scientist—perhaps a sociologist—might study the river's contribution to a riverfront society and that society's dependence upon the river for transportation of goods and services. An historian, who often bridges the gap between the social sciences and the humanities, might report on the importance of the Mississippi and other American waterways to our westward expansion and the development of America. A humanist—for example, a novelist—might write about the actual experiences people had on or near the Mississippi. Mark Twain, for instance, wrote his autobiographical novel *Life on the Mississippi* to share with his readers what he had *felt* as a youth learning the trade of riverboat pilot on a Mississippi steamboat. Without such a work of imaginative literature, we would have a hard time understanding what it was really like to be a youth on the river during Twain's time. Such a work of literature contributes to our understanding by putting us in a different time and place from our own, thus broadening our horizons in a manner that is somewhat different from either the natural or social sciences. The sciences attempt to give us the outside, external knowledge of a phenomenon, whereas the humanistic disciplines attempt to give us the inside, internal knowledge of a phenomenon.[10] Both make important contributions to our understanding of the world.

The Importance of Texts in the Humanities

Written texts in the humanities are generally of three types: (1) creative writing (literature, poetry, and drama); (2) interpretive writing (literary and art criticism); and (3) theoretical writing (historical and social theories of literature and art).

Creative writing produces numerous literary texts that provide us with an aesthetic experience and capture new insights into humanity. Creative writing is comparable to other creative, artistic endeavors in that it often has this twofold objective: the aesthetically pleasing (or emotionally moving) and the imaginative reenactment of human experience. We ask a work of art to move us and to mean something to us, to show us a way of looking at ourselves and the world that we may not otherwise have seen.

As we receive creative art and literature as an audience, interpretive questions arise, such as, What sort of work is it? and How are we to respond to it? Much of the writing connected with the humanities is interpretive, since the audience tries to understand both the meaning and significance of a particular creative work. Often, an interpretive critic will attempt to disclose the particular intention of the artist: the novelist's attitude toward the heroine, for example, or the intended aesthetic impact of a dance. Interpretive critics will research their claims by using the evidence found in the work itself to support the hypothesis—that is, the particular "reading" of the text or work of art.

The third kind of humanistic writing is theoretical. For the theorist, creative art and literature are important insofar as they exemplify more general social and historical principles. The theorist, for example, looks for connections between a particular work of art and its social and historical context, or for relationships among different artistic media, such as fresco painting and architecture in medieval Europe. Theorists provide links between our understanding of art and literature and other subjects such as history, sociology, or psychology. Finally, theorists take a step back from a particular work of art or literature in an attempt to get a broader view. In looking at the entire social and historical context, they ask such questions as, How has photography affected portrait painting? and What is the role of the devil in the American novel?

Research in the Humanities

The humanist deals in significance, insight, imagination, and the meaning of human experience. What does it mean, then, to research in the humanities? Interpreting and critiquing art and literature is one type of research conducted by humanists. Interpreters and theorists in the humanities attempt to "talk sense" about a work of art or literature in order to make the audience see what the artist or author meant, and to link the work with other, larger human events and experiences. A second kind of humanistic research involves reconstructing humanity's past, reconstructing both the ideas (philosophical research) and the events that have occurred over time (historical research). All three types of humanistic research (literary and art criticism, philosophical research, and historical research) contribute to our understanding of the meaning of human experience.

Literary and Art Criticism

Critical researchers necessarily use their own subjective interpretations of a work of art or literature in critiquing it. But those subjective interpretations are based on experience and reflective thought, and they are expressed in well-chosen language. Criticism in the humanities is not just a string of personal opinions. The critical researcher builds a solid argument to substantiate his or her interpretation or theory. Such an argument is based on research involving a close reading of the text itself (in literary criticism), or a close analysis of the work of art (in art criticism). The argument will also take into account social and historical factors that bear upon the interpretation of the literary text or work of art. It will incorporate research involving other related texts or works of art by the same author or artist, or secondary criticism influencing the critic's own argument. A piece of good interpretive criticism will be both insightful and true to life. A piece of good literary or art criticism will be complete and comprehensive; it will offer the audience a sound theory that fits with the experience of audience members and that ties together related threads in their understanding. A critical reseacher will investigate the complex context from which a work of art or literature has come in order to provide an understanding of how it fits into the larger realm of human experience. In this way, the critical researcher is much like an historical or a social science researcher.

One example of a critical researcher who combined techniques of criticism with historical scholarship is John Livingston Lowes, who began with the question of what sources influenced the poetry of Samuel Coleridge, a nineteenth-century English poet and critic.[11] In an attempt to elucidate Coleridge's poetry, Lowes traced the sources the poet used in writing such poems as "The Rime of the Ancient Mariner" and "Kubla Khan." Richard Altick calls Lowes's book "the greatest true-detective story ever written."[12] Lowes began his research with Coleridge's *Gutch Memorandum Book,* a notebook containing the suggestions for reading that Coleridge had jotted down as he looked for ideas to translate into poetry. Next, Lowes looked at the library records from the Bristol Library that showed the books Coleridge had borrowed. Following these and numerous other leads, Lowes was able to virtually reconstruct how certain of Coleridge's greatest poems took shape in the author's mind and took form on the written page.

Philosophical Research

The philosophical researcher investigates the truths and principles of being, knowledge, and human conduct. Alfred North Whitehead, in his book *Process and Reality,* describes the process of research in speculative philosophy:

> The true method of discovery is like the flight of an aeroplane. It starts from the ground of particular observation; it makes a flight into the thin air of imaginative generalization; and it again lands for renewed observation rendered acute by rational interpretation.[13]

Here Whitehead is describing the general process of inquiry that we have been discussing. As he says, the success of any imaginative speculation is the verification of it through extended application. He sees the work of philosophical research as an attempt to frame a coherent, logical system of the general ideas of humanity. In Whitehead's work, he presents a scheme that can be used to interpret or frame the "cosmology." He shows how his philosophical scheme can be used for "the interpretation of the ideas and problems which form the complex texture of civilized thought."[14] Thus, the philosophical laws are verified in their application to actual philosophical problems encountered in human experience.

Historical Research

Historical researchers proceed in much the same fashion as philosophy researchers, except that historical researchers investigate events as well as ideas. An historian researches the events that have occurred in a person's life or at a particular time. Then, the historian weaves those events and ideas into a narrative that recounts and interprets the past. As in all the humanities, historians attempt to understand and interpret life itself. Historians also use the data gathered by social scientists—the surveys and statistical counts conducted by sociologists, economists, or political scientists. However, historians often present their understanding of the past in a story form intended to give the reader a picture of the past events, describing and recreating what those events were like for the participants. It is in this way that the study of history bridges the gap between the social sciences and the other humanities such as literature and the arts.

The research process used by historians is much like that of the literary theorists. The historian investigates the facts and data available about an individual or a period of time. Through those facts, carefully verified for their accuracy, the historian recreates the past in order to capture the truths that reside there. The historian is not reluctant to make individual judgments about the meaning and importance of past events. As in all humanities, the historian verifies those judgments by gauging their ring of truth, their resemblance to what is known intuitively about life, and their explanatory power.

One example of an historical researcher at work is Frank Maloy Anderson.[15] Anderson was confronted with the problem of who wrote the important "Diary of a Public Man," a document of questioned authorship that first appeared in 1879 in the *North American Review*. Many historical, little-known facts about Abraham Lincoln were revealed in the diary. Anderson spent nearly thirty-five years trying to identify the document's author, using every historical clue he could find. He searched congressional records, hotel registries, business documents, and newspaper subscriptions. Out of this extensive search, he posited two hypotheses: (1) the diary was a fiction, or (2) it was a combination of fiction and truth. Anderson decided upon the second hypothesis, because he could find nothing that was provably false in the document. He arrived at a probable author in Sam Ward, but could never prove this beyond all doubt. Nevertheless, Anderson's historical case is a good one, based as it is on intuitive speculation combined with factual evidence.

Acceptable Evidence in the Humanities

In the humanities, there is no objective proof that leads unerringly to a particular interpretation or theory. Rather, the humanist will make a claim and argue for that claim. What is demanded in the humanities is not proof, but sensitivity and perceptiveness. The way of knowing required in the humanities can be cultivated by hard work and study.

The evidence that is acceptable in literary and art criticism or interpretation comes from the interpreter's sensibility, from the work of art or literature itself, and from the context. Some interpretations and theories may seem more insightful than others—they cast the work into a new light or integrate it into a wholeness we had not originally perceived. The claim or hypothesis made by a theorist is accepted as valid if it "fits" the work and helps the audience understand it. Critical and theoretical research can expand our consciousness, deepening and broadening our sensitivity to experiences. We could say, as did William James, that the performance of a piece of violin music is "the scraping of the hair of a horse over the intestines of a cat."[16] Though the description is true enough, as Meiland points out it is not all there is to violin music; in fact, the remark leaves out just about everything that is really important in the performance of a violin piece. A valid interpretation illuminates a work in a way that makes it more meaningful to us.

The evidence that is acceptable in historical and philosophical re-search is that which is based either on verifiable facts or adequate inter-pretations that fit known human experience. As Barzun and Graff put it, "The researcher who does historian's work can at least preserve his sense of truth by concentrating on the tangle of his own stubborn facts."[17] But in addition to those facts, the historian is also "aware of his duty to make individual judgments" regarding the meaning or significance of those facts.[18] As Whitehead states, the application of his philosophical scheme to life "at once gives meaning to the verbal phrases of the scheme by their use in the discussion, and shows the power of the scheme to put the various elements of our experience into the consistent relation to each other."[19] In both cases, these humanistic researchers insist upon the role of the researcher's insight and imagination in elucidating human experience and in describing and predicting what human beings are and how they think and act. Acceptable evidence in all the humanities is evidence that supports those imaginative and insightful descriptions and interpreta-tions.

QUESTIONS FOR DISCUSSION

1. What is the general goal of inquiry in the humanities?
2. How are written texts used in the humanities? Why are they impor-tant?
3. What three kinds of research are common in the humanities? How are they alike or different?
4. What constitutes acceptable evidence in the humanities?

EXERCISES

1. Obtain a copy of an undergraduate catalog. In the catalog, find refer-ences to the academic disciplines and notice how they are classified. Are there differences in the categories you find in the catalog and those outlined in this chapter? In a paragraph, describe the major divi-sions of disciplines in the catalog.

2. In an undergraduate catalog, look up a discipline you are considering as a major (e.g., prelaw, history, or mathematics). In addition to courses in that discipline, what other courses are required (e.g., foreign languages, liberal arts, laboratory sciences)? In a paragraph, describe those "core" requirements and speculate on why they are included as a part of an undergraduate education.

3. In your classes in high school or prior to the courses you are currently taking in college, you have probably studied sciences, social sciences, and humanities. Describe in a short essay how classes in these three areas were similar or different.

4. For each problematical situation below, propose a solution and suggest in a short report how you would go about verifying that solution:

   A. In your dorm, you are in charge of collecting the money for a favorite charity. You must organize the collection drive.

   B. As president of your student association, you are in charge of getting your fellow students to voluntarily comply with the no-smoking rule in the college cafeteria.

   C. Your college newspaper has assigned you to write an article on pollution and the environment. The editor wants you to report how students on your campus really feel about pollution and other environmental issues.

5. Recall a problematical experience that you have had or a social situation that troubles you (such as racism, pollution, or sex discrimination). Is there any way to eliminate the problem you have identified? If so, how would you go about it? In a short essay, describe the problem and your suggested solutions.

■ Notes

[1] Adapted from *Rhetoric: Discovery and Change*, by Richard Young, Alton Becker, and Kenneth Pike. © 1970 by Harcourt Brace Jovanovich, Inc. Reprinted by permission of the publisher.

[2] Charles Nicolle, "The Mechanism and Transmission of Typhus," in René Taton, *Reason and Chance in Scientific Discovery* (New York: Philosophical Library, 1957), pp. 76–78. Reprinted by permission of the Philosophical Library, Inc.

[3] Taton, p. 85.

[4] Taton, p. 88.

[5] Stanley Milgram, *Obedience to Authority: An Experimental View* (New York: Harper & Row, 1974).

[6] Milgram, p. 6.

[7] Sigmund Freud, *Civilization and Its Discontents*, edited and translated by James Strachley (New York: W. W. Norton, 1961).

[8] Freud, p. 62.

[9] Jacques Barzun and Henry F. Graff, *The Modern Researcher*, rev. ed. (New York: Harcourt Brace and World, 1970), p. 245.

[10]Jack Meiland, *College Thinking: How to Get the Best Out of College* (New York: Mentor, 1981), p. 174.

[11]John Livingston Lowes, *The Road to Xanadu: A Study in the Ways of the Imagination* (London: Pan Books, 1978). Originally published in 1927.

[12]Richard Altick, *The Art of Literary Research* (New York: W. W. Norton, 1963), p. 100.

[14]Frank Maloy Anderson, *The Mystery of "A Public Man": A Historical Detective Story* (Minneapolis: University of Minnesota Press, 1948).

[15]As found in Jack Meiland, *College Thinking: How to Get the Best Out of College* (New York: Mentor, 1981), p. 186.

[16]Barzun and Graff, p. 250.

[17]Barzun and Graff, p. 251.

[18]Whitehead, p. xi.

CHAPTER 2

Primary Research Methods

■ INTRODUCTION

In all disciplines, the primary research methods are the customary ways in which investigators in a particular field gather information and search for solutions to problems they have posed. When conducting primary research, researchers are gathering and analyzing data. Secondary research, in contrast to primary research, involves studying and analyzing the primary research of others as it has been reported in books and journals. Many research projects are based on a combination of primary and secondary research methods.

In this chapter, we will discuss primary research methods used by researchers in the sciences, social sciences, and humanities. We will begin with a discussion of primary research methods in the natural and physical sciences, since primary research in many fields is based on the scientific method.

■ PRIMARY RESEARCH IN THE SCIENCES

Lab Experiments and Reports

Central to an understanding of research in the sciences is an understanding of the scientific method. In the sciences, the *method* by which an experimenter solves a problem is as important as the *result* the experimenter achieves. Guided by the scientific method, researchers investigate the laws of the physical universe by asking and answering questions through empirical research. The scientific method begins with a scientist formulating a question and developing a hypothesis that may answer the question posed. On the basis of the hypothesis, the scientist predicts what should be observed under specified conditions and circumstances in the laboratory. Next, the scientist makes and records observations, generally using carefully designed, controlled experiments. Finally, the scientist either accepts or rejects the hypothesis, depending upon whether or not the actual observations corresponded with the predicted observations.

As you may have discerned from this description of the scientific method, writing plays a role at every step. A researcher must describe in great detail both the method used in the experiment and the results achieved. A report of the experimental findings will be based on the laboratory notes taken during the experiment. All researchers must keep written records of their research. In the natural sciences, such records generally take the form of a laboratory notebook. In this notebook the researcher keeps a complete, well-organized record of every experiment and each experimental variable (phenomena that are not constant in the experiment). The researcher must record this information in a clear, easy-to-understand format so that he or she (and co-workers) will have easy access to it when it is time to draw conclusions from the experiment.

In your undergraduate science courses, you will be expected to conduct scientific experiments and record your method and results in a laboratory notebook. You may also be expected to report your experiments in a systematic way. A good laboratory report will introduce the experiment, describe the materials and methods used in collecting the data, explain the results, and draw conclusions from those results.

Your scientific experiments will necessarily be connected with laboratory work, and it is beyond the scope of this book to lead you through an actual scientific experiment. However, it is important for you to realize that the scientific method employed by researchers necessitates the careful, organized, and complete presentation of methods and results through written reports.

Observation and Reports

In some scientific disciplines, empirical or experimental work is supplemented by field observations that occur outside the laboratory. In this section, we will discuss a field experiment and report assigned to students in a physical geography laboratory.[1] This field experiment will illustrate one approach to problem solving that incorporates both scientific data and field observation.

The students in the physical geography lab at Texas Tech University study landforms. In their laboratory research assignment, students are asked to investigate the urban flood hazard in Lubbock, Texas, and to report their findings. The students work in groups of four or five to gather the necessary data. It is not unusual in the scientific community for researchers to work in teams, collaborating on both the actual research and the written report of the research. For this assignment, the teacher provides important background readings to help students identify the potential problem of urban flooding. Students must apply general knowledge obtained in the class discussions and course readings to the particular problem of urban flooding in the city where they are attending college.

In this assignment, students are using a common approach to problem solving. They are given a potential problem by the instructor, and their first step is to identify and define that problem carefully. In the outline below, notice the similarity to the inquiry steps discussed in Chapter 1 (preparation, incubation, illumination, verification) and to the scientific method.

Students must

1. Clearly identify and define the problem.
2. Define an objective or goal that might lead them to a solution to the problem.
3. Gather information from their own backgrounds and from books, printed matter, media, other people, observations, and laboratory experiments.
4. Define the constraints that might limit the solution; generate possible solutions (hypotheses).
5. Evaluate all the possible solutions to determine which is most likely to solve the problem, which satisfies the basic objective, and which is the most feasible, practical, economical, safe, legal, and so on.
6. Prepare a written report that describes the problem, the experimental and field-data-collection methods, and the proposed solution to the problem. In the report, the evidence gathered is used to support the proposed solution.

Throughout this experiment, students use primary research methods—observation, experimentation, and report. They also use secondary research methods, by incorporating the ideas they find in the pertinent books and articles they read. What follows is an excerpt from a student report on urban flooding in Lubbock, Texas. As you read this report, notice how the students have followed the approach to problem solving outlined above. Also, notice how they have used the various sources as evidence to support their position.

```
              Geography Report—Group 5

                    Leslie Bayer

                   Kim Springer

                Charlotte Wedding

                    Pat Cates


The main objective of this report is to present a flood
hazard reduction plan for Maxey Park in Lubbock, Texas.
```

Within this scope we plan to:

1. Determine the specific boundaries around the park that would be flooded with a heavy rain.
2. Conduct discussions with other individuals who can give in-depth information about Lubbock's existing flood-management program.
3. Establish satisfactory or possible solutions for the flooding around Maxey Park.

To begin, a description of the location and nature of the flood problem in Lubbock is in order. Lubbock is located on the Texas South Plains. This area is relatively flat with only minor changes in elevation, which decreases the ability of water to drain easily. Because of this, Lubbock's drainage system is designed around what are known as playa, or man-made lakes. These lakes receive run-off, which is channeled mainly by streets and other man-made drainage channels. Therefore, Lubbock's flooding type is called inflooding, because the lakes within the city fill up and overflow the surrounding areas.

The specific area of consideration, Maxey Park, is located in the western central part of Lubbock. The park and the immediate surrounding residential and commercial areas lie in a slightly depressed area, which increases the likelihood of flooding around this particular park. [Students included drainage-basin analysis data from laboratory experiments.]

Three other problems that increase flooding are that (1) Lubbock is a semiarid region, which somewhat reduces infiltration capacity; (2) Lubbock streets are squared off, increasing flood peaks because run-off has reduced time to occur; and (3) Lubbock's rainfall is short and intense, increasing the demand on the drainage system.

The present flood problems facing Lubbock are definitely more acute than those of the past. Such a situation is caused by increased urbanization as a result

of years of growth. The only time in the past during which
Lubbock has had a rainfall close to the 6.4 inch rainfall
of October, 1983, was in 1967, when 5.7 inches fell. An
interview with Emory Potts, a Lubbock City Engineer,
suggests that the flood in October, 1983, was between a
50- and 100-year flood. Regarding the amount of rainfall
(6.4 inches) during a 24-hour period, the flood was closer
to a 50-year flood. However, the total accumulation over
the 4-day period was 9-10 inches, which classifies the
flood as a 100-year flood.

From the above facts, it is evident that Lubbock has a
serious problem regarding flooding. The city has
implemented several measures to curb flooding. Its
primary action has been to pass a Lakes ordinance to
protect residential and commercial areas. This ordinance
is designed to decrease flooding of these areas by
building parks around natural playa lakes so that no homes
or buildings will be constructed within the immediate
area. The city's second measure has been the construction
of a storm sewer system that empties into the Canyon
Lakes. Unfortunately, this system is not very extensive.
[Students went on to describe the city's current
storm-sewer and flood-prevention systems.]

One possible solution to alleviate flooding around
Maxey Park is to dredge the accumulation of silt in Maxey
Lake. This action would probably allow the lake to hold
more water and possibly increase the natural percolation.
Another solution is to build the homes and buildings on a
higher or elevated foundation to help protect them from
the water. However, Mr. Potts (city engineer) also
emphasized that very little can be done to ''counteract
mother nature.''

Because of the potential flooding situation around
Maxey Park, with few possible solutions to the problem,
none of the members of our group would want to purchase a
house immediately adjacent to the area. However, those
who own homes in the area should acquire adequate flood

insurance. Owners should also be prepared to sandbag the
lawn, plan alternate routes of travel, and have a plan for
safe and quick evacuation if it should become necessary.

[Students included charts and graphs illustrating the
Maxey Lake area and its flood problems.]

QUESTIONS FOR DISCUSSION

1. What are the stated objectives of the report?
2. What is the nature of the flooding problem described by the report?
3. Where did the group get its information? What kinds of primary and secondary sources did the students use? Did they acknowledge those sources?
4. What possible solutions were posed for lessening the hazard? What measures should home owners take to reduce the flood problem?

EXERCISE

To help you understand the process of observation and report, this exercise will lead you through a problem-solving task similar to but less complex than the physical-geography problem discussed above. You will use the same steps to problem solving outlined above as you explore possible solutions to a traffic hazard that you have identified in your community. For this exercise, work in groups of four or five people. Be sure that you divide the work evenly among the members of your group.

A. Identify the traffic hazard that you have observed in your community. Perhaps it is an intersection where accidents occur frequently or a school crossing zone that has no painted crosswalk. Describe the problem as carefully as you can, giving the location of the problem area (maps might be appropriate).

B. Define an objective or goal that might lead to the solution of the problem. Perhaps a stoplight, a painted crosswalk, or a crossing guard would eliminate the traffic hazard.

C. Gather information from your own background and from books, printed matter, media, other people, and observations. You may want to attend a meeting of the local traffic commission or study the commission's long-range plans for the community. Or you may want to speak to the principal of an elementary school about a school traffic hazard.

D. While gathering data, generate possible solutions and define the constraints that might limit them. Perhaps the city budget precludes installing any more traffic lights. In such a case, you might look for alternative sources of funding that the city has not yet explored.

E. Evaluate the possible solutions you have posed in D. to determine which is most likely to solve the problem, which satisfies the objective, which is the most feasible, practical, economical, safe, legal, and so on.

F. Prepare a report three to five pages long that describes the problem, the data-collection method, and the proposed solutions. In the report, use the evidence gathered to support the proposed solution.

■ PRIMARY RESEARCH IN THE SOCIAL SCIENCES

The social sciences have incorporated many of the research techniques of the natural and physical sciences and have developed some research methods of their own as well. Remember, as we discussed in Chapter 1, the primary aim of the social sciences is to study human beings and their interaction within societies. Social scientists seek to help us understand the events that happen around us and to communicate that understanding to others. Systematic inquiry is essential in the social sciences. Because researchers must communicate the social knowledge they acquire through their research, they need a clear written form for transmitting their insights.

As in the natural and physical sciences, researchers in the social sciences employ a version of the scientific method. The following steps (discussed in detail below) are generally followed in the researching of a social scientific question:

1. choosing the research problem and stating the hypothesis
2. formulating the research design and method of gathering data
3. gathering the data
4. analyzing the data
5. interpreting the results of the data analysis in order to test the hypothesis

Step 1—Problem and Hypothesis

Obviously, the first step must be preceded by extensive study and preparation in the discipline under investigation. To choose a research problem that is significant, fresh, and researchable, the social scientist must have an intimate knowledge of the field of study. Often, researchers will choose a problem based on the prior research of other social scientists, or they will seek to test their hypotheses of reality against actual social reality. It is crucial for researchers to keep abreast of the current research in their fields by reading professional journals, attending national meetings of professional societies, and maintaining contacts with other researchers doing similar studies. Research problems and hypotheses are not formulated in a vacuum. The first two inquiry steps discussed in Chapter 1, preparation and incubation, precede the actual formulation of a hypothesis.

Step 2—Research Design

The researcher must decide how to test the hypothesis posed in step 1. To do this, he or she needs to determine which concepts or events being studied are constant and which are variable. *Variables* are phenomena that change or differ. Temperature, for example, is a variable that differs by degrees. Thus, the variable "temperature" contains the idea of more or less heat, and this variable influences the physical world. Similarly, the social variable "religion" may be expressed differently: Protestant, Catholic, Muslim, and so on. Just as temperature influences physical nature, a social variable such as religion influences human nature. Public opinion polls have discovered that Protestants and Catholics differ predictably in their preference for political parties. Thus, the variable "religion" influences social behavior.

Once the variables have been identified, the researcher must decide how best to measure them. The methods used by the social scientists include the following (discussed in detail below):

1. experimental method
2. surveys and questionnaires
3. interviews
4. observation and description

Step 3—Gathering the Data

The researcher gathers data based upon the research design chosen as most appropriate for testing the hypothesis. Social science researchers pay close attention to matters of accurate sampling and the accurate recording of data. The accompanying table, taken from FBI Crime Reports, illustrates the kind of data often gathered by social scientists.[2]

Step 4—Analyzing the Data

Researchers analyze their data quantitatively (using numbers) to discern its relationship to the hypothesis. Depending on the research method used, the researcher will rely to a greater or lesser degree on statistical analyses of the data. Often researchers will "code" their data to make it suitable for machine processing. Computers can quickly and accurately process data and correlate variables. As an example of data analysis, students in a political science class were asked to analyze the crime statistics data in the table to find new calculations. First, the students were asked to

TABLE 2.1   FBI Uniform Crime Reports, *Crime in the United States* (per 100,000 population)

	Murder				Forcible Rape			Violent Crime[a]
	1962	1974	1977	1979	1969	1974	1979	1979
Abilene	5.4	6.1	10.0	8.1	9.3	22.2	28.0	218
Amarillo	1.9	11.7	13.2	11.7	16.7	16.9	33.3	440
Baltimore	7.5	16.8	10.2	13.7	9.3	35.7	41.0	1088
Boston	2.4	5.6	3.6	4.7	5.4	18.5	22.6	648
Brownsville—								
Harlingen	4.0	11.3	14.8	6.6	7.3	12.0	53.1	442
Chicago	7.0	15.9	18.7	14.3	27.2	34.8	24.6	569
Cleveland	3.5	17.2	14.2	16.7	3.5	27.8	32.6	687
Dallas—								
Ft. Worth	9.9	14.5	15.2	18.3	9.3	40.8	42.2	694
Detroit	4.3	20.2	14.1	13.8	13.5	45.7	47.5	896
Houston	8.5	18.7	18.0	30.0	19.8	31.6	45.9	673
Los Angeles	4.5	12.9	16.0	20.0	26.0	54.5	64.9	1205
Lubbock	11.3	16.8	19.1	22.0	15.5	47.9	47.9	592
Midland	16.2	9.0	14.3	11.8	13.3	14.9	18.6	429
New York	5.0	16.3	17.1	19.8	8.6	42.8	42.8	1497
Philadelphia	3.6	11.9	8.9	10.6	14.6	28.1	27.2	529
Pittsburgh	2.7	3.1	4.8	5.6	6.1	19.8	20.9	363
Washington, D.C.	6.0	15.4	10.3	9.3	9.9	41.0	36.1	693

[a]Violent Crime Index is a total of indices for murder, forcible rape, robbery, and aggravated assault.

calculate the percentage of annual change for each type of violent crime from 1974 to 1979. Then, they were asked to rank the cities from 1 to 17 for 1962 and 1979. By being submitted to different kinds of analysis in this way, the same data can be made to yield different information, which may or may not be significant.

Step 5—Interpreting the Results

The relationship among variables suggested by the hypothesis is tested at this stage in the research, often through statistical measures. In the social sciences, a hypothesis can never be proven or disproven "beyond the shadow of a doubt." However, researchers can statistically calculate the probability of error for the hypothesis and thus can strongly suggest the truth or validity of the hypothesis. The following introductory paragraph is taken from a student report on the FBI crime statistics cited in the crime-statistics table. As part of a political science assignment, the student interprets the data and tries to explain the alarming increase in violent crime.

Conclusions Drawn from Crime Statistics
of Selected U.S. Cities

by Kenneth Nershi

The average incidence of murder per 100,000 population
for the selected U.S. metropolitan areas was 6.0 in 1962
and rose to 13.9 in 1979, less than two decades later. The
occurrence of forcible rape also increased sharply for
these cities during this period; beginning with an index
of 12.1 in 1962, it tripled to an average index of 36.8 in
1977. These statistics from the FBI Uniform Crime Reports
are indeed troubling to the concerned U.S. citizen and
project an ominous trend of increased crime rates for the
1980s. There are, I believe, three major factors that
caused these alarming statistics: plea bargaining due to
an overcrowded judicial system, the bail system and delay
of trial, and the deterioration of neighborhood
structures in the large U.S. cities.

Outlined below are the research methods most commonly used by social science researchers. Each method has both advantages and disadvantages. Researchers must keep the relative merits of each method in mind as
they design a research project.[3]

Experimental Method

The social scientific experiment is a highly controlled method of determining a direct link between two variables—for example, between high
temperature and riots. The researcher must have control over the research
environment so that no external variables can affect the outcome. Unlike
experimental methods in the sciences, in social scientific research it is
often difficult to control the research environment totally. A researcher
who is interested in the causes of riots should not attempt to create a riot
in the laboratory for study. However, social science researchers can study
the behavior of laboratory animals and make certain hypotheses about human behavior based on their experimental results. For example, to test the
hypothesis that overcrowding can cause riots, some researchers studied

populations of rats and varied the population density to test their hypothesis. They found that for the rat populations, overcrowding did indeed cause antisocial behavior. From this result, the researchers hypothesized that a similar phenomenon exists for people—that is, overcrowded cities can contribute to antisocial behavior. Though experimental research is the best means of definitively establishing causal links (variable A *causes* variable B; overcrowded living conditions *cause* antisocial behavior), experiments may be narrow in focus. In the case of the above experiment, people may or may not behave as rats do.

Surveys and Questionnaires

Ideally we would study an entire population to gain insights into its society. Finding out how *all* Americans intend to vote in an upcoming election would accurately predict the outcome. However, polling an entire population is seldom feasible, so pollsters sample small segments of the entire population at random. Researchers have refined sampling techniques to the point where polls can be quite accurate. Thus, CBS news can announce the outcome of a presidential election hours before the returns are in for much of the country.

One particular kind of survey is the questionnaire, a form that asks for responses to a set of questions. Large numbers of people can be polled for their opinions by means of questionnaires. The researcher must design the questionnaire carefully so that it is valid (measures what it claims to measure), reliable (measures the same thing each time), and complete (each question is answered). The following questionnaire was designed by a student to discover the attitudes toward weight held by a group of college women. For an example of how this questionnaire was analyzed and interpreted, see the model research paper in Chapter 7.

Interviews

Interview studies are one particular type of survey. Their advantages over the questionnaire include flexibility (the questioner can interact with the respondent), response rate (the questioner immediately knows the respondent's answer), and nonverbal behavior (the questioner can gather nonverbal clues as well as verbal). There are other advantages of interviews as well, but the disadvantages are also great. Primarily, the time and expense of interviews makes them difficult to conduct. Consequently, fewer responses can be gathered. In addition, the interview is actually a complex interaction between individuals and thus can hinge on the characteristics of the individuals involved. If a respondent is put off by the interviewer, his or her interview answers will be affected. Nevertheless, interviewing is an important research method in the social sciences that results in rich, high-quality data. The following interview questions were used by a student to discover her peers' political attitudes on the abortion issue prior to an election. She used the answers she gathered as the basis for a paper on student opinion about abortion.

QUESTIONNAIRE

1. Are you a member of a college sorority?   yes   no
2. Are you happy with your present weight?   yes   no
3. Is weight gain or loss a strong determining factor in your moods?   yes   no
4. Do you feel you have succeeded in completing a major task when you lose weight?   yes   no
5. Have you ever used laxatives or diuretics to control your weight?   yes   no
6. Have you ever used self-inflicted vomiting to control your weight?   yes   no
7. Have you ever stopped your menstrual cycle from weight loss?   yes   no
8. If you were thinner, would it help you fit in with your peers?   yes   no
9. If you were thinner, would it help your dating problems?   yes   no
10. Do you feel guilty or angry after overeating or binge eating?   yes   no
11. Are you happy with your present weight?   yes   no
12. Do you wish you weighed more or less than you do?   more   less
13. Please indicate your present height and weight.   height: weight:
14. Please list the three magazines you most frequently read.
    1
    2
    3
15. Please indicate your parents' income level (per year).
    _____ $0–10,000
    _____ $10–20,000
    _____ $20–50,000
    _____ over $50,000

RESULTS ON ABORTION INTERVIEW

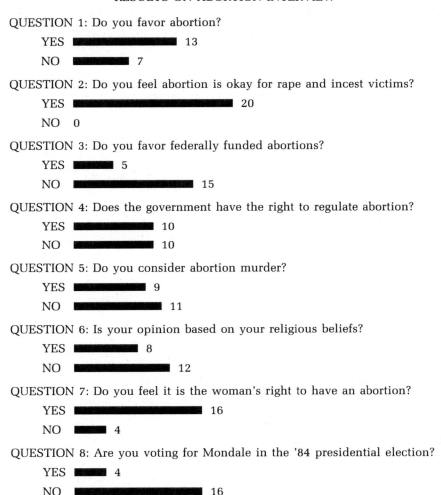

QUESTION 1: Do you favor abortion?

YES ██████████ 13

NO ██████ 7

QUESTION 2: Do you feel abortion is okay for rape and incest victims?

YES ████████████████ 20

NO 0

QUESTION 3: Do you favor federally funded abortions?

YES ████ 5

NO ████████████ 15

QUESTION 4: Does the government have the right to regulate abortion?

YES ████████ 10

NO ████████ 10

QUESTION 5: Do you consider abortion murder?

YES ███████ 9

NO █████████ 11

QUESTION 6: Is your opinion based on your religious beliefs?

YES ██████ 8

NO █████████ 12

QUESTION 7: Do you feel it is the woman's right to have an abortion?

YES █████████████ 16

NO ███ 4

QUESTION 8: Are you voting for Mondale in the '84 presidential election?

YES ███ 4

NO █████████████ 16

Observation and Description

The survey method is important for obtaining a person's opinion on a particular issue. The observation, on the other hand, is best suited to the collection of nonverbal data. In this method, the observer takes notes on people behaving in customary ways in a particular environment or setting. In this way, the researcher accumulates "field notes," which are used to analyze trends and discern customary behaviors. The disadvantages of observation include lack of control over the environment, lack of quantifiable data, and small sample size. Also, whenever an observer enters the environment to observe people, the participants' behavior may no longer be natural.

The goal of social research based on observation and description is a general one: to describe and perhaps evaluate a culture or subculture in as much detail as possible. An example of this type of observational research is sociologist Margaret Mead's book *Coming of Age in Samoa*. In this book, Dr. Mead describes the complex culture of the Samoan island, paying particular attention to customs surrounding the transition from adolescence to adulthood.

The following excerpt from a report written for a speech communications course illustrates an observation and description of a particular cultural setting—the country singles' bar.[4] The researcher was observing particular nonverbal behaviors exhibited by the patrons of the bar. As you read the report, notice the descriptions and categorizations of the patrons in this "subculture."

Red Raider Romances

by Lee Guyette

The following study was conducted at the Red Raider Club in Lubbock, Texas. The study is a brief survey of the nonverbal communication displayed in this particular club. The following observations were made by me not only in the recent few days, but also over a seven-month period in which I worked as a cocktail waitress there. I made my observations from the standpoint of a nonperson/waitress and from the person/female customer. The Red Raider Club is a Country and Western club that caters primarily to a crowd of people between the ages of 25 to 50. It is for the most part a blue-collar, lower-middle-class crowd.

Body Types, Shapes, and Sizes

Attractiveness:

A majority of the people, both male and female, were only average in appearance. There were a few exceptionally attractive males and females, and they did seem to get preferential treatment; for example, the attractive men were turned down less when they asked a woman to dance, and the attractive women were asked to dance more frequently.

Body Image and Appearance:

Many of the individuals were slightly overweight. They did not seem to be very aware of or satisfied with their bodies. Their body concept seemed low. In the more attractive individuals, the reverse was true. The attractive individuals were more aware of their bodies; they noticed what they were doing with their bodies, and they smiled more and seemed in general more comfortable with themselves. I did notice that the less attractive people seemed to worry less about their unsightly bodies as they became intoxicated.

Body Messages:

Most of my subjects were definitely endormorphic, and they certainly seemed viscerotonic. Most of the men were slightly overweight. There were women as tall as six feet and men as short as five feet. Nearly all my subjects were white. Perhaps 2 percent were Hispanic and there were no blacks. Many of the men had beards and moustaches, perhaps to indicate masculinity. Most of the women wore their hair either long and curly or short and straight.

Clothing and Personal Artifacts

Function of Dress:

The main function of dress in this club was cultural display more than comfort or modesty. Nearly all of the subjects of both sexes wore jeans. The men wore Wranglers and most of the women wore designer jeans. Chic, Lee, Wrangler, Sergio, and Vanderbilt were the most commonly worn for the women. A few women wore western dresses. I did not see any man not wearing cowboy boots and most of the women also wore cowboy boots. A few women wore high-heeled shoes. All of the women wearing dresses wore heels. Most of the people, both female and male, wearing jeans and boots also had their names on the back of their belts. For the men, it was their last names on the belt; for the women their first names.

Communication Components of Dress:

It is difficult to say whether or not these people were intentionally or unintentionally communicating messages through dress. They all seemed to communicate their preference for western dress. They did not wish to communicate, however, that they were from a lower socioeconomic background by wearing western dress. Although this conception has changed in recent years, it still is thought that lower—middle—class people wear western clothes.

Personality Correlates of Dress:

It is extremely difficult to assess personality types of a large group just from their clothing styles. However, I did notice that most of the women in dresses were there with dates. I also noticed that women wearing ruffled western blouses danced more frequently. For the most part, both men and women dressed conservatively. The colors were usually solid black, brown, and white for the men, and red, purple, or blue for the women.

Perception of Dress:

Most of the people were dressed in the conventional stereotype of western dress. Indeed, it was almost as if there were an unspoken dress code. The young attractive girls, wearing red and purple blouses with ruffles, tight jeans, boots, belts, and wearing their hair long, seemed to be thought the sexiest and most likeable. They were asked to dance more frequently than any others. The young attractive men with beards and moustaches wearing black or white western cut shirts seemed to be the most popular with the women. No one wore very much jewelry of any kind. A few women had small earrings or hair barettes. Nearly everyone smoked cigarettes continuously. I saw no pipes or cigars.

The Effects of Dress:

The main effect I observed was that everyone seemed able

to identify with each other and feel a sense of belonging
to the group because of their similar style of dress.

[Researcher goes on to describe behaviors observed
according to the following categories: body movements and
gestures; facial expressions and eye behavior; responses
to environment; personal space, territory, and crowding;
touching behavior; voice characteristics; taste and
smell; culture and time.]

Discussion

I feel that the nonverbal communication that I have
described may be representative of lower—middle—class
America in Lubbock, Texas. The nonverbal communication
described in this report may illustrate
lower—middle—class values: the tendency to be slightly
overweight in both sexes; the conservative, traditional,
western—style dress; the traditional use of male/female
regulators and posture; the overcontrol of masculine
expressions of emotion and the lack of control in feminine
emotional expressions; the environment, with its tacky
chairs and dirty carpet; the use of territory by the men;
the fact that women have no true territory, personal
space, or value (the women are treated as possessions and
property and they have only as much value as they are
granted by men); the way in which the men have absolute
control over when and how they will be touched, but the
women have very little to say about when or how the men
will touch them; the way the women plead with soft cooing
pitch at the end of their voice or remain silent while the
men speak loudly and uninterruptedly; the use of
substandard speech; the accepted deception on the part of
the males; the overwhelming smell of tobacco and liquor
and stale urine in the restrooms; the taste of cheap
wines, beer, and whisky; the time being measured by the
sets the band plays. All of these things are often
associated with lower—middle classes. Women and men may

be poorly educated and thus rely on tradition and myth. I
felt that the nonverbal communication that I observed was
representative of this particular subculture.

QUESTIONS FOR DISCUSSION

1. What is the relationship between the observer and those she is observing?
2. Name some trends and customary behaviors reported by the observer in this particular setting.
3. Does the writer overgeneralize from a small sample—that is, does she jump to conclusions based on insufficient data? Why or why not?
4. Is it likely that the observer's presence changed the dynamics of the situation so that her subjects' behavior was no longer natural? Why or why not?

EXERCISES

1. To understand observing and reporting, begin by observing the behavior of a particular group or subculture and report on that observation. As in the sample paper above on the country singles' bar, first choose subjects in a "field" to observe. Some possibilities include customers at a fast-food restaurant, patrons at a theatre, participants in a sport, spectators at a rock concert, students in a dorm, customers in a department store elevator, and so on.

   Procedure:
   A. Identify the field you have chosen to observe. Describe the setting, location, and the time you spent observing. Describe your research method. (Are you an observer or participant?)
   B. Take field notes as you observe the behaviors of the individuals in your chosen group. Look for verbal and nonverbal behaviors.
   C. Categorize your field notes into related behaviors and personality types.
   D. Speculate on the meaning of the behaviors you observed. What did you learn about the people in your study and how they act? Give possible reasons for why they behaved as they did.
   E. Write up your field observations in a report three to five pages long.

2. To understand the processes of interviewing and reporting, conduct an actual interview, working by yourself or with a classmate.

Procedure:

A. Find someone in your intended major field. Write or phone the person to introduce yourself. Set up an interview with that person, explaining that you want to find out what a person in your chosen career actually *does*.

B. Prior to the interview, draw up a list of interview topics similar to the following:

- education and background
- job title and general description of the job
- description of the company or organization
- years at the job
- prior positions within the same company
- tasks performed in the job
- tools used in the job (e.g., computers, books, etc.)
- future career plans or aspirations
- job satisfaction
- advice for someone just beginning in the career field

Use this topic list as a model only in developing your questions. The questions you ask will vary in accordance with your career choice. It is important to think through the questions you intend to ask your informant very carefully. If you want to tape the interview, be certain to ask for permission.

C. Once you have collected your data, analyze and categorize it into a report three to five pages long. Someone reading your report should be able to discern what the career is like for participants.

■ PRIMARY RESEARCH IN THE HUMANITIES

Just as in the sciences and social sciences, researchers in the humanities employ standard research methods. Since the goal of the humanities is to explore and explain the human experience, humanities researchers make extensive use of written records of that experience. Such written records are called *primary texts* and can include literary texts (poems, stories, novels, plays), other kinds of texts (letters, diaries, journals), and historical records (court proceedings, governmental records, etc.). All of these texts provide the raw data from which the researcher in the humanities works.

Using Primary Texts

Research in the humanities often begins with a primary text of particular interest to the researcher. The researcher must read the text very carefully as preparation, noting any significant events, themes, characters, and so on. After finishing the close reading, much as researchers in the social sciences do, the humanities researcher posits a hypothesis—that is, a plausible interpretation of the work and its significance. Then, the researcher collects evidence from the text itself and from other, related sources: works written by the same author, sources used by the author, and historical works on events occurring during the period when the work was written. These related sources are used to help verify or refute the initial hypothesis. Ultimately, the humanities researcher seeks to explain and interpret a primary text in such a way that its richness of meaning is increased for its readers.

Life-History Interviewing

The methods of humanities research may at times approximate the methods in social science research even more closely than the above description suggests. Historical research, for example, may include surveys and interviews of participants in a significant historical event, and very often historical research relies on the statistics gathered by social scientists.

One example of a humanities researcher is Studs Terkel, author of the book *Hard Times: An Oral History of the Great Depression*, which chronicles life during the 1930s.[5] Terkel's primary sources for his work were people who had lived through the Depression. He interviewed people from various walks of life and parts of the country, inquiring into their own life histories. The interviews were taped and transcribed. From the transcripts, Terkel wrote his version of the life history of each individual, bringing his own interpretations and explanations to the interview data. Terkel presented these explanations to readers in story form; the pieces describe and recreate events in each informant's life and together give a composite picture of life during the Depression.

The following excerpts show how Terkel transformed the taped material from his interview with Emma Tiller into a "story." As you read these excerpts, notice the differences between the taped original and Terkel's narrative. What kinds of changes did he make? Why do you think he made the changes he did?

Emma Tiller (transcribed tape)

by Studs Terkel

(used by permission of the author)

a white in the south is like they is i guess in most other

places they will not give and help especially the ones who

is turned out to be tramps and hoboes uh they come to their

---

door for food they will drive them away white tramps they
will drive them away but if a negro come they will feed him
they always go and get something another and give him
something to eat and they'll even give them a little do you
smoke or do you you dip snuff or uh or any do you use
anything like that yes ma'am yes ma'am well they would uh
give him a quarter or uh fifty cents you know and give him a
little sack of food and a bar of soap or something like
that well uh but they own color they wouldn't do that for
them then the negro woman would uh uh say you know well
we've got some cold food in there we'll give you she said
oh no i don't give them nothing he'll be back tomorrow you
know so so they won't dispose it [Terkel: Oh, you mean the
Negro woman who works] yes [for the white] yes [mistress]
yes [the white − −] she would take food and put it in a bag
and sometimes wrap it in newspaper and ah we would hurry
out and sometimes we'd have to run down the alley because
he'd be gone down the alley and holler at him hey mister
and he would stop you know and say come here and he'd come
back and said look you come back by after while and i'll
put some food out there in a bag and i'll put it down side
the can so that you don't see it if we could see soap we'd
swipe a bar of soap and face rag or something or you know
and stick it in there for them negroes always would feed
these tramps even sometimes we would see them on the
railroad track picking up stuff and we would tell them you
know come to our house and give them the address and tell
him to come back that we would give him a old shirt or a
pair of pants or some old shoes and some food we always
would give them food many times i have gone in in my house
and taken my husband's old shoes and his coat and some of
them he he needed them hisself but i didn't feel he needed
them as bad as that man needed them because that man to me
was in a worser shape than he was in regardless of whether
it was negro or white i would give them to him.

'Emma Tiller' (pages 60–61)

When tramps and hoboes would come to their door for food,
the southern white people would drive them away. But if a
Negro come, they will feed him. They'll even give them
money. They'll ask them: Do you smoke do you dip snuff?
Yes, ma'am, yes, ma'am. They was always nice in a nasty way
to Negroes. But their own color, they wouldn't do *that* for
'em.

   They would hire Negroes for these type jobs where they
wouldn't hire whites. They wouldn't hire a white woman to
do housework, because they were afraid she'd take her
husband.

   When the Negro woman would say, 'Miz So-and-So, we got
some cold food in the kitchen left from lunch. Why don't
you give it to 'im?' she'll say, 'Oh, no, don't give 'im
nothin'. He'll be back tomorrow with a gang of 'em. He
ought to get a job and work.'

   The Negro woman who worked for the white woman would take
food and wrap it in newspapers. Sometimes we would hurry
down the alley and holler at 'im: 'Hey, mister, come
here!' And we'd say, 'Come back by after a while and I'll
put some food in a bag, and I'll sit down aside the garbage
can so they won't see it.' Then he'd get food, and we'd
swipe a bar of soap and a face razor or somethin', stick it
in there for 'im. Negroes would always feed these tramps.

   Sometimes we would see them on the railroad tracks
pickin' up stuff, and we would tell 'em: 'Come to our
house.' They would come by and we would give 'em an old
shirt or a pair of pants or some old shoes. We would always
give 'em food.

   Many times I have gone in my house and taken my husband's
old shoes—some of 'em he needed hisself, but that other
man was in worser shape than he was. Regardless of whether
it was Negro or white, we would give to 'em.

From *Hard Times: An Oral History of the Great Depression,* by Studs Terkel, Copyright © 1970 by Studs Terkel. Reprinted by permission of Pantheon Books, a Division of Random House, Inc.

QUESTIONS FOR DISCUSSION

1. What do you think Emma Tiller's job was?
2. Compare Emma's description of the treatment of hoboes by whites with that by blacks.
3. What attitude towards poor people does Emma exemplify?
4. What role do you think compassion played during the Depression?
5. How does Terkel use language to illustrate Emma Tiller's character?
6. Choose one line from the original transcript and compare it to Terkel's rendition of the same line. What changes did Terkel make? Why do you think he made those changes?
7. Which version is easier to read? Why?
8. How does Emma Tiller's story help make life during the Depression vivid and real?
9. Relate Terkel's work *Hard Times* to what you have learned about humanities research. Does Terkel's approach satisfy the goals of humanities research?

EXERCISE

In this exercise, you will use some of the tools and procedures of researchers in the humanities as you research and write an autobiographical report.

Procedure:

A. First, locate a primary text. In this case, locate a newspaper that was printed on the day you were born. Old newspapers are probably kept in your library on microfilm, so you will need to learn how to use the microfilm readers. If possible, choose a newspaper from a city near where you were born. For example, if you were born in the East, you could read the *New York Times* or the *Washington Post.*

B. Read the newspaper completely, looking for significant events, people, and ideas. Take notes about any important events, people, or ideas that you find in the newspaper.

C. Once you have finished reading and taking notes, formulate a hypothesis that tells something about the times in which you were born. For example, you might hypothesize that very little has changed in the kinds of news stories written then and now. Or you might find that prices are drastically different and speculate about the reasons for the change. Or you might find a significant article (on a political event or a social issue, such as the first busing for desegregation in a major city and the consequent rioting) that would provide the basis of your paper. Whatever the idea or event you choose, the task is to determine its significance and interpret it for your readers.

D. Write a short autobiographical account illustrating the times in which you were born. If possible, include your own experiences as a point of departure for your paper.

■ Notes

[1] I am indebted to Professor Judy Davidson of the Texas Tech University geography department for this assignment and student response.

[2] I am indebted to Professor Neale Pearson of the Texas Tech University political science department for pointing out this table and for allowing me to use the subsequent assignment and student report.

[3] Information for this section of the chapter is adapted and reprinted with the permission of The Free Press, a Division of Macmillan, Inc., from *Methods of Social Research*, by Kenneth D. Bailey. Copyright © 1982 by The Free Press.

[4] I am indebted to Professor John Deethardt of the Texas Tech University speech communications department for passing on to me this assignment and student response.

[5] Studs Terkel, *Hard Times: An Oral History of the Great Depression* (New York: Pantheon Books, 1970).

CHAPTER 3

Library Resources

■ INTRODUCTION

Your library contains many important general research tools that you need to become familiar with to conduct any research project. Also in your library are specific resources that are important for research in particular disciplines. This chapter covers information on both general library resources and specific library resources used in the sciences and technology, social sciences, humanities, and business.

■ LIBRARIES AND GENERAL LIBRARY RESOURCES

The Library Reference Area

Librarians themselves are excellent resources when you need help finding information in the library. However, you need to know enough about libraries to ask the librarian to help you, just as you need to know enough about your car to tell an auto mechanic what to look for when your car needs repair. It is not productive to walk up to an auto mechanic and simply ask for help. You need to explain the specifics of your particular problem and describe the make, model, age, and condition of your car. Similarly, you need to tell a librarian what kind of project you are working on, what information you need, and in what form that information is likely to be stored. So that you can ask the right questions, you must first take the time to learn your way around the library. Working your way through this chapter is a good place to begin.

Librarians customarily use terminology that you should become familiar with. Particular terms will be defined later in this chapter. We will start by looking at some major library sources and what distinguishes them.

In the heading to this section of the chapter you saw the word *refer-ence*. As you might suspect, a reference is something that refers to something else. In your library there will be an area designated the reference area and a person called the reference librarian. The reference area may be a separate room or simply a section of the library. In the reference area you will find books containing brief factual answers to such questions as, What is the meaning of a particular word? What is the population density of a particular state? and What is the birthplace of a certain famous person? Also in the reference area are books that refer you to other sources. These library tools—bibliographies and indexes—will help you find particular articles written about particular subjects. The reference area of the library is usually the place to begin any research project you may have. Reference sources include the following general types of works:

Dictionaries	Provide information about words
Encyclopedias	Provide concise information about people, places, ideas, specific subjects
Bibliographies	List books or articles about particular subjects
Biographies	Provide information on the life and work of famous people, living and dead
Indexes	Provide access to larger units of information such as journals and magazines, newspapers, parts of books
Serials	Magazines that are published at specific intervals and scholarly journals that contain articles and research reports in a specific field
Abstracts	Short summaries of larger works
Reviews	Comments on particular works such as films, novels, and even scientific research

General Reference Works

In most research projects, you will need to discover the general information relevant to your research. The most commonly used general reference works are dictionaries, encyclopedias, and biographies. Depending upon your project, you may also need to consult atlases, almanacs, handbooks, and directories.

Dictionaries

Dictionaries provide information about words: definitions, pronunciations, usage, origin, and changes of meaning. It is essential that you have a good desk dictionary to consult for all your writing. Some good ones include

> *American Heritage Dictionary of the English Language,* 2nd college ed. Boston: Houghton-Mifflin, 1982.
>
> *Webster's New Collegiate Dictionary,* 9th ed. Springfield, Mass.: Merriam, 1983.

More comprehensive dictionaries are to be found in the reference area of your library. These include

> *Oxford English Dictionary* (OED), 13 vols. London: Oxford University Press, 1933, with supplements. The OED traces the chronological history of words and describes and illustrates with examples the changes in the meaning of words through the years.
>
> *Webster's Third New International Dictionary of the English Language.* Springfield, Mass.: Merriam, 1981. This unabridged (complete) dictionary gives definitions of spoken as well as standard written English. It is a complete source of words in the English language.

Encyclopedias

Encyclopedias provide concise information on people, places, subjects, events, and ideas. Encyclopedias are particularly useful for general background information on a specific subject or person. Look in the encyclopedia's index for references to related subtopics and articles within the encyclopedia. Both general and specialized encyclopedias exist. The specialized encyclopedias—for example, the *Encyclopedia of American History*—cover information in particular disciplines or fields. These encyclopedias often contain bibliographies, which can lead you to other sources in your research. (For specialized encyclopedias, see "Discipline-Specific Resources," below.) Some general encyclopedias include the following:

> *Collier's Encyclopedia.* New York: Macmillan, 1977.
>
> *Encyclopaedia Britannica.* Chicago: Encyclopaedia Britannica, 1979.
>
> *Encyclopedia Americana.* New York: Americana, 1977.
>
> *Academic American Encyclopedia.* Danbury, Conn.: Groliers, 1983.

Biographies

Biographies provide information on the lives and work of famous people. As with the encyclopedias, there are both general and specialized biographies. (The specialized biographies are covered in "Discipline-Specific Resources," below.) General biographies include the following:

Current Biography. New York: Wilson, 1940–present. Covers important living people from all fields, including popular figures. Published monthly with bound annual cumulation (Yearbook).

Dictionary of American Biography, 21 vols. New York: Scribner's, 1943. Covers famous Americans who are no longer living. Includes biographies of all noteworthy persons from America's colonization on.

The McGraw-Hill Encyclopedia of World Biography. New York: McGraw-Hill, 1973. Covers famous men and women both living and dead. A good place to find biographies on persons not traditionally covered in other works— for example, women and minority groups.

Who's Who. New York: St. Martin's Press, 1948–present. Covers living people who are prominent in their fields. Primarily a source of information on famous British citizens. *Who Was Who* contains the biographies of those no longer living but previously selected for *Who's Who*.

Who's Who in America. Chicago: Marquis, 1899–present. Covers living Americans who are noted for exceptional contributions to their fields. *Who Was Who in America* provides biographies of those no longer living but previously selected for *Who's Who in America*.

Bibliographies

Bibliographies are lists of books or articles about particular subjects. Some bibliographies are found at the end of articles or books; others are entire books in themselves. General bibliographies include the following:

Bibliographic Index. New York: Wilson, 1938–present. Lists bibliographies found in other sources, including bibliographies in books, journals, and single volumes.

Guide to Reference Books, by Eugene P. Sheehy, 9th ed. Chicago: American Library Association, 1976. Lists and describes reference works that can provide access to other works.

A World Bibliography of Bibliographies, by Theodore Besterman, 4th ed., 5 vols. Lausanne: Societas Bibliographica, 1965. Lists available bibliographies.

Locating Books and Resources: The Card Catalog

Cards that record the library's holdings are generally found in the card catalog. (Note: Library catalogs differ from institution to institution. Many libraries use card catalogs, but others use on-line computer access systems or microforms.) Each card lists a single work, and each work is represented by its author, title, and subject entries. Your library's card catalog may be divided into author/title cards and subject cards, and these may be filed together in one file or separately.

Each work has a unique number, the *call number*, in the upper left-hand corner of the catalog card. There are two major systems of cataloging in the United States—the Dewey decimal system and the Library of Congress system—and your library will most likely use one of them. Both systems use call numbers, which provide you access to the particular item in the library. The accompanying examples use the Library of Congress system. (If they used the Dewey decimal system, the call numbers would be somewhat different.) On author cards the author's name is at the top, on title cards the title is at the top, and on subject cards the subject heading is at the top.

Author Card

```
  1.
 PR
 461    2. Buckley, Jerome Hamilton.
 B75    3.   The Victorian temper : a study in literary culture
 1981        / by Jerome Hamilton Buckley. -- 4. 1st pbk. ed. --
        5. Cambridge [Cambridgeshire] : Cambridge University
           Press, 1981, c1951.
        6.   x, 282 p. ; 22 cm.
        7.   Includes bibliographical references and index.


        8.   1. English literature--19th century--History and
           criticism. I. Title

 TxLT    bo                              ILUUnt    81-6142
```

1. *Call Number*
2. *Author's Name*
3. *Work's Title*
4. *Edition*
5. *Imprint (place of publication, publisher, date of publication)*
6. *Number of pages, size of book*
7. *Special features*
8. *Tracings*

Title Card

```
                     1. The Victorian temper
 PR
 461    Buckley, Jerome Hamilton.
 B75    2. The Victorian temper : a study in literary culture /
 1981   by Jerome Hamilton Buckley. -- 1st pbk. ed. --
        Cambridge [Cambridgeshire] : Cambridge University
        Press, 1981, c1951.
           x, 282 p. ; 22 cm.
        Includes bibliographical references and index.


           1. English literature--19th century--History and
        criticism. I. Title

 TxLT    bo                              ILUUnt    81-6142
```

1. *Title*
2. *Complete Title*

Subject Card

```
                        ENGLISH LITERATURE 19th C
                        HISTORY AND CRITICISM
       PR
       461     Buckley, Jerome Hamilton.
       B75       The Victorian temper : a study in literary culture /
       1981    by Jerome Hamilton Buckley. -- 1st pbk. ed. --
               Cambridge [Cambridgeshire] : Cambridge University
               Press, 1981, c1951.
                 x, 282 p. ; 22 cm.
                 Includes bibliographical references and index.


                 1. English literature--19th century--History and
               criticism. I. Title

       TxLT    bo                              ILUUnt      81-6142
```

You will find the subject cards particularly useful when you search for information on a topic. However, sometimes it is difficult to predict which terms will be used as subject headings in the subject catalog. A useful guide to the appropriate subject headings is the *Library of Congress Subject Heading* list *(LCSH)*. This large, two-volume work is usually kept near the subject catalog or in the reference area of the library. Below is an excerpt from the *LCSH* list. The terms in boldface type are the subject headings used in the subject card catalog. Terms following *sa* or *xx* are additional subject headings that can be used to find information on a specific topic. Terms following x are not used as headings.

> **Cartons** *(Commerce. HF5770: Manufacture. TS1200)*
> *sa* Egg carton craft
> Paper box machinery
> *x* Paper boxes
> *xx* Boxes
> Paper box industry
> Paper containers
> Paper products
> Paperboard

Many libraries have converted their catalogs into computerized catalog access systems to provide their patrons with the most up-to-date information. There are two major computerized cataloging systems: microforms and on-line.

Microforms
Your library's holdings might be organized on microforms rather than catalog cards. Microforms are either microfilm or microfiche. Microform

readers are necessary to read either form. Information stored on microform is similar to that on traditional cataloging cards. If your library uses this cataloging system, check with the reference librarian for instructions about using the microform readers.

On-line Systems

Some libraries provide users with catalogs that are stored on computers. Library patrons enter key words (for example, the author's name or a book title) by typing them onto the keyboard. The computer's response is displayed on the terminal screen. In this way, library users gain access to the most up-to-date information on library holdings. If your library uses such a system, it is important that you learn to use it as soon as possible.

Locating Articles in Serials: Periodicals

Periodicals are magazines and newspapers printed at regular intervals: daily, weekly, monthly, quarterly, and so on. The reference section of your library will contain several indexes to articles found in periodicals. Two important indexes of general-interest periodicals are

Magazine Index. Los Altos, Calif.: Information Access, 1978–present.

Reader's Guide to Periodical Literature. New York: Wilson, 1901–present.

Both sources index articles in popular magazines. The *Reader's Guide* is available in chronologically bound volumes, each containing an alphabetical listing of articles from a particular year. (The current issues are paperbound.) The *Magazine Index* is available on microform and on-line computer systems. This index is extremely useful for very current topics, because it indexes about twice as many articles as *Reader's Guide.* In both sources, entries are arranged both by subject and author.

Newspapers

Your library will probably store back issues of newspapers on microform. To gain access to articles in the *New York Times,* use the *New York Times Index,* which lists all major articles from the *Times* from 1913 to present. The *Newspaper Index* lists articles from the *Chicago Tribune, Los Angeles Times, New Orleans Times-Picayune,* and *Washington Post.* Both indexes are arranged by subject. For business news, use the *Wall Street Journal Index.*

Finding Periodicals

In the appropriate index, you will find titles of articles related to your particular research topic. When researching your topic, you need to write down the complete *citation* of any relevant article. The citation includes the author (if given) and title of the article, the name of the magazine, the volume number, the issue number, the date, and the pages of the article.

For example, suppose you were researching the dismissal of a Stanford football coach. You might turn up these entries:

Football, College
'83 college football preview. il *Sport Mag* 74:23-6+ S '83
All-South '83 [special section] il *South Living* 18:99+ S '83
The band played on and on [Stanford coach P. Wiggin dismissed after loss to California] R. Fimrite. il por *Sports Illus* 59:96-8 N 28 '83
Barry: It's 1:30. Do you know where your players are? [M. Dupree leaves Oklahoma] D. S. Looney. il por *Sports Illus* 59:50-2+ O 24 '83
A big day for the D [Nebraska vs. Oklahoma] J. Mc-Callum. il *Sports Illus* 59:55-6+ D 5 '83
But how 'bout them Lions? [Penn State vs. Georgia in the Sugar Bowl] J. Papanek. il *Sports Illus* 58:14-20 Ja 10 '83
Cal picks up right where it left off [victory over Texas A&M] N. B. Clark. il *Sports Illus* 59:50 S 12 '83
Carolina's cookie crumbled again [Maryland vs. North Carolina] J. McCallum. il *Sports Illus* 59:25-7 N 7 '83
The Cats are sharpening their claws [Kentucky] J. Diaz. il *Sports Illus* 59:78-80 O 3 '83

You would write down this citation:

> The band played on and on [Stanford coach P. Wiggin dismissed after loss to California] R. Fimrite. il por *Sports Illus* 59:96–8 N 28 '83

The title of the magazine is usually abbreviated in the index. To find the full name of the magazine, look in "Abbreviations of Periodicals Indexed," usually found at the front of each volume of the index.

Your library will have a particular system for listing magazine and newspaper holdings. This listing may appear in a separate catalog, in the main card catalog, on computer printouts, or on microform. Consult your librarian to determine which system your library uses. The serials listing will tell you which periodicals your library subscribes to, where they are located in the library, the inclusive dates of the issues your library has, and whether the issues are in bound or unbound volumes or on microform.

Once you have obtained the call number of the magazine containing your article from the serials listing, you will be able to find the magazine itself, whether it is in a bound volume, in the current-periodicals section of the library, or on microform.

Evaluating Periodicals

If you find the title of a magazine but are unsure of its nature or scope, a useful evaluative tool is Katz's *Magazine for Libraries*, 4th ed. (New York: Bowker, 1982). This work describes and explains magazines. Katz's guide will give you some insight into the magazine's purpose, reputation, and scope.

Locating Articles in Serials: Professional Journals

When you are researching a technical subject, you will want to refer to articles written on the subject by professionals in the field. Professional journal articles are indexed in much the same way as periodicals. However, numerous specialized indexes exist for professional articles, and each index covers a particular discipline or subject area. "Discipline-Specific Resources," below, lists discipline-appropriate indexes for sciences and technology, social sciences, humanities, and business.

Once you have located an appropriate index, begin looking up your topic in the most recent volume first. If you were researching the topic "anorexia nervosa," here is an example of what you might find in the *Social Sciences Index:*

Anorexia nervosa
Anorexia nervosa in a patient with an infiltrating tumor of the hypothalamus. R. A. Weller and E. B. Weller. Am J Psych 139:824-5 Je '82
Cerebrospinal fluid opioid activity in anorexia nervosa. W. H. Kaye and others. Am J Psych 139:643-5 My '82
Comparative analysis of primary anorexics and schizophrenics on the MMPI. A. C. Small and others. bibl J Clin Psychol 37:733-6 O '81
Diagnosis of anorexia nervosa in children and the validity of DSM-III. M. Irwin. Am J Psych 138:1382-3 O '81
Geometric model of anorexia and its treatment. J. Callahan. il Behav Sci 27:140-54 Ap '82
Homeostatic regulation and Pavlovian conditioning in tolerance to amphetamine-induced anorexia. C. X. Poulos and others. bibl J Comp & Physiol Psychol 95:735-46 O '81
Locus of control as a measure of ineffectiveness in anorexia nervosa. J. Hood and others. bibl J Consult & Clin Psychol 50:3-13 F '82
Paradoxical intention in the treatment of chronic anorexia nervosa. L. K. George and S. Lieberman. Am J Psych 139:650-3 My '82
Treatment of ego deficits in anorexia nervosa. C. L. Zeller. Am J Orthopsych 52:356-9 Ap '82

For articles that sound promising, copy down the complete citation (author, title, and publication data) in the working bibliography in your research notebook and/or on your bibliography cards. To find the full version of abbreviated journal names, turn to "Abbreviations of Periodicals Indexed," usually at the front of the index volume. Then, locate the particular journal by using your library's listing of serial holdings, just as you did for magazines and newspapers. Professional journals will be stored in bound or unbound volumes (the latter for very recent editions) or on microform. The citation you have obtained from the index is your key to finding a particular article. Thus, it is crucial that you copy down the citation information accurately and completely. Many of the indexes to scholarly journals follow the format of the *Social Sciences Index* (see the example above). However, there are variations in the index formats. Take the time to get acquainted with the arrangement of each index by reading the explanation in the index's preface. If you are still confused about how an index is organized, ask your reference librarian for help.

The Impact of Technology on Libraries

Already in this chapter we have discussed some technological advances affecting libraries: computerized card catalogs and the computerized *Magazine Index*. A third technological advance involves on-line database searching for information (see example on page 61). For approximately the past ten years, information has been stored in computerized databases for easy access and retrieval. Many of these computerized databases correspond to printed indexes, and most of the information retrieved from an on-line search is also available in print. An on-line search, then, is generally an alternative way of finding sources on a subject. Depending on your particular research project and the research capabilities of your library, a traditional search using printed indexes may still be the best way to find sources. For example, if you are researching an event that occurred during World War II and need articles written at that time, an on-line search may not uncover many relevant sources, since computer databases are relatively new—primarily listing sources published in the past ten years.

Furthermore, on-line searching may be expensive. Your library will pass on to you the cost of maintaining access to and using the computer database. Thus, an on-line search can cost as much as $75.00 per hour of computer use. Because of the expense, on-line searches are most cost effective for large research projects. Most research projects conducted by undergraduates do not require on-line searching, but in some degree programs students must produce major research projects in the discipline. For such projects, an on-line search may be appropriate. It is important for you to be aware of computer databases, therefore, so that you can discuss with your computer-search librarian the feasibility of doing an on-line search for a particular research project. Some of the major computer databases are listed by discipline in "Discipline-Specific Resources," below.

EXERCISES

1. In the reference section of the library, find a major biographical work. To become familiar with biographical sources, look up information on a famous person who is or was important in your major field. (Be sure to look in an appropriate biography in accordance with whether the person is living or dead, American or British, etc.) Take notes on that person's life and work. Write a one-page report on some aspect of the person that seems interesting to you. You may wish to consult more than one biography and compare their entries.

2. In your library's card catalog, look up a subject area that interests you as a possible research topic. (For ideas, browse through the *Library of Congress Subject Headings* list.) Write down the author, title, and call number of any book that seems interesting. Using the call number, find the book in the library stacks. Write a complete citation for the

PRINTS User: U0020650 28Sep84 PRINT 13/5/1-117

DIALOG File 1: ERIC -- 66-84/Sep

EJ299965 HE518071
Many Colleges Limit Students' Use of Central Computers for
Writing.
  Turner, Judith Axler
  CAUSE/EFFECT, v7 n3 p6-7 May 1984
  Available from: UMI
  Language: English
  Document Type: POSITION PAPER (120); PROJECT DESCRIPTION (141)
  Journal Announcement: CIJSEP84
  Allocating limited resources to an unlimited demand is an issue
faced by data processing management in higher education. Use of
the central computer for word processing is creating a demand at
many institutions that is stretching and exceeding the available
computing resources. (Author/MLW)
  Descriptors: *College Students; *Computers; Data Processing;
Higher Education; *Time Management; Use Studies; *Word
Processing; *Writing (Composition)
  Identifiers: *Computer Centers; Yale University CT

EJ298427 IR512505
A Dyslexic Can Compose on a Computer.
  Arms, Valarie M.
  Educational Technology, v24 n1 p39-41 Jan 1984
  Available from: UMI
  Language: English
  Document Type: PROJECT DESCRIPTION (141)
  Journal Announcement: CIJAUG84
  Describes the strategies used by a technical writing teacher
who encouraged a dyslexic university engineering student to use a
microcomputer as an aid in composition writing, and discusses how
a word processing program was used to make the writing process
easier and increase the student's self-confidence. (MBR)
  Descriptors: College Students; Computer Assisted Instruction;
*Dyslexia; Higher Education; Learning Disabilities; Learning
Motivation; *Microcomputers; *Teaching Methods; *Word
Processing; *Writing (Composition)

EJ298270 FL515801
Computer-Assisted Text-Analysis for ESL Students.
  Reid, Joy; And Others
  CALICO Journal, v1 n3 p40-42 Dec 1983
  Language: English
  Document Type: PROJECT DESCRIPTION (141); POSITION PAPER (120)
  Journal Announcement: CIJAUG84
  Reports an investigation into possibilities of using word
processors and text analysis software with English as second
language (ESL) students to determine (1) if foreign students can
learn to use computer equipment, (2) if students feel time
invested is worthwhile, and (3) if ESL students' problems with
writing American academic prose can be remedied by this type of
assistance. (SL)
  Descriptors: Comparative Analysis; *Computer Assisted
Instruction; *English (Second Language); Grammar; Modern

Language Curriculum; Second Language Learning; *Student
Participation; Vocabulary Development; *Word Processing;
*Writing Skills

EJ298267 FL515798
Computer-Assisted Language Learning at the University of
Dundee.
  Lewis, Derek R.
  CALICO Journal, v1 n3 p10-12 Dec 1983
  Language: English
  Document Type: NON-CLASSROOM MATERIAL (055); POSITION PAPER
(120)
  Journal Announcement: CIJAUG84
  Presents an overview of activities in field of
computer-assisted language learning at the University of Dundee
(Scotland). These include (1) use and testing of a
self-instructional teacher's package, (2) development of the
computer-controlled tape recorder, (3) cloze-type gapping
exercises, and (4) projects aimed at the word processing
component of a microcomputer to improve composition and
translation skills of undergraduates. (SL)
  Descriptors: *Cloze Procedure; *Computer Assisted Instruction;
Foreign Countries; *Language Tests; Modern Language Curriculum;
*Second Language Instruction; *Student Participation;
Translation; Undergraduate Students; *Word Processing; Writing
Skills
  Identifiers: Dundee University (Scotland)

EJ297923 CS729605
Pitfalls in Electronic Writing Land.
  Oliver, Lawrence J., Jr.
  English Education, v16 n2 p94-100 May 1984
  Available from: UMI
  Language: English
  Document Type: POSITION PAPER (120)
  Journal Announcement: CIJAUG84
  Discusses the drawbacks of computer assisted instruction in the
composition classroom. (FL)
  Descriptors: *Computer Assisted Instruction; *Computers;
Elementary Secondary Education; Higher Education; *Problems;
*Teacher Role; *Word Processing; *Writing Instruction

EJ297016 IR512399
'Writing to Read'--Challenging an Age-Old Tradition.
  Electronic Education, v3 n5 p21-22 Feb 1984
  Language: English
  Document Type: PROJECT DESCRIPTION (141)
  Journal Announcement: CIJJUL84
  Describes Dr. John Henry Martin's theory of how children can
learn to write phonetically before learning to read and how this
theory developed into a computer-based teaching system
(cont. next page)

book, including the author's full name, the title and edition of the book, and the publication data. Then, write a one-paragraph annotation describing the book. (An annotation is a short critical or explanatory note.)

3. Using one of the indexes to periodicals, look up the subject you looked up in question 2 above. Again, note one article listed in the index that sounds interesting. Find the article itself in the library by using your library's serials listing of magazine holdings and their locations. Make a photocopy of the article. On your copy, underline key ideas in the article. Turn in your underlined copy.

4. Look up the magazine you used in question 3 in Katz's *Magazines for Libraries*. Write down the information you find about the magazine. (Note: If your library does not have Katz's work, find out if it carries a similar work, such as Farber's *Classified List of Periodicals for the College Library*.)

5. Using the *Social Sciences Index*, look up a current social problem—for example, alcoholism, child abuse, or prison reform. In the index, find one current article in a scholarly journal. Write down the citation from the index, find the complete journal name in the front of the index, and using that information find the journal article in your library. Remember, you will need to look up the journal name in the serials listing just as you did for a popular magazine. Make a photocopy of the article. On your copy, underline key ideas. Then construct an outline of the article. Turn in the photocopy with your outline.

6. Find any information your library has about on-line computer searches and discuss computer searching in your particular field with the librarian responsible for computer searches.

■ DISCIPLINE-SPECIFIC RESOURCES

So far in this chapter, we have discussed general resources available in the library and practiced using those resources. This part of the chapter lists specialized library resources for various disciplines. In general, the same types of resources are covered: dictionaries and handbooks, encyclopedias, biographies, indexes, bibliographies, abstracts, and computer databases.

Science and Technology

General Sources and Guides to Literature

Reference Sources in Science and Technology, by E. J. Lamsworth. Metuchen, N.J.: Scarecrow, 1972. A guide to locating and using reference sources in sciences.

Science and Engineering Literature: A Guide to Current Reference Sources, by H. R. Malinowsky et al., 3rd ed. Littleton, Colo.: Libraries Unlimited, 1980. Lists and annotates reference works in various scientific fields.

Science and Technology: An Introduction to the Literature, by D. J. Grogan, 3rd
  ed. Hamden, Conn.: Shoe String Press, 1976. A guide to sources in
  sciences, including dictionaries, encyclopedias, handbooks, microforms,
  and computerized sources.

Dictionaries

Chamber's Dictionary of Science and Technology. T. C. Collocott and A. B.
  Dobson, eds. Edinburgh: W & R Chambers, 1974. Concise dictionary of
  science and technology—a good source for definitions of terms.

The Condensed Chemical Dictionary, 10th ed. New York: Van Nostrand Reinhold, 1981. Provides definitions of chemical terms and information on
  pharmaceuticals.

Dictionary of Inventions and Discoveries, by E. F. Carter, 2nd ed. New York:
  Crane Russak, 1976. Catalogs and describes major scientific inventions
  and discoveries.

McGraw-Hill Dictionary of Scientific and Technical Terms, 2nd ed. New York:
  McGraw-Hill, 1978. Provides clear definitions of terminology.

*Ocran's Acronyms: A Dictionary of Abbreviations and Acronyms Used in Sci-
  entific and Technical Writing,* by E. B. Ocran. Boston: Routledge & Kegan
  Paul, 1978. A useful dictionary of abbreviations and scientific code
  words.

Handbooks

Handbook of Chemistry and Physics, 58th ed. Cleveland: Chemical Rubber,
  1913–present. Provides facts and data on chemistry and physics.

Materials Handbook, by G. S. Brady. New York: McGraw-Hill, 1929–present.
  Describes characteristics (nature and property) of commercially available
  materials.

Encyclopedias

The Cambridge Encyclopedia of Astronomy. S. Milton, ed. Cambridge, England: Institute of Astronomy, 1977. Provides a survey of current thinking
  in the field of astronomy.

The Encyclopedia of Biological Sciences, 2nd ed. Peter Gray, ed. New York:
  Van Nostrand Reinhold, 1970. Concise summaries of information in biology, geared for a nontechnical audience.

The Encyclopedia of Computer Science and Engineering. Anthony Ralston, ed.
  New York: Van Nostrand Reinhold, 1983.

The Encyclopedia of Physics. R. G. Lerner and G. L. Trigg, eds. Reading, Mass.:
  Addison-Wesley, 1980. Provides background information on major principles and problems in physics.

Grzimek's Animal Life Encyclopedia. B. Grzimek, ed. New York: Van Nostrand Reinhold, 1972–present. Provides an overview of the animal king-
  dom with illustrations.

Grzimek's Encyclopedia of Ecology. B. Grzimek, ed. New York: Van Nostrand
  Reinhold, 1976. Provides general information on the study of ecology.

McGraw-Hill Encyclopedia of Environmental Science, 2nd ed. S. P. Parker, ed. New York: McGraw-Hill, 1980. Provides information on the earth's resources and how they have been used.

McGraw-Hill Encyclopedia of Science and Technology, 5th ed. New York: McGraw-Hill, 1980. Provides concise, current background information on scientific and technical topics; an excellent place to begin a science research project, since the articles are not written for specialists.

McGraw-Hill Yearbook of Science and Technology. New York: McGraw-Hill, annual. Updates the encyclopedia (listed above) every year. Consult the yearbook for the most recent developments in a particular field.

Van Nostrand's Scientific Encyclopedia, 15th ed. New York: Van Nostrand Reinhold, 1976. Provides concise background information on a variety of scientific disciplines.

Biographies

American Men and Women of Science, 13th ed. J. Cattell, ed. New York: Bowker, 1976. Provides information on living, active scientists in the fields of economics, sociology, political science, statistics, psychology, geography, and anthropology.

Dictionary of Scientific Biography. New York: Scribner's, 1970–1981. Provides information on scientists from classical to modern times. Covers only scientists who are no longer living.

National Academy of Sciences, Biographical Memoirs. Washington, D.C.: National Academy of Sciences, 1877–present. Provides information on American scientists.

Who's Who in Science in Europe. Guernsey, B. I.: Francis Hodgson, 1972. Provides information on European scientists.

Indexes and Abstracts

Applied Science and Technology Index. R. Manofsky, ed. New York: Wilson, 1958–present. Provides access to articles in engineering, technology, and applied chemistry, geology, and physics. A good source for general science topics.

Biological Abstracts. Philadelphia: Biosciences Information Services, 1980–present (continues *Bioresearch Index*, 1967–1979). Provides concise summaries of important articles in biology.

Biological and Agricultural Index. New York: Wilson, 1919–present. Provides access to articles in biology and agriculture.

Cumulative Index to Nursing and Allied Health Literature. Glendale, Calif.: Glendale Advertisement Medical Center, 1977–present. Provides access to articles related to nursing and the other health professions.

Engineering Index. New York: Engineering Index, 1906–present. Provides access to articles and other publications in all fields of engineering.

General Science Index. New York: Wilson, 1978–present. Covers general science periodicals and is a good reference source for undergraduates and novices in the sciences.

Index Medicus. Prepared by the U.S. Department of Health and Human Services, N.I.H. Publications. Washington, D.C.: National Library of Medicine, 1960–present. Monthly index to periodicals and journals related to medicine.

Index to Scientific and Technical Proceeding. Philadelphia: Institute for Scientific Information, 1978–present. Includes subject indexes to important published conference proceedings.

Science Citation Index. C. Garfield, ed. Philadelphia: Institute for Scientific Information, 1982. An index to professional journals in all scientific fields. The citation index lists articles connected to subsequent works that have cited those articles. By using the citation index, one can search forward from a known key source to other works that build upon it.

Science and Technology Databases

- Agricola (agriculture)
- Biosis Previews (biology, botany)
- CA search (chemistry)
- Compendix (engineering)
- Geoarchive (geology)
- Mathfile (mathematics)
- NTIS (science and technology)
- SPIN (physics)

Social Science

General Sources and Guides to Literature

A Bibliographical Guide to Educational Research, by D. M. Berry. Metuchen, N.J.: Scarecrow, 1975. A guide to sources for education topics.

Guide to Library Research in Psychology, by J. E. Bell. Dubuque, Iowa: W. C. Brown, 1971. A useful source for undergraduate research.

The Information Sources of Political Sciences, by F. L. Holler, 2nd ed. Santa Barbara, Calif.: ABC-Clio, 1975. Lists and annotates reference sources, including specific areas of political science.

The Literature of Political Science: A Guide for Students, Librarians, and Teachers, by C. Brock. New York: Bowker, 1969. A guide to sources for political science topics.

Sources of Information in the Social Sciences, by C. M. White, 2nd ed. Chicago: American Library Association, 1973. A guide to references in all the social sciences, including an introduction to each discipline.

The Student Anthropologist's Handbook, by C. Frantz. Cambridge, Mass.: Schenkman, 1972. A guide to the discipline, including research materials.

The Student Sociologist's Handbook, by P. Bart and L. Frankel, 2nd ed. Morristown, N.J.: General Learning Press, 1976. Useful source for undergraduate research.

The Study of International Politics: A Guide to the Sources for the Student, Teacher and Researcher, by D. F. LaBarr and J. D. Singer. Santa Barbara, Calif.: ABC-Clio, 1976. A guide for students of international politics.

Dictionaries and Almanacs

The Almanac of American Politics, by M. Barone. G. Ujifusa, ed. Washington D.C.: National Journal, 1984. Provides facts and data on American politics.

Congressional Quarterly Almanac. Washington, D.C.: Congressional Quarterly, 1945–present. Summarizes the yearly activities of Congress, including voting records and major legislation.

Dictionary of Behavioral Sciences. B. B. Wolman, ed. New York: Van Nostrand Reinhold, 1974. Provides simple and concise definitions of terms in psychology and related fields.

A Dictionary of Politics, by W. Z. Laqueur. New York: The Free Press, 1974. A concise dictionary of political terms. Contains entries on political figures.

Dictionary of Psychology, by J. P. Chaplin. New York: Dell, 1975. Provides concise definitions of psychological terms.

United States Government Manual. Washington, D.C.: U.S. Government Printing Office, 1935–present. Provides current information on all aspects of the federal government.

Encyclopedias

Encyclopaedia of the Social Sciences. E. R. Seligman, ed. New York: Macmillan, 1930–1935. Provides historical information on topics of interest in the social sciences. About half the articles are biographical.

The Encyclopedia of Education. L. C. Deighton, ed. New York: Macmillan, 1971. Provides excellent background information on educational topics: history, theory, research, philosophy.

The Encyclopedia of Human Behavior. R. M. Goldenson, ed. Garden City, N.Y.: Doubleday, 1970. Contains terms, theories, treatment techniques, and biographies of important figures in psychology, psychiatry, and mental health.

Encyclopedia of Psychology, by H. J. Eysenck et al. New York: Herder and Herder, 1972. Provides an overview of important terms and concepts in psychology.

Encyclopedia of Social Work. New York: National Association of Social Workers, 1965–present. Provides general information on a variety of topics related to social work. Includes both articles and biographies.

Encyclopedia of Sociology. Guilford, Conn.: Dushkin Publishing Group, 1981. Describes terms, concepts, major ideas, major theorists in sociology.

International Encyclopedia of Higher Education. A. S. Knowles, ed. San Francisco: Jossey-Bass, 1977. Provides background information on topics related to higher education (education beyond high school).

International Encyclopedia of Psychiatry, Pychology, Psychoanalysis, and Neurology. B. B. Wolman, ed. New York: Van Nostrand Reinhold, 1977. Provides concise information on psychology and related fields.

International Encyclopedia of the Social Sciences. D. L. Sills, ed. New York: Macmillan, 1968. Provides analyses of current topics and issues in the social sciences. Includes a biographical supplement published in 1979.

Biographies
See Biographies (pages 53–54), Biographies for sciences (page 64), and Encyclopedias, above.

Indexes and Abstracts
Current Index to Journals in Education (CIJE). New York: CCM Information Sciences, 1969–present. An important current index to articles and publications in education and related fields.

Education Index. New York: Wilson, 1929–present. More selective index than *CIJE*, but covering a larger time period. Good for historical education topics.

Psychological Abstracts (also available on computer). Lancaster, Pa.: American Psychological Association, 1927–present. Provides brief summaries of important articles and books related to psychology. Since this index is selective, not all articles will be covered. However, it provides detailed information on each article indexed.

Public Affairs Information Service (PAIS, also available on computer). New York: Public Affairs Information Service, 1915–present. Provides access to public sources on current events, such as taxes, copyright laws, social concerns, and politics.

Resources in Education (RIE), currently known as *Educational Resources Information Center (ERIC,* also available on computer). Washington, D.C.: U.S. Government Printing Office, 1975. Provides access to publications and documents related to education but not published in journals.

Social Sciences Citation Index. Philadelphia: Institute for Scientific Information, 1973–present. Provides access to work in social sciences; interdisciplinary and international in scope. Like the *Science Citation Index,* this index provides access to sources written after a known source, thus building forward in time.

Social Science Index. New York: Wilson, 1974–present. Provides access to works in all the social sciences. A good index to start with for a general social science topic.

Social Work Research and Abstracts. New York: National Association of Social Workers, 1977–present. Provides concise summaries of important works related to social work fields.

Sociological Abstracts (also available on computer). New York: Sociological Abstracts, 1952–present. Provides brief summaries of important work in social sciences related to sociology and current social issues.

Women's Studies Abstracts. Rush, N.Y. Women's Studies, 1972–present. Provides brief summaries of recent publications related to women.

Social Science Databases

- ERIC (education)
- NICEM (nonprint educational materials)
- PAIS (political science)
- Psychinfo (psychology)
- Psychological Abstracts
- Social Scisearch (multidisciplinary social science)
- Sociological Abstracts

Humanities

General Sources and Guides to Literature

Art Research Methods and Resources: A Guide to Finding Art Information, by L. Jones. Dubuque, Iowa: Kendall-Hunt, 1978. A guide to sources in art.

A Field Guide to the Study of American Literature, by H. Kolb. Charlottesville, Va.: University of Virginia Press, 1976. A guide to selected sources in American literature.

Guide to Historical Literature, by the American Historical Association. New York: Macmillan, 1961. A guide to sources in American history.

Harvard Guide to American History, rev. ed. F. Freidel, ed. Cambridge, Mass.: Harvard University Press, 1974. A guide to sources in American history; contains an introduction to the discipline.

Literary History of the United States, 4th ed., by R. E. Spiller et al. New York: Macmillan, 1974. A history of U.S. literature from colonial times to 1960s.

New Cambridge Modern History. Cambridge, England: Cambridge University Press, 1957–1970. An introduction to history from the Renaissance through the modern period.

Oxford History of English Literature. F. P. Wilson and B. Dobree, eds. Oxford, England: Oxford University Press, 1969–1977. An introduction to English literature from early to modern times. Includes extensive bibliographies.

Philosopher's Guide to Sources, Research Tools, Professional Life and Related Fields. R. DeGeorge, ed. Lawrence, Kan.: Regents Press of Kansas, 1980. A guide to sources in philosophy, religion, social science, fine arts, literature, and other related fields.

A Reader's Guide to the Great Religions. C. J. Adams, ed. New York: The Free Press, 1977. Introduces major religions and discusses sources.

Dictionaries

A Dictionary of Comparative Religions. S. G. Brandon, ed. New York: Scribner's, 1970. Provides information on the world religions.

Dictionary of Contemporary American Artists, by P. Cummings. New York: St. Martin's Press, 1982. Provides concise information on living American artists.

Encyclopedic Dictionary of Religions. P. K. Meagher, ed. Washington, D.C.: Corpus Publications, 1979. Provides complete background information on the world's great religions.

Funk & Wagnalls' Standard Dictionary of Folklore, Mythology, and Legend. M. Leach, ed. New York: Funk & Wagnalls, 1972. Provides concise information on myths and legends.

Harvard Dictionary of Music, by W. Apel, 2nd ed. Cambridge, Mass.: Harvard University Press, 1969. Contains valuable information on all aspects of music, including musical terminology.

McGraw-Hill Dictionary of Art. B. Myers, ed. New York: McGraw-Hill, 1969. Provides information on all aspects of art: artists' lives and careers, styles, periods, buildings, museums, terms.

The New Grove Dictionary of Music and Musicians. S. Sadie, ed. London: Macmillan, 1980. Provides information on musical topics from ancient to modern times.

Encyclopedias

Britannica Encyclopedia of American Art. Chicago: Encyclopaedia Britannica, 1973. Provides concise information on all facets of American art. Contains many illustrations.

Cassell's Encyclopaedia of World Literature, rev. ed. J. Buchanan-Brown, ed. New York: Morrow, 1973. Provides concise background information on the world's great literature and authors.

Encyclopedia of American History, by R. B. Morris. New York: Harper & Row, 1976. Valuable overview of American history; contains brief biographies of famous Americans.

Encyclopedia of Bioethics. W. T. Reich, ed. New York: The Free Press, 1978. Provides information on philosophy and religion.

Encyclopedia of Philosophy. P. Edwards, ed. New York: Macmillan, 1967. Complete reference work on philosophical thought, both Eastern and Western.

Encyclopedia of World Art. New York: McGraw-Hill, 1958–1968. Provides information on the world's art and artists.

An Encyclopedia of World History: Ancient, Medieval, and Modern. W. L. Langer, ed. Boston: Houghton-Mifflin, 1972. Lists major world events from earliest times to 1970. (*The New Illustrated Encyclopedia of World History* is essentially the same work with illustrations.)

Historical Atlas, by W. R. Shepherd, New York: Barnes & Noble, 1964. Provides maps that illustrate world history.

The New College Encyclopedia of Music, by J. A. Westrop and F. L. Harrison; rev. by C. Wilson. New York: Norton, 1976. Provides concise information on all aspects of music.

Princeton Encyclopedia of Poetry and Poetics. A. Preminger, ed. Princeton, N.J.: Princeton University Press, 1974. Provides concise information on poetry and poetics through time, covering history, theory, technique, and criticism of poetry.

Biographies

American Novelists Since WWII. J. Helterman and R. Layman, eds, Dictionary of Literary Biography Series, vol 2. Detroit: Gale, 1978. Provides illustrated biographical entries on recent American novelists.

American Poets Since WWII. D. Greiner, ed. Dictionary of Literary Biography Series, vol 5. Detroit: Gale, 1980. Provides illustrated biographical entries on recent American poets.

Contemporary American Composers: A Biographical Dictionary, by R. Anderson. Boston: G. K. Hall, 1976. Provides information on American composers born since 1870.

Contemporary Authors: A Biographical Guide to Current Authors and Their Works. Detroit: Gale, 1962–present. Provides information on current American authors.

Directory of American Scholars, 8th ed. New York: Bowker, 1982. A biographical directory that includes information on notable scholars still active in their fields.

(See also Biographies, pages 53–54, and Encyclopedias, above.)

Indexes, Bibliographies, and Abstracts

Abstracts of English Studies. Urbana, Ill: NCTE, 1958–present. Provides summaries of important articles on all literature in English.

America: History and Life. Santa Barbara, Calif.: Clio Press, 1964–present. Provides access to works on American history. Entries since 1974 include abstracts.

Art Index. New York: Wilson, 1930–present. Provides access to works in archaeology, architecture, art history, crafts, fine arts, design, photography, and related topics.

Articles on American Literature, 1900–1950. Compiled by Lewis Leary. Durham, N.C.: Duke University Press, 1954. Lists articles on major and minor American authors.

Arts and Humanities Citation Index (also available on computer). Philadelphia: Institute for Scientific Information, 1982–present. An index to professional journals in the arts and humanities. The citation index provides listings of articles connected to subsequent works that have cited those books and articles.

Cambridge Bibliography of English Literature, and *New Cambridge Bibliography of English Literature* (an updated version). F. W. Bateson, ed. Cambridge, England: Cambridge University Press, 1940–1977. Lists significant literary works in English; arranged by genre (fiction, poetry, drama) and chronology. Includes citations of books and articles written about each work indexed.

Film Literature Index. Albany, N.Y.: Filmdex, 1974. Provides access to articles on film, including articles in general periodicals.

Historical Abstracts (also available on computer). Santa Barbara, Calif.: Clio Press, 1955–present. Provides brief summaries of articles on world history (1450–present). In 1964–present editions, American history is excluded, since it is covered in *America: History and Life.*

Humanities Index. New York: Wilson, 1974–present. Provides access to works from all humanities fields: archaeology, classics, folklore, history, language and literature, criticism, arts, philosophy, religion, and related topics.

Index to Book Reviews in the Humanities. Detroit: P. Thomson, 1960–present. Provides access to book reviews in the humanities. Organized by the author of the work being reviewed.

International Index of Film Periodicals. New York: Bowker, 1973. Provides access to works on film; the best and most comprehensive coverage of film studies.

MLA (Modern Language Association) International Bibliography of Books and Articles on Modern Languages and Literatures (also available on computer). New York: Modern Language Association of America, 1963–present. Comprehensive index to works related to literary and language studies: the first place to look in a study of literature or linguistics.

Music Index. Detroit: Information Coordinator, 1949–present. Provides access to works on music in general periodicals.

New York Times Film Reviews, 1913–1968. New York: N.Y. Times and Arno Press, 1970 (with updates). Provides access to film reviews as they appeared in the *New York Times.*

The Philosopher's Index (also available on computer). Bowling Green, Ohio: Philosophy Documentation Center, Bowling Green State University, 1967 –present. Provides access to works on philosophy.

Religion Index I: Periodicals. F. Dickerson, ed. Chicago: American Theological Library Association, 1977–present. Provides access to works in religious periodicals.

Selective Bibliography for the Study of English and American Literature, 6th ed., by R. Altick and A. Wright. New York: Macmillan, 1979. Lists materials available to students researching a literary topic. A limited listing, but a good place to start on most literary topics.

Year's Work in English Studies. London: Murray, 1919–present. Selected articles on English literature are described. Since 1954 each volume contains a chapter on American literature.

Humanities Databases

■ Arts and Humanities Citation Index

■ MLA Bibliography (1976–present)

■ Philosopher's Index

■ Historical Abstracts

Business and Economics

General Sources and Guides to Literature

Business Information Sources, by L. M. Daniells. Berkeley, Calif.: University of California Press, 1976. A guide to sources in business.

Economics and Foreign Policy: A Guide to Sources, by M. R. Amstutz. Detroit: Gale, 1977. A bibliography of books and articles—annotated.

Research Guide in Economics, by C. E. Helppie, J. R. Gibbons, and D. W. Pearson. Morristown, N.Y.: General Learning Press, 1974. A guide to research in economics for undergraduates.

Standard and Poor's Industry Surveys. New York: Standard and Poor's, 1959– present. A useful source for investment research. Detailed information on American industry.

Dictionaries

A Dictionary for Accountants, by E. L. Kohler. Englewood Cliffs, N.J.: Prentice-Hall, 1975. Defines key terms and concepts in accounting.

Dictionary of Advertising Terms. L. Urdang, ed. Chicago: Tatham-Laird and Kudner, 1977. Defines key terms and concepts in advertising.

Dictionary of Business and Economics, by C. Ammer and D. S. Ammer. New York: The Free Press, 1977. Defines key terms and explains major economic theories.

Mathematical Dictionary for Economics and Business Administration. W. Skrapek et al., eds. Boston: Allyn & Bacon, 1976. Defines mathematical terms and concepts important for business and economics.

McGraw-Hill Dictionary of Modern Economics: A Handbook of Terms and Organizations. New York: McGraw-Hill, 1973. Provides concise definitions of key terms and concepts in economics.

Encyclopedias

Encyclopedia of Accounting Systems. Englewood Cliffs, N.J.: Prentice-Hall, 1976. Provides concise analyses of accounting systems for various types of industry.

Encyclopedia of Banking and Finance, by M. Glenn. Boston: Bankers, 1973. Provides concise information on all aspects of banking and finance.

Encyclopedia of Business Information Sources. Detroit: Gale, 1976. Provides concise information and access to sources in business.

Encyclopedia of Management, 3rd ed. C. Heyel, ed. New York: Van Nostrand Reinhold, 1982. Concise information on many current business topics.

Biographies (see Biographies, pages 53–54).

Indexes and Abstracts

Accountant's Index. New York: American Institute of Certified Public Accountants, 1920–present. Index to pamphlets, books and government publications related to accounting.

Business Index. Menlo Park, Calif.: Information Access, 1979–present. Provides access to current information on business topics as found in today's newspapers and periodicals.

Business Periodicals Index. New York: Wilson, 1958–present. Provides access to works in business: advertising, finance, marketing, management, and so on.

Economic Titles/Abstracts (also available on computer). The Hague: Nijoff, 1974–present. Provides access to books, reports, journals on economics.

Wall Street Journal Index. New York: Dow Jones, 1958–present. Provides access to corporate news by company name; includes general news about products.

Business and Economics Databases

- ABI/INFORM
- Econ Abstracts International
- Labor Statistics
- Management Contexts
- Standard and Poor's News

EXERCISES

1. Locate a general source or guide to literature from your major field or a field that interests you. Browse through the work, noting its organization and coverage. Write down a complete citation for the work and then write a one-paragraph abstract describing the work. (An abstract is a very short summary that condenses the essential meaning of the source. See Chapter 5 for a discussion of abstracts.)

2. Locate a specialized dictionary from your major field or a field that interests you. Browse through the dictionary. Look up one key idea, term, or event. Paraphrase the information you find. Be sure to record complete citation information for the dictionary.

3. Locate a specialized encyclopedia from your major field or a field that interests you. Look up one key idea, person, or event. Summarize in your own words the information that you find. Give complete citation information from the encyclopedia, including author's name, if provided.

4. Locate a specialized index from your major field or a field that interests you. Browse through the index to become familiar with its organization and format. Record one subject heading and the first article citation under that heading. At the front of the index, look up the full name of the journal recorded in your citation. Then, using your library's serials listing, locate the journal and article you noted from the index. Make a photocopy of the article. Write a one-page summary of the article and turn in your photocopy with your summary.

CHAPTER 4

Library Research Methods

■ INTRODUCTION

Successful research depends on knowing what library resources are available, but it also depends on knowing how to find and use those resources. Developing a search strategy will help you to find materials on your research topic and to use library resources efficiently. First, you need to use library tools to locate source materials; then, you must evaluate those sources and interpret them so that they will be useful to your particular research project.

■ PREPARATION AND INCUBATION

As a college student, you are uniquely prepared to begin a research project. Your experiences and prior schooling have given you a wealth of information to draw from. The research project you are about to start may have begun in one of two ways: you may have been assigned to do a research paper in a particular college class or you may have discovered an interesting question or problem on your own that you decided to investigate. Though the former impetus, a course assignment, might seem artificial or contrived at first, in reality it will give you the opportunity to discover something about your world that has always intrigued you. Perhaps something you read about in your textbook or in a popular magazine seemed interesting to you. Or perhaps you have had a puzzling experience. Whatever the particular motivation, any research project begins with a starting question that will guide the research.

For example, Randy Elder, whose research paper appears in Chapter 6, had an interest in computer crime. He was assigned to write a research paper in a college course, and in response decided to pursue his interest. His starting question was something like "What exactly is computer crime and what is being done to prevent it?'' In order to answer this question, Randy had to devise a systematic research approach. He needed particular materials for recording his research, and he needed a search strategy for guiding the research process.

Gathering Research Materials

For your research, you need to obtain a notebook to serve as your "research notebook." In the notebook, record your library search strategy and your list of sources (working bibliography). Also in your research notebook, keep track of your own understanding of the answer to your starting question as it evolves through your research. It is crucial that as you investigate your topic you record your impressions and comments in your research notebook.

Your research notebook, then, will be the place for recording your entire research process: the starting question, the search strategy, the sources you will use in your search, your evaluative comments on the sources, the answer you will propose to your starting question written in the form of a thesis statement, an outline and organizational plan for your paper, and all preliminary drafts of your paper. Some students even like to take notes from sources in their research notebooks instead of on notecards, in order to keep all their research information in a single convenient place. If you decide on this approach, be sure to record your notes and evaluative comments in separate parts of the notebook. I suggest to my students that they leave a blank page for comments in their notebooks adjacent to each page of notes. Also, remember to reserve a place in your notebook for recording any primary research data (such as interview, survey, or questionnaire data) that you collect in connection with your research project.

Notecards are also important for most research projects. Many students and teachers like to record information from library sources onto notecards. If you choose this method, you will develop two sets of cards: bibliography cards and notecards. You will use the bibliography cards to record bibliographical information from the source (author, title, and publication data). And you will use the notecards to record actual notes (either paraphrased or directly quoted) from the source. Below find examples of two bibliography cards and a notecard that Randy Elder used in his research on computer crime.

The Bibliography Card for a Book

On the bibliography card for a book, write down the library call number of the book (in case you need to look up the book again), the author(s) of the book (if known), the complete title and edition number of the book, and the publication data (place of publication, publishing company, and date). The author, title, and publication data is called the book's *citation*.

```
QA                                                    3
76.15
E 48
The Encyclopedia of Computer Science
and Engineering, 2nd ed. Anthony Ralston,
ed. N.Y.: Van Nostrand Reinhold, 1983.
```

The Bibliography Card for a Serial

The bibliography card for a serial (magazine or journal) article includes the library call number; the author(s) and title of the work; the
serial's name, issue, and volume number; the date of publication (month
and year); and page number or numbers of the article. The information on
the author, title, and publication data makes up the article's citation.

```
Q                                                     4
1
D57
Browne, M.W. "Locking Out the Hackers,"
Discover. 15 (Sept. 1980) 31-40.
```

Notecards

Each notecard contains a descriptive title and the notes themselves. To
paraphrase material in your source, you will need to be careful to transcribe the meaning without using the author's wording. To quote directly,
be sure to mark words or phrases from the original with quotation marks.
Provide a page reference for all notes, both quotations and paraphrases.

3. 1

Crime and Computer Security
Origin

When computers began to be used for
classified government documents, the
need for security was recognized
(p. 426).

A number appears in the upper right-hand corner of both the bibliography card and the notecard. This is the *control number*. It allows you to match the notes with the source. On the notecard above, the number 3 tells you that this note was found in the third source, *Encyclopedia of Computer Science and Engineering*. The number 1 in 3.1 indicates that this note was the first one taken from source 3. Notes are numbered consecutively for each source. It is important that you number every notecard in this way, since you will be relying on this system later in documenting the source of your information.

The Working Bibliography

Whether you are using a research notebook and notecards together or simply a research notebook alone, you will need to begin a working bibliography. Start the working bibliography a few pages from the back of your notebook, leaving yourself enough room to record all the sources. A bibliography, as you learned in Chapter 2, is a list of books and articles on a particular subject. Your working bibliography will be your preliminary list of sources. It will grow as your research progresses, as one source leads you to another. It is called a "working" bibliography—as opposed to the finished bibliography—because it may contain some sources that you ultimately will not use in your paper.

A working bibliography need not be in final bibliographic form, but it is important to record accurately all the information you will eventually need to make the final bibliography for your research paper. The information for each source on your working bibliography is the same as that listed above for bibliography cards (books and articles). Though they contain the same kinds of information, your working bibliography and your bibliography cards differ in function. You make and use the cards when you actually find a source and begin taking notes from it. In the working bibliography, on the other hand, you will note down all sources that you run across—in bibliographies of books, for instance—whether or not your library has them and whether or not they turn out to be relevant to your topic.

Developing a Search Strategy

Once you have decided on a starting question and have gathered the necessary research materials, you are ready to outline a search strategy. Many library research projects begin in the reference area of the library, since the library tools that refer you to other sources are kept there. Often you will begin with reference works (dictionaries, encyclopedias, and biographies) and proceed to more specific reference works (abstracts, indexes, and databases). To make your library search an orderly and thorough process, you will need to design a search strategy. In most fields, a search strategy includes the following major components:

1. general sources—dictionaries and encyclopedias (both general and specific)
2. biographies (may be omitted for some topics)
3. reviews of literature and research reports
4. indexes and bibliographies (for access to source materials)
5. card catalog and/or serials listing (for location of source materials)
6. primary research (may be omitted for some topics)

Randy Elder designed the following search strategy to help him answer his starting question on computer crime:

1. Look up computer crime in dictionaries and encyclopedias, including *Chamber's Dictionary of Science and Technology* and the *Encyclopedia of Computer Science and Engineering*.
2. Look up any reviews already done on computer crime, using *Index to Scientific Reviews* and *Current Contents*.
3. Use the *Applied Science and Technology Index* to look up current works on computer crime. Check headings to be sure that the key word is *computer crime*. [Note: Randy discovered that this particular index listed articles on computer crime under the heading *Electronic Data Processing—Security Measures*.] Use the *Science Citation Index* for a forward search on key sources.
4. Look up *computer crime* in the *LCSH (Library of Congress Subject Heading)* list to determine if it is the subject heading used in the card catalog. Then, look up *computer crime* and other related headings in the subject listing of the card catalog to find books and other materials on computer crime.

You may need to change or modify your search strategy as you go along; do not feel that the strategy must be rigid or inflexible. However, using a search strategy enables you to proceed in an orderly, systematic fashion with your research. On your working bibliography, list each source you encounter in your search. As you read in the general and specialized encyclopedias, for example, you may find related references listed at the end of articles. Write down complete citations for any references that look promising so that you can look them up later. Similarly, as you look through the reviews, the indexes, and the card catalog, write down the citations to any promising sources. In this way, you will build your working bibliography during your library search.

EXCERCISES

To begin preparation for your own research project, follow these steps:

1. Select and narrow a research topic—that is, limit the topic in scope so that it is of a manageable size.
2. Articulate a starting question.
3. Gather your research materials—notebook and notecards.
4. Reserve space in your research notebook for notes from sources and evaluative comments.
5. Reserve space for your working bibliography pages, starting about four pages from the back of the notebook; title the first page "Working Bibliography."
6. Outline your search strategy (refer to Chapter 3 for specific library tools to use in your search and to Chapters 6, 7, 8, or 9 for a sample search in your chosen discipline).

Outlining a Time Frame

After writing down your search strategy, you will have a better idea of how long your research will take. Now is the time to sit down with a calendar and create a time frame for your entire research project. Your teacher may have given you some deadlines, and if so, they will help you decide on a time frame. If not, you will have to set your own dates for accomplishing specific tasks so that you can proceed in an orderly fashion toward the completion of the project. If you have never done a research project before, you might be overwhelmed at the thought of such a large task. However, if you break the job down into smaller parts, it will seem more manageable.

Allow yourself three to four weeks for locating, reading, and evaluating sources. As you begin to work in the library, you will see that a library search is a very time-consuming process. Just locating sources in a large library takes time. Sometimes a book you want will have been checked out by another library patron; in such a case you will have to submit a "recall notice" to the librarian asking that the book be returned and reserved for you. You may also find that you need to obtain materials from another library through an interlibrary loan, another time-consuming process. Plan to spend two to three hours in the library each day for the first month of your research project. After that you will spend less time in the library.

If your research project involves primary research, begin to plan for that research while you are writing your search strategy. Allow approximately one to two weeks for conducting your primary research, depending on its nature and scope.

Schedule one to two weeks for preliminary writing. To make sense of your subject and answer your starting question, you will need to spend time and effort in studying and writing about your sources. Eventually, you will be able to express your understanding of the subject in a thesis statement, which will help control the shape and direction of the research paper.

Finally, give yourself enough time to plan, organize, and write the research paper. You will need to outline your paper and to arrange your source information in order to present your findings in a meaningful way. Allow yourself one to two weeks for organizing and writing a rough draft of your paper and an additional week for revising, polishing, and editing your draft. If you intend to hire a typist, allow an extra week for the typing of the paper.

As you can see from this overview, most research projects take an entire college term to complete. Recall from Chapter 1 the stages in the research process: preparation, incubation, illumination, and verification. You need to consider all four stages as you plan your research project. Allow time for your library search, time for ideas to incubate in your subconscious, time for arriving at an understanding of your topic, and time to verify that understanding in writing.

What follows is a sample time frame:

Week 1	Select research topic; Articulate starting question; Gather and organize research materials; Draw up search strategy; Plan research time frame; Read general background sources.
Week 2	Build working bibliography; Locate sources in library.
Week 3	Read and evaluate sources; Take notes on relevant sources; Comment on sources in research notebook.
Week 4	Conduct any primary research; Complete reading of sources; Identify gaps in research and find more sources if necessary.
Week 5	Preliminary writing in research notebook—summary, synthesis, critique activities; Begin to define an answer to the starting question.
Week 6	Write a thesis statement; Plan and outline the research paper.

Week 7   Write a rough draft of the research paper; Keep careful track of sources used (quotes and paraphrases).

Week 8   Revise and polish draft; Check correct use and documentation of sources.

Week 9   Type and proofread final copy.

EXERCISES

1. Outline the time frame of your research project; refer to a current academic calendar from your school and to any deadlines provided by your teacher.
2. Plan any primary research you intend to conduct for your research project.

Locating Sources

After defining your search strategy and outlining a time frame for your research project, you can begin the actual research process in the library. Refer to the relevant section of Chapter 3, "Library Resources," to find sources for your topic.

EXERCISE

Begin your library search, writing down source citations in your working bibliography. Refer to the relevant section of Chapter 3 and to the model search outlined in Chapter 6, 7, 8, or 9 for explicit direction in the process of research for your chosen discipline.

Reading for Meaning

The sources you locate in your library search are the raw material for your research paper. You might supplement these sources with primary data, but generally your research paper will be based on information from written secondary sources. Your job is to read carefully and actively. Reading is not a passive process by which the words float into your mind and become registered in your memory. If you read passively, you will not comprehend the author's message. You have probably had the experience of rereading a passage several times and still not understanding a word of it. In such cases, you were not reading actively. Perhaps you have fallen asleep while reading—again, you were not reading actively. In active reading, the reader is engaged in a dialogue with the author.

To be fair in your interpretation of what you are reading, you must first be receptive to what the author is saying. Therefore, you must approach anything you read with an open mind. Before actually beginning to read, look at any nontextual materials that accompany the source, including information about the author, the publisher, the origin of the work, the title, and the organizational plan or format of the work.

The Author

Questions to consider about the author include the following: Who is the author? Is the author living or dead? What is the author's nationality? What other works did the author write? What are the author's qualifications and/or biases on this particular topic?

The Publication

You should look at the publication information for the source. What was the date of publication? Would the particular context help you understand the work? It is also important to evaluate the medium in which the work appears. Was this an article published in a popular magazine, such as *Ladies' Home Journal*, or was it a paper in a scholarly journal, such as *College and Research Libraries*? The title of the work itself may reveal some important information. Does the title seem significant? Does it indicate the probable conclusions or main points of the article or book? Does it provide a clue to some controversy? Authors provide titles as indicators of what the work will contain, so we should be sensitive to the title of any work we read.

The Organization

Finally, before you read the work, look at the author's organizational plan. For a book, look at the table of contents, the chapter headings, and the major subdivisions. Judging from these clues, ask yourself what the author's main points are likely to be. What does the author seem to consider important about the subject? For articles, look at any subdivisions or headings. These will help you to understand the overall structure of the article.

Active Reading

Once you have completed your preliminary overview of the work, you are ready to begin the actual reading process. Plan to read a work that you need to understand thoroughly at least twice. During the first reading, go through the work at a relatively quick pace, either a section or a chapter at a time. If an article is relatively short, you can read it through entirely at one sitting. As you go along, pay attention to key words or phrases and try to get a general idea of the author's main points. This reading will be more than a skimming of the work; you should be able to generally understand what you have read on this first time through.

Then, read the work again, carefully and slowly. Use a highlighter or a pencil to underline key ideas and to write in the margins of your own books or photocopied articles. Of course, if you are borrowing a book from the library, you will not be able to underline on the book itself. In that case, record key ideas on your notecards or in your research notebook. The second time you read, stop frequently to absorb the information and interpret it in your own mind. For each paragraph or section of the article or chapter, jot down on the page itself or on notecards a sentence or two that captures the main idea. Be sure that these marginal notes are *in your own words*. It is crucial that you paraphrase the author's points rather than simply reiterating them in his or her words. The examples below show acceptable and unacceptable paraphrasing:

Original Passage

During the last two years of my medical course and the period which I spent in the hospitals as house physician, I found time, by means of serious encroachment on my night's rest, to bring to completion a work on the history of scientific research into the thought world of St. Paul, to revise and enlarge the *Question of the Historical Jesus* for the second edition, and together with Widor to prepare an edition of Bach's preludes and fugues for the organ, giving with each piece directions for its rendering. (Albert Schweitzer, *Out of My Life and Thought*. New York: Mentor, 1963, p. 94.)

A Poor Paraphrase

Schweitzer said that during the last two years of his medical course and the period he spent in the hospitals as house physician he found time, by encroaching on his night's rest, to bring to completion several works. [Note: This paraphrase uses too many words and phrases from the original.]

A Good Paraphrase

Albert Schweitzer observed that by staying up late at night, he was able to finish several major works while still attending medical school and serving as a "house physician." [Note: This paraphrase is appropriate because it does not use the author's own words, except in one instance, which is acknowledged by quotation marks.]

Making Section-by-Section Summaries

After completing each section or chapter by making marginal notes, write a brief (three- or four-sentence) summary on your notecards or in your notebook of what you read. Again, use your own words when writing these summaries. If the material is particularly difficult, you may need to stop and summarize more frequently than after each section or chapter. If it is relatively simple to understand or not particularly pertinent to your topic, take fewer notes and write shorter summaries. At any rate, be certain that you are internalizing what you read—the best gauge of your understanding of the material is your ability to put it into your own words in the form of paraphrases and short section-by-section summaries.

Underlining

Underlining is an important component of the reading process, but only when you underline discriminately. Underline important ideas or arguments only. If you underline everything, or if you underline information that is unimportant, it will do more harm than good. Also, make sure that you understand an entire paragraph or section before underlining it or you may highlight the wrong information.

Reviewing

After completing your marginal notes and summaries, go back and review the entire piece, taking time to think about what you read. Evaluate the significance of what you learned by relating the work to your own project and starting question. Your research notebook is the place to record the observations and insights gained in your reading. How does the work fit in with other works you read on the same topic? What ideas seem particularly relevant to your own research? Does the work help to answer your starting question? Answering such questions in your research notebook will help you to put each work you read into the context of your own research.

Perceiving the Author's Organizational Plan

In writing, you should attempt to make your organizational plan clear to your potential readers. Similarly, while reading, you should attempt to discern the organizational plan of the author. One of the best ways to understand the author's plan is to try to reconstruct it through outlining. For an article or book that seems especially important to your research project, you may want to understand the material in a more complete and orderly way than that gained through notetaking or summarizing. You can accomplish this goal by constructing an outline of what you have read.

In a well-written piece, the writer will have given you clues to important or key information. Your summaries should identify main ideas that are most likely to be the main points of the outline. However, you will still need to go back to the work to identify the author's secondary, supporting points, including examples, illustrations, and supporting arguments used to make each individual argument clearer or more persuasive. In outlining a key source, you can come to understand it more fully. Again, be sure that all the points in your outline have been stated in your own words rather than the words of the author.

EXERCISE

The following article has been included to illustrate how to go about underlining, annotating, summarizing, and outlining a key source. Read the article carefully, noticing which ideas have been underlined and which annotated. Do you agree with my identification of key ideas? The final third of the article has not been underlined, summarized, or included on the outline that follows. Try out these four techniques (underlining, annotating, summarizing, outlining) by finishing the interpretation of the article, beginning immediately after the quotation from Paul Dirac:

A. Underline key ideas.

B. Annotate the article by putting notes in the margins that paraphrase the author's words.

C. Summarize in your own words the main ideas of the last section of the article, as you would on a notecard or in your research notebook (three to four sentences).

D. Complete the outline following the article.

The Scientific Aesthetic
By K. C. Cole

"Poets say science takes away from the beauty of the stars—mere globs of gas atoms. Nothing is 'mere.' I too can see the stars on a desert night, and feel them. But do I see less or more? The vastness of the heavens stretches my imagination—stuck on this carrousel, my little eye can catch one-million-year-old light . . . For far more marvelous is the truth than any artists of the past imagined! Why do the poets of the present not speak of it? What men are poets who can speak of Jupiter if he were like a man, but if he is an immense spinning sphere of methane and ammonia must be silent?"

Beauty and creativity in science

This poetic paragraph appears as a footnote in, of all places, a physics textbook: *The Feynman Lectures on Physics* by Nobel laureate Richard Feynman. Like so many others of his kind, <u>Feynman scorns the suggestion that science strips nature of her beauty,</u> leaving only a naked set of equations. Knowledge of nature, he thinks, deepens the awe, enhances the appreciation. But Feynman has also been known to remark that the only quality art and theoretical physics have in common is the <u>joyful anticipation that artists and physicists alike feel when they contemplate a blank piece of paper.</u>

What is the kinship between these seemingly dissimilar species, science and art? Obviously there is some—if only because so often the same people are attracted to both. The image of Einstein playing his violin is only too familiar, or Leonardo with his inventions. It is a standing joke in some circles that all it takes to make a string quartet is four mathematicians sitting in the same room. Even Feynman plays the bongo drums. (He finds it curious that while he is almost always identified as the physicist who plays the bongo drums, the few times that he has been asked to play the drums, ''the introducer never seems to find it necessary to mention that I also do theoretical physics.'')

One commonality is that art and science often cover the same territory. A tree is fertile ground for both the poet and the botanist. The relationship between mother and child, the symmetry of snowflakes, the effects of light and color, and the structure of the human form are studied equally by painters and psychologists, sculptors and physicians. The origins of the universe, the nature of life, and the meaning of death are the subjects of physicists, philosophers, and composers.

Art and science cover same ground

Yet when it comes to approach, the affinity breaks down completely. Artists approach nature with feeling; scientists rely on logic. Art elicits emotion; science makes sense. Artists are supposed to care; scientists are supposed to think.

Differing approaches art = emotion science = logic

At least one physicist I know rejects this distinction out of hand: ''What a strange misconception has been taught to people,'' he says. ''They have been taught that one cannot be disciplined enough to discover the truth unless one is indifferent to it. Actually, there is no point in looking for the truth unless what it is makes a difference.''

The history of science bears him out. Darwin, while sorting out the clues he had gathered in the Galapagos Islands that eventually led to his theory of evolution, was hardly detached. ''I am like a gambler and love a wild experiment,'' he wrote. ''I am horribly afraid.'' ''I trust to a sort of instinct and God knows can seldom give any reason for my remarks.'' ''All nature is perverse and will not do as I wish it. I wish I had my old barnacles to work at, and nothing new.''

The scientists who took various sides in the early days of the quantum debate were scarcely less passionate. Einstein said that if classical notions of cause and effect had to be renounced, he would rather be a cobbler or even work in a gambling casino than be a physicist. Niels Bohr called Einstein's attitude appalling, and accused him of high treason. Another major physicist, Erwin Schroedinger, said, ''If one has to stick to this damned quantum jumping, then I regret having ever been involved in this thing.'' On a more positive note, Einstein spoke about the universe as a ''great, eternal riddle'' that ''beckoned like a liberation.'' As the late Harvard professor George Sarton wrote in the preface to his *History of Science,* ''There are blood and tears in geometry as well as in art.''

Instinctively, however, most people do not like the idea that scientists can be passionate about their work, any more than they like the idea that

Artists and scientists are both passionate and in control of their work

poets can be calculating. <u>But it would be a sloppy artist indeed who worked without tight creative control, and no scientist ever got very far by sticking exclusively to the scientific method.</u> Deduction only takes you to the next step in a straight line of thought, which in science is often a dead end. "Each time we get into this log jam," says Feynman, "it is because the methods we are using are just like the ones we have used before . . . A new idea is extremely difficult to think of. It takes fantastic imagination."

<u>The direction of the next great leap is as often as not guided by the scientist's vision of beauty.</u> Einstein's highest praise for a theory was not that it was good but that it was beautiful. His strongest criticism was "Oh, how ugly!" He often spoke about the aesthetic appeal of ideas. "Pure logic could never lead us to anything but tautologies," wrote the French physicist Henri Poincaré. "It could create nothing new; not from it alone can any science issue."

Poincaré also described the role that aesthetics plays in science as "a delicate sieve," an arbiter between the telling and the misleading, the signals and the distractions. Science is not a book of lists. The facts need to be woven into theories like tapestries out of so many tenuous threads. Who knows when (and how) the right connections have been made? <u>Sometimes, the most useful standard is aesthetic:</u> Erwin Schroedinger refrained from publishing the first version of his now famous wave equations because they did not fit the then-known facts. "I think there is a moral to this story," Paul Dirac commented later. "Namely, that it is more important to have beauty in one's equations than to have them fit experiment . . . It seems that if one is working from the point of view of getting beauty in one's equations, and if one has really a sound insight, one is on a sure line of progress."

Sometimes the connection between art and science can be even more direct. Danish physicist Niels Bohr was known for his fascination with cubism—especially "that an object could be several things, could change, could be seen as a face, a limb, and a fruit bowl." He went on to develop his philosophy of complementarity, which showed how an electron could change, could be seen either as a particle or a wave. Like cubism, complementarity allowed contradictory views to coexist in the same natural frame.

Some people wonder how art and science ever got so far separated in the first place. The definitions of both disciplines have narrowed considerably since the days when science was natural philosophy, and art included the work of artisans of the kind who build today's fantastic particle accelerators. "Science acquired its present limited meaning barely before the nineteenth century," writes Sir Geoffrey Vickers in Judith Wechsler's collection of essays *On Aesthetics in Science.* "It came to apply to a method of testing hypotheses about the natural world by observations or experiments . . ." Surely, this has little to do with art. But Vickers suspects the difference is deeper. People want to believe that science is a rational process, that it is describable. Intuition is not describable, and should therefore be relegated to a place outside the realm of science. "Because our culture has somehow generated the unsupported and improbable belief that everything real must be fully describable, it is unwilling to acknowledge the existence of intuition."

There are, of course, substantial differences between art and science. Science is written in the universal language of mathematics; it is, far more than art, a shared perception of the world. Scientific insights can be tested by the good old scientific method. And scientists have to try to be dispassionate about the conduct of their work—at least enough so that their passions do not disrupt the outcome of experiments. Of course, sometimes they do: "Great thinkers are never passive before the facts," says Stephen Jay Gould. "They have hopes and hunches, and they try hard to construct the world in their light. Hence, great thinkers also make great errors."

But in the end, the connections between art and science may be closer than we think, and they may be rooted most of all in a person's motivations to do art, or science, in the first place. MIT metallurgist Cyril Stanley Smith became interested in the history of his field and was surprised to find that the earliest knowledge about metals and their properties was provided by objects in art museums. "Slowly, I came to see that this was not a coincidence but a consequence of the very nature of discovery, for discovery derives from aesthetically motivated curiosity and is rarely a result of practical purposefulness."

Outline

I. Introductory quote from physics book

    A. Feynman rejects the idea that science makes nature ugly

    B. Creativity is in both science and art

II. How art and science are similar and different

    A. Common subjects or themes

B. Differing approaches to subject matter

C. Both science and art include emotions and logic

III. The importance of control and creativity

A. Great breakthroughs in science often come from the scientist's ''vision of beauty''

B. Aesthetics serve as ''a delicate sieve'' for science

IV. Connections between art and science

[Continue outline]

■ ILLUMINATION AND VERIFICATION

An essential part of your research is the evolution of your understanding of the subject. As you read and evaluate your sources, you will be seeking a solution to your starting question. Several preliminary writing tasks can help you evaluate your sources and understand your topic.

Evaluation

In your working bibliography, you record the information needed to find a source in the library. Once you have located a source, you need to evaluate it for its usefulness to your particular research project and to your starting question. Every library search will entail the systematic interaction of examination, evaluation, and possibly elimination of material. It is not unusual for an article with a promising title to turn out to be totally irrelevant. Do not be discouraged by dead ends of this sort—they are an accepted and expected part of the library search. You must not hesitate to eliminate irrelevant or unimportant information. As you read each source, consider the following criteria (see also the section on active reading above).

Evaluative Criteria

1. The relevance of the work to your topic and starting question
2. The timeliness or recency of the work (particularly important in scientific research projects)
3. The author of the work (based on all available information)
4. The prestige or nature of the journal (scholarly or popular press)
5. The controversial nature of the source (whether it agrees with or contradicts other sources)

As you encounter new sources, you will be the best judge of whether or not a particular source contains useful information for your research project. Record your evaluative comments in your research notebook.

EXERCISE

Write an evaluation of one book or article you have located in your library search (or an article assigned by your teacher). Use the above criteria for evaluating the source.

Preliminary Writing from Sources

Reading actively and taking accurate and careful notes are the first important techniques for writing from sources. Your reading notes will form the basis for all your subsequent writing about that particular source. In this section, we will discuss three important approaches to source books and articles that result in three different kinds of writing. These are (1) summarizing the main points of the source book or article in condensed form, (2) synthesizing the information found in two or more related sources, and (3) critiquing the information found in one or more sources.[1] These three kinds of writing differ from each other in the approach the writer takes to the source in each instance. Your purpose for writing summaries will be different from your purpose for writing syntheses or critiques. Although the source or subject may remain the same, your approach to that source or subject can change, depending on your purpose. Using different approaches to the same sources will help you to understand those sources better.

Summarizing

When *summarizing*, the writer takes an entirely objective approach to the subject and the source. The writer of summaries is obliged to accurately record the author's meaning. To do this, of course, the summarizer must first understand the source and identify its key ideas during active reading. The marginal notes and section-by-section summaries will provide the basis for the written summary of the source. In general, a summary will be about one-third as long as the source itself.

To write a summary, first transcribe your short marginal reading notes onto a separate sheet of paper. Read these over and decide what you think the author's main point was. Write the main point in the form of a *thesis statement* that encapsulates the central idea of the whole article. Be sure not to use the author's words; rather, paraphrase the author's central idea in your own words. Then, by combining the thesis sentence with the marginal notes, you will have constructed the first outline of your summary. Revise the outline for coherence and logical progression of thought.

Next, write the first draft of your summary, following your outline rather than the source. Use your own words, not the words of the author, paraphrasing and condensing his or her ideas. If you want to use the author's own words for a particular passage, use quotation marks to indicate the author's exact words and insert a page reference in parentheses:

> Cole observes that "a tree is fertile ground for both the poet and the botanist" (p. 54).

In the first few sentences of your summary, introduce the source book or article and its author:

> In the article "The Scientific Aesthetic" (*Discover*, Dec., 1983), the author, K. C. Cole, discusses the relationship of aesthetics and science.

Follow this context information with the thesis statement, which reflects the author's position, and then with the summary itself.

> Thesis: Cole thinks that there are close connections between science and art that stem from the creative spirit of humanity.

Do not insert your own ideas or opinions into the summary. Your summary should reflect the content of the original as accurately and objectively as possible.

When you have completed the first draft of your summary, review the source to be certain that it is complete and accurate. Then reread your summary to determine if it is clear, coherent, and concise. Next, revise the summary for style and usage, making your sentences flow smoothly and correcting your grammar and punctuation. Finally, write and proofread the final draft. Remember, your summary will recount objectively and in your own words what someone else wrote.

Synthesizing

When *synthesizing*, you will approach your material with an eye to finding the relationships among sources. Your purpose will be to discern those relationships and present them coherently and persuasively to your potential readers. Again, the process begins with the active reading of the sources. As you read, highlight and summarize key ideas from your sources in the margins. But instead of simply summarizing the information in one source, look for relationships between ideas in one source and those in another. The sources may be related in one or more of the following ways:

- They may provide *examples* of a general topic, or one source may serve to exemplify another.
- They may *describe* or *define* the topic you are researching.
- They may present information or ideas that can be *compared or contrasted.*

You must decide in what way or ways your sources are related. When you have decided upon the relationships among the sources, write a thesis sentence that embodies that relationship. This thesis sentence should indicate the central idea of your synthesis.

Write an outline of your synthesis paper based on the organizational plan suggested by the thesis statement. This outline should articulate the relationship you have discerned among the sources. For example, if the passages you read all served to *describe* the same topic (perhaps life in colonial New England), the structure might look like this:

I.   Opening paragraph with contextualizing information about the sources and the particular situation, life in colonial New England.

II.   Thesis statement describing the relationship to be discussed: Life in colonial New England is *described* by historians and participants as rigid in its social structure.

III.   Description 1 (based on source 1: an historical work about the New England colonies).

IV.   Description 2 (based on source 2: a diary or journal written by an early colonist).

V.   Description 3 (based on source 3: a sermon written by a colonial preacher).

VI.   Conclusion: All the sources combined contribute to a description of the rigid social structure in colonial New England.

After outlining your synthesis, write the first draft of your paper. In the introductory section of your synthesis, just as in the summary, introduce the sources and their authors. Follow the introduction of sources with your thesis expressing the relationship among the sources. As you write your first draft, keep your thesis in mind, selecting from your sources only the information that develops and supports that thesis. You may want to discuss each source separately, as in the example above, or you may prefer to organize your paper to present major supporting points in the most logical sequence, using information from the sources to develop or support those points. Be sure that you acknowledge all ideas and information from your sources each time you use them in your synthesis.

Upon completion of your first draft, review the sources to be sure you have represented the authors' views fairly and cited source ideas and information properly. Reread your first draft to make sure it is organized logically and that it supports your thesis effectively. Be certain that you have included sufficient transitions between the various sections of your synthesis. Revise your synthesis for style and correctness. Finally, write and proofread the final draft of your synthesis. In general, a synthesis should give the reader a persuasive interpretation of the relationship you have discerned among your sources.

Critiquing

In the third kind of writing from sources, *critiquing*, the writer takes a critical or evaluative approach to a particular source. When writing critiques, you argue a point that seems important to you based on your own evaluation of the issues and ideas you have encountered in your sources. Critiques are necessarily more difficult to write than summaries or syntheses, because they require that you think critically and come to an independent judgment about a topic. However, critiques are also the most important kind of writing from sources to master, because in many research situations you are asked to formulate your own opinion and critical judgment (as opposed to simply reporting or presenting the information written by others).

As in the other forms of writing from sources, critiquing begins with active reading and careful notetaking from a source. You must objectively identify the author's main ideas and points before you can evaluate and critique them. Once you understand the source and the issues it addresses, you are in a position to appraise it critically. Analyze the source in one or more of the following ways:

- What is said, by whom, and to whom?
- How significant are the author's main points and how well are the points made?
- What assumptions does the author make that underlie his or her arguments?
- What issues has the author overlooked or what evidence has he or she failed to consider?
- Are the author's conclusions valid?
- How well is the source written (regarding clarity, organization, language, etc.)?
- What stylistic or rhetorical features affect the source's content?

Other questions may occur to you as you critique the source, but these will serve to get you started in your critical appraisal. To think critically about a source, look behind the arguments themselves to the basis for those arguments. What reasons does the author give for holding a certain belief? In addition, try to discern what assumptions the author is making about the subject. Do you share those assumptions? Are they valid assumptions? It is your job to evaluate fairly but with discerning judgment, since this evaluation will be the core of your critique. Formulate a thesis that states your evaluation. Do not feel that your evaluation must necessarily be negative; it is possible to make a positive critique, a negative critique, or a critique that cites both kinds of qualities.

Write an outline of your critique, including the following:

1. An introduction of the subject you wish to address and the source article you wish to critique. Be sure to include a complete citation for the source.
2. A statement of your judgment about the issue in the form of a thesis. In that thesis statement, give your own opinion, which will be supported in the critique itself.
3. The body of the critique. First briefly summarize the source itself. Then review the issues at hand and explain the background facts and assumptions that your readers must understand to share your

judgment. Use the bulk of your critique to review the author's position in light of your judgment and evaluation.

4. Your conclusion, which reminds the reader of your main points and the reasons you made them.

After completing your outline, write the first draft of your critique, using your outline as a guide. Make certain that all your points are well supported with specific references to the source. Also, make certain that your main points are related to each other and to the thesis statement.

Review the source to be sure you have represented the author's ideas accurately and fairly. Reread your first draft to determine whether your thesis is clearly stated, your paper logically organized, and your thesis adequately and correctly supported. Revise your critique for content, style, and correctness. Finally, write and proofread the final draft of your critique.

Unfortunately, because critiques are subjective, it is not possible to be any more explicit in guiding your writing of them. The substance of the critique will depend entirely upon the judgment you make about the source. Remember, though, that a critique needs to be well supported and your opinion well justified by evidence drawn from the source itself. In the exercises that follow, you will have the opportunity to practice writing summaries, syntheses, and critiques. It will also be valuable to write summaries, syntheses, and critiques of sources you are using in your research project as a way to better understand that topic. Do all such preliminary writing in your research notebook.

EXERCISES

1. *Summary*

    Carefully read, underline, and annotate one of the articles that follow. Using the procedure described above, write a summary of the article you have chosen.

2. *Synthesis*

    A. Use two or more of the following articles as the basis for an extended *definition* of sexual harassment. The articles that are particularly relevant to definition are Linenberger, "What Behavior Constitutes Sexual Harassment?" and Renick, "Sexual Harassment at Work: Why It Happens, What to Do About It."

    B. Use two or more of the following articles to *compare and contrast* the solutions to sexual harassment presented by the authors. The articles that are particularly relevant are Renick, "Sexual Harassment at Work: Why It Happens, What to Do About It"; and Saunders, "Sexual Harassment."

    C. Use the illustrations and examples from two or more of the following articles to *describe* sexual harassment in the workplace.

3. *Critique*

Choose one of the following articles and write an evaluative critique. Remember, in a critique it is appropriate to include your opinions and experiences as well as your reactions to the article itself. Some issues you might want to focus on are (1) the fairness of the definition of sexual harassment to men in the office, (2) the fairness of making women provide proof of harassment, (3) the relationship of harassment to office politics in general, and (4) the assumption that sexual harassment only happens to women.

What Behavior Constitutes Sexual Harassment?
By Patricia Linenberger

Patricia Linenberger is an Associate Professor of Business Administration (Business Law) at the University of Wyoming.

SEXUAL HARASSMENT in employment promises to be one of the most complex and controversial issues facing business in the next decade. Although courts have repeatedly found it to be a violation of Title VII of the 1964 Civil Rights Act and a basis for tort liability,[1] business people are still in a quandary, not knowing exactly what behavior is prohibited. One commentator remarked, "The simple truth is that, with the exception of blatant instances, both employers and employees may expect a period of uncertainty in determining just what conduct constitutes sexual harassment."[2]

There are several reasons for this uncertainty. First, the courts thus far have dealt only with the most blatant kinds of behavior. The conduct complained of in past cases was so aggravated that there was no question of its social acceptability. And, of course, the courts have not specified the types of conduct which, in the future, might result in liability for sexual harassment.

Second, because the EEOC Guidelines are broadly based, they are of limited use in determining prohibited behavior. They include many phrases such as "conduct of a sexual nature" and "intimidating, hostile, or offensive working environment," which must be defined on a case-by-case basis.[3]

Third, research studies reveal that there is a wide divergence of perceptions as to what words or actions should result in liability for sexual harassment. Employers and employees are aware that two well-intentioned people could thoroughly misread each other's signals. What one person intends or views as a compliment might be classified by another as sexual harassment. This uncertainty has caused concern among those involved in employee relations. People are confused and unsure of what is acceptable or unacceptable in their individual relations with business colleagues.

It is the purpose of this article to aid personnel executives and their legal counsel in recognizing the behavior which is likely to

---

[1] This article will not attempt to discuss all possible tort actions. For more complete coverage see Montgomery, "Sexual Harassment in the Workplace: A Practitioner's Guide to Tort Actions," 10 *Golden Gate L. Rev.* 879 (1980).

[2] Siniscalco, "Sexual Harassment and Employer Liability: The Flirtation that Could Cost a Fortune," 6 *Employee Relations L. J.* 277 (1980), p. 286.

[3] 45 *Fed. Reg.* 74677 (1981) (codified in 29 CFR 1604.11).

be interpreted as sexual harassment. The article will review the judicial treatment of sexual harassment, and the factual situations in both Title VII cases and tort actions will be described in some detail in order to illustrate the behavior that the courts have found to be clearly unacceptable. The problem of recognizing the more subtle kinds of sexual harassment will be investigated. The EEOC Guidelines, various governmental agency definitions, and two research projects will be examined for guidance in identifying the less blatant types of sexual harassment. The latter part of the article will present and consider ten factors which should be analyzed by employers and employees when evaluating behavior for potential sexual harassment liability.

Title VII Court Decisions

Although the issue has not yet been addressed by the United States Supreme Court, sexual harassment has been recognized as a cause of action under Title VII in the decisions of four federal circuit courts.[4] To date there is no circuit court which has denied the Title VII cause of action.

Courts hearing Title VII cases have had no difficulty in ascertaining whether sexual harassment had actually occurred. Most courts have dealt with factual situations which exhibited very aggravated sexual harassment. In most of the cases, the women's employment was terminated when they refused the undesired sexual advances of their

male superiors.[5] Typically, the male supervisors would invite the women to lunch or to after work social events, make sexual remarks, and suggest that sexual affairs would enhance the women's employment status by creating more satisfactory working relationships. When the sexual advances were rebuffed many of the women were fired or denied promotions and raises.

In other cases women employees brought suit because their working conditions were made intolerable by offensive sexual conduct.[6] Examples of the offensive conduct were: lewd sexual comments, innuendos, and gestures[7]; sexually derogatory statements[8]; requests for women to remove their clothes[9]; teasing with photographs of nude women and placing obscene cartoons at a woman's place of work;[10] public speculation on the virginity of female workers[11]; and grabbing women in intimate areas of their bodies.[12]

Because the decisions did not specifically state what comments were judged to be lewd or sexually derogatory, there is still

---

[4] *Tomkins v. Public Service Electric & Gas Co.*, 422 FSupp 553 (DC NJ, 1976), 12 EPD ¶11,267, rev'd 568 F2d 1044 (CA-3, 1977), 15 EPD ¶7954; *Garber v. Saxon Industries, Inc.*, 552 F2d 1032 (CA-4, 1977), 14 EPD ¶7587; *Miller v. Bank of America*, 418 FSupp 233 (DC Cal, 1976), 13 EPD ¶11,357, rev'd and rem'd 600 F2d 211 (CA-9, 1979), 20 EPD ¶30,086; and *Barnes v. Train* (DC DofC, 1974), 13 FEP 123, rev'd and rem'd sub nom *Barnes v. Costle*, 561 F2d 983 (CA DofC, 1977), 14 EPD ¶7755.

[5] *Miller*, cited at note 4; *Williams v. Saxbe*, 413 FSupp 654 (DC DofC, 1976), 12 EPD ¶11,130, rev'd on other grounds sub nom *Williams v. Bell*, 587 F2d 1240 (CA DofC, 1978), 17 EPD ¶8695, decision on remand *Williams v. Civiletti*, 487 FSupp 1387 (DC DofC, 1980), 23 EPD ¶30,916; *Tomkins*, cited at note 4; *Barnes*, cited at note 4; *Heelan v. Johns-Manville Corp.*, 451 FSupp 1382 (DC Colo, 1978), 16 EPD ¶8330; *Munford v. James T. Barnes & Co.*, 441 FSupp 459 (DC Mich, 1977), 77 LC ¶8233; *Rinkel v. Associated Pipeline Contractors (DC Alas, 1978)*, 16 EPD ¶8331; and *Stringer v. Commonwealth of Pennsylvania Department of Community Affairs*, 446 FSupp 704 (DC Pa, 1978), 17 EPD ¶8565.

[6] *Brown v. City of Guthrie* (DC Okla, 1980), 30 EPD ¶33,031; *Kyriazi v. Western Electric Co.*, 461 FSupp 894 (DC NJ, 1978), 18 EPD ¶8700; and *Continental Can Co. v. State of Minnesota*, 297 NW2d 241 (Minn SCt, 1980), 23 EPD ¶30,997 (decided under state statute similar to Title VII).

[7] *Brown*, cited at note 6.

[8] *Continental Can*, cited at note 6.

[9] *Brown*.

[10] *Kyriazi*, cited at note 6.

[11] *Ibid*.

[12] *Continental Can*.

doubt as to what activity courts will determine to be prohibited behavior. However, many of the physical abuses complained of were so outrageous that reasonable people would be likely to agree that they constituted sexual harassment.

In several instances courts have ruled that sexual harassment is only actionable under Title VII if acquiescence is a condition of continued employment.[13] These courts have required the plaintiffs to show that acquiescence to the sexual harassment was required in exchange for employment opportunities such as promotion, raises, or retention of the job. In one of the cases the court stated that it was not the supervisor's frequent advances that violated Title VII but the termination of the employment when the victim refused to acquiesce to the advances.[14]

Similarly, when a woman was harassed by a male coworker another court declined to grant relief.[15] The coworker made sexual advances and remarks but did not have the power to promise her anything with respect to her employment, nor was he in a position to refuse her any employment opportunities. Since acquiescence to the sexual harassment was not impliedly or expressly required as a condition of employment her claim was denied.

In contrast, two courts have liberally construed "condition of employment" to refer to the overall quality of the working environment.[16] They allowed actions for sexual harassment in situations where frequent and emotionally disturbing sexual demands were made but were not made as requirements for employment benefits or continued employment. The courts acknowledged that the harassment created an impermissible condition of employment by creating an intimidating, hostile, or offensive working environment. One court noted that Title VII must protect people who are sexually harassed but suffer no direct employment consequences.[17] Otherwise, employers would be free to allow sexual harassment with no liability, as long as no employment opportunity was denied an employee who refused to participate.

An examination of the recent court decisions reveals a variety of standards for determining the level of employer culpability required to incur Title VII liability for sexual harassment. The courts have taken several different positions.

The rule most burdensome for plaintiffs imposes employer liability for sexual harassment perpetrated by its employees only when: the offensive conduct contravened company policy; it occurred with the employer's knowledge; and the consequences were not rectified when discovered.[18] A similar but slightly less restrictive standard requires the employee to show that the employer had actual or constructive knowledge of the harassment at the time of its occurrence.[19] A third standard allows recovery when the employer fails to investigate and appropriately deal with a claim of sexual harassment.[20]

Lastly, one court has adopted the most expansive standard for employer liability by applying the doctrine of respondeat superior.[21] It allowed a cause of action for sexual harassment based solely upon the premise that an employer is vicariously responsible for the acts of a supervisor, its agent, which were committed within the scope of employment. Vicarious liability was imposed even though the employer had no knowledge of the supervisor's alleged sexual harassment and had a policy forbidding such conduct.

---

[13] *Heelan,* cited at note 5; *Clark v. World Airways* (DC DofC, 1980), 24 EPD ¶31,385; and *Smith v. Rust Engineering Co.* (DC Ala, 1978), 18 EPD ¶8698.

[14] *Heelan.*

[15] *Smith,* cited at note 13.

[16] *Brown; Bundy v. Jackson,* 641 F2d 934 (CA DofC, 1981), 24 EPD ¶31,439.

[17] *Bundy,* cited at note 15.

[18] *Barnes.*

[19] *Tomkins* (CA-3, 1977), cited at note 4.

[20] *Munford,* cited at note 5.

[21] *Miller* (CA-9, 1979).

Tort Actions

Although sexual harassment has received a great deal of attention in the legal and employment literature, very little has been written about the use of tort actions to remedy the problem. There are numerous possible tort actions which could be appropriate. They include, but are not limited to, assault and battery, intentional infliction of emotional distress, intentional interference with contractual relationships, fraud, false imprisonment, slander, libel, and invasion of privacy.

Although they are separate torts almost all cases of sexual harassment involve both assault and battery. Assault has been defined as an "intentional, unlawful offer to touch the person of another in a rude or angry manner under such circumstances as to create in the mind of the party alleging the assault a well-founded fear of an imminent battery coupled with the apparent present ability to effectuate the attempt."[22] In an assault the victim is put in "imminent apprehension" of a harmful or offensive contact with another person, although no actual contact occurs.[23]

When only verbal sexual harassment occurs it is doubtful if recovery in tort would be allowed. Unaccompanied by some show of physical force, words alone generally do not support a cause of action for assault. Even repeated and constant demands for sexual affairs would not be actionable.

In one instance an employer had made statements such as: "[T]his is going to be our year. I sincerely plan on going to bed with you so be thinking about when and where." He gave the woman employee a list of "the qualifications necessary for his secretary, [including] willing to go to bed with Supt." The court determined that, because the words were directed at future

events and did not create imminent apprehension, they did not constitute assault.[24]

However, when the words are combined with gestures, movement toward the woman, and actual battery, the reasonable apprehension of imminent offensive contact is created. Courts have found the requisite "imminent apprehensions" in two sexual harassment cases. In the first case the defendant extended his hand toward the plaintiff and made suggestive remarks.[25] In the second case the defendant repeatedly stopped his car within a few feet of a woman and moved the lower part of his body back and forth, creating a reasonable apprehension that he was planning to get out of his car and "inflict upon her immediately bodily harm. . . ."[26]

Prosser defines battery as an "intentional and unpermitted [contact] with the plaintiff's person."[27] Because of its offensive and insulting nature, battery exists even when the physical contact does not result in actual harm. The combined torts of assault and battery have been the cause of action in several sexual harassment cases. In various cases the plaintiffs have alleged that their employers, supervisors, and coemployees committed the following acts: "A supervisor grabbed plaintiff in [the supervisor's] office, pulled her towards him and kissed her . . . put his hand on plaintiff's leg and attempted to reach under her skirt . . . put his arms around plaintiff and his hands on her breasts."[28]

Several employees and officers "attacked, beat, struck, [and] assaulted [a female employee] by approaching her and threatening to forcibly kiss and embrace her

---

[22] *Western Union Tel. Co. v. Hill*, 26 Ala App 540 (1933), 150 So 709.

[23] *Restatement (Second) of Torts* Sections 21, 27 (1977).

[24] *Peter v. Aiken*, No. L-13891-77 (NJ SupCt, filed Dec. 8, 1977), amended complaint at 2, cited in Montgomery, cited at note 1, p. 901.

[25] *Western Union*, cited at note 22.

[26] *State v. Allen*, 245 NC 185 (1956), 95 SE2d 526.

[27] W. Prosser, *Law of Torts*, 4th ed. (1971), p. 34.

[28] *Peter v. Aiken*, cited at note 24, amended and supplemental complaint pp. 2–3, as cited in Montgomery, p. 901.

and forcibly kissing and embracing her.''[29] An employer ''with the use of force and violence placed his hands upon the private parts of the plaintiff herein and made efforts to seduce and offend the dignity of the plaintiff.''[30] Another supervisor asked ''how bad do you want your job?'' and then attempted to kiss the female employee ''while forcibly pinning her in her seat with one arm and fondling her breast. . . .''[31]

Recently courts have been more inclined to allow recovery for the infliction of emotional distress in sexual harassment cases. According to the *Restatement of Torts,* emotional distress includes ''fright, horror, grief, shame, humiliation, embarrassment, anger, chagrin, disappointment, and worry.''[32] To be actionable the defendant's conduct must be ''so outrageous in character, and so extreme in degree, as to go beyond all possible bounds of decency, and to be regarded as atrocious [and] utterly intolerable in a civilized community.''

Courts have acknowledged a cause of action in two cases. In one, a man repeatedly phoned a woman to suggest that she meet him for illicit sexual purposes. He also sent her obscene photographs of himself.[33] In the other, a man repeatedly phoned a woman, soliciting her for sex, and came to her home to expose himself.[34]

Definitions

Although there is some inconsistency and confusion in the judicial treatment of sexual harassment, there is one common element in the cases. They generally in-

---

[29] *Meyer v. Graphic Arts International Union Locals 63-A and 63-B,* 88 Cal App 3d 176 (1979), 151 Cal Rptr 597.

[30] *Skousen v. Nidy,* 90 Ariz 215 (Ariz, 1962), 367 P2d 248.

[31] *Gomez v. Construction & General Laborers Union,* No. H-5777 2-6 (Cal SupCt, Alameda County, filed Dec. 20, 1979), complaint, p. 5.

[32] *Restatement,* cited at note 23, Section 46, comment (j).

[33] *Mitran v. Williamson,* 21 Misc2d 106 (NY SupCt, 1960), 197 NYS2d 689.

[34] *Samms v. Eccles,* 11 Utah 2d 289 (1961), 358 P2d 344.

volved such offensive conduct that reasonable people would be likely to agree that the behavior involved was indeed sexual harassment. But personnel managers do not always have the luxury of such clear factual situations. They have to evaluate the day-to-day conduct in the workplace and make the often difficult determination of what behavior constitutes sexual harassment.

The article now will explore the sexual harassment recognition problem. It first will look at various possible definitions of sexual harassment and then review the sexual harassment perception difficulties as revealed in two surveys.

Sexual harassment has been defined by numerous employers, governmental agencies, civil rights groups, and commentators. Typical definitions will be examined for guidance in recognizing prohibited behavior.

The definition included in the EEOC Guidelines is the one most likely to be utilized in the future. The EEOC has defined sexual harassment as: ''Section 1604.11 Sexual harassment. a) Harassment on the basis of sex is a violation of Sec. 703 of Title VII. Unwelcome sexual advances, requests for sexual favors, and other verbal or physical conduct of a sexual nature constitute sexual harassment when (1) submission to such conduct is made either explicitly or implicitly a term or condition of an individual's employment, (2) submission to or rejection of such conduct by an individual is used as the basis for employment decisions affecting such individual, or (3) such conduct has the purpose or effect of unreasonably interfering with an individual's work performance or creating an intimidating, hostile, or offensive working environment.''[35]

Parts of this definition have been explained to a certain extent by the courts. They have given some indication of what constitutes a ''condition of employment,'' and examples of an ''intimidating, hostile,

---

[35] *Fed. Reg.* 74677, cited at note 3.

or offensive working environment'' have been discussed in several cases.

However, there have been no judicial interpretations of ''unwelcome sexual advances, requests for sexual favors, and other verbal and physical conduct of a sexual nature. . . .'' To be sure, the EEOC very intentionally wrote a broad, general definition so all possible forms of sexual harassment would be covered. But the problem with the definition is that it leaves management with the responsibility of recognizing sexual harassment on a day-to-day basis as it occurs. Management must determine what a sexual advance is and when it is unwelcome. What behavior constitutes verbal or physical conduct of a sexual nature?

In response to these questions the Guidelines answer as follows: ''b) In determining whether alleged conduct constitutes sexual harassment, the Commission will look at the record as a whole and the totality of the circumstances, such as the nature of the sexual advances and the context in which the alleged incidents occurred. The determination of the legality of a particular action will be made from the facts, on a case by case basis.''

Perhaps an examination of other definitions would clarify the issues. One commentator suggests that sexual harassment ''can be any or all of the following: staring at, commenting upon, or touching a woman's body; requests for acquiescence in sexual behavior; repeated nonreciprocated propositions for dates; demands for sexual intercourse; and rape.''[36] Although it is more specific than the EEOC definition, it is still very subjective. It more clearly indicates how to tell an unwelcome sexual advance from a welcome one. The unwelcome advance is persistent and nonreciprocated. But someone still has to make a factual determination of what particular stares and comments are inappropriate.

Governmental entities have made a studied effort to define sexual harassment but have had no more success than the EEOC or commentators. Two governmental definitions are included for comparison. The Michigan Employment Security Commission offers this definition: ''(1) sexual contact or threat of sexual contact which is not freely entered into and mutually agreeable to both parties; (2) the continual or repeated abuse of a sexual nature including, but not limited to, graphic commentaries on the victim's body, sexually degrading words used to describe the person, propositions of a sexual nature, or the display of sexually offensive pictures and objects; or (3) the threat or insinuation that the lack of sexual submission will adversely affect the victim's employment, wages or other conditions which affect the victim's livelihood.''[37]

The Mayor's Order for the District of Columbia defines sexual harassment as the: ''Exercise or attempt to exercise by a person of the authority of power of his or her position to control, influence, or affect the career, salary, or job of another employee or perspective employee in exchange for sexual favors. Sexual harassment may include, but is not limited to: (1) verbal harassment or abuse; (2) subtle pressure for sexual activity; (3) unnecessary patting or pinching; (4) constant brushing against another employee's body; (5) demanding sexual favors accompanied by implied or overt threat concerning an individual's employment status; (6) demanding sexual favors accompanied by implied or overt promise of preferential treatment with regard to an individual's employment status.''[38]

Note that in the District of Columbia ''*unnecessary* patting or pinching [emphasis added]'' is sexual harassment. It is inter-

---

[36] L. Farley, *Sexual Shakedown* (1978), pp. 14–15.

[37] February 23, 1979, memorandum from Commission Director S. Martin Taylor as cited in White, ''Job Related Sexual Harassment and Union Women: What Are Their Rights?'', 10 *Golden Gate L. Rev.* 929 (1980), p. 936.

[38] Mayor's Order for the District of Columbia No. 79–89 (May 24, 1979) amending Section 2 of Mayor's Order No. 75-230 (Oct. 31, 1975), cited in White, cited at note 37, p. 937.

esting to speculate on the situation where patting or pinching would be necessary.

It is apparent that the difficulty in defining sexual harassment is with the more subtle "working environment" type of harassment. The outrageous physical abuses are immediately perceived as offensive, but the daily, repeated subtle forms of sexual harassment can have as great or greater emotional impact on the victim.

Perceptions

Previously, it was concluded that, no matter what definition is used, factual determinations still have to be made to identify the specific behavior constituting sexual harassment. Unfortunately, research indicates that the factual determinations will be extremely difficult because most people cannot agree on what is impermissible conduct.

Many commentators believe that the victim defines the offense.[39] The perception of the recipient is the key factor in deciding what specific actions, words, or conduct actually constitute sexual advancement. They argue that in a sexual harassment case the perception of the perpetrator should be irrelevant.

If this is the correct approach there are other unanswered questions raised. Perceptions of what is intimidating, hostile, or offensive varies with the individual. Should these determinations be made on a subjective or objective basis? Must the workplace environment be suitable for the most sensitive employee or for the average employee? Can each potential victim determine what offends him or her and then hold the employer liable?

The variation in perceptions of what behavior constitutes sexual harassment was illustrated in the results of two surveys. The first, a survey of *Harvard Business Review*

subscribers, reveals that "The biggest issue is not defining sexual harassment but recognizing it when it occurs."[40] Collins summarized: "Too much of whatever harassment and/or sexual activity that occurs between employees is subject to interpretation. While employees who are clearly harassing others can be disciplined, I suspect that clear-cut cases will be hard to identify or prove."[41]

Respondents to the survey (approximately 2,000 managers and executives) agreed which extreme situations constitute sexual harassment but differed over the more subtle situations.[42] A large majority defined blatant behavior, such as constant pinching or patting or a lost promotion if a woman ended an affair with a supervisor, as sexual harassment. But the male and female respondents disagreed when defining the subtler visual and verbal harassment such as leering, ogling, joking, and innuendo.[43]

Male executives are generally unwilling to define sexual horseplay and subtle advances as clear-cut harassment. Subtle harassment is thought to be pervasive, but it is not easily recognized because it does not have such immediate consequences. With both male and female executives the seriousness of the harassment seems to depend on who is making the advance.[44] A supervisor's behavior was perceived as more threatening and serious than a coworker's.

The second survey was conducted by the Federal Merit Systems Protection Board to determine the nature and extent of sexual

---

[39] Zemke, "Sexual Harassment: Is Training the Key?", *Training/HRD* (February 1981), p. 22; Hubbartt, "Sexual Harassment: Coping with the Controversy," *Ad. Management* (August 1980), p. 34; and Comment, "Sexual Harassment and Title VII," 51 *N. Y. U. L. Rev.* 148 (1976), p. 162.

[40] This was a joint survey conducted by *Redbook* magazine and *Harvard Business Review*. The results were written up in both periodicals. Safran, "Sexual Harassment: The View from the Top," *Redbook* (March 1981), p. 45; Collins and Blodgett, "Some See It . . . Some Won't," *Harv. Bus. Rev.* (March–April 1981).

[41] Collins, cited at note 40, p. 92.

[42] *Ibid.*, p. 80.

[43] *Ibid.*, p. 81.

[44] *Ibid.*, p. 80.

harassment in the federal government.[45] Approximately 20,000 male and female federal employees participated in the survey. As with the *Harvard Business Review* survey, respondents had different perceptions of what behavior constituted sexual harassment depending upon who was the perpetrator.

The federal employee respondents agreed that supervisors should be held to a higher standard of conduct; however, the majority of both men and women considered the following to be sexual harassment whether done by a supervisor or a coworker. Uninvited and deliberate touching, leaning over, cornering, or pinching; uninvited pressure for sexual favors; or uninvited letters, phone calls, or materials of a sexual nature were classified as the "severe behavior."

The following behaviors, classified as "less severe," were considered to be sexual harassment by both men and women respondents only if the perpetrator was a supervisor. If the perpetrator was only a coworker the majority of women still considered the behavior sexual harassment, but the majority of the male respondents did not: uninvited sexual teasing, jokes, remarks or questions; uninvited sexually suggestive looks or gestures; or uninvited pressure for dates.

The problems both executives and employees have in recognizing sexual harassment have been outlined. Even if there were a way to accurately describe prohibited behaviors in words the problem of individual perception would still exist. The next section of the article is designed to aid employees and personnel managers in the difficult process of recognizing sexual harassment.

The Factual Determination

As indicated by the Guidelines and by the case law a factual determination must be

made on a case-by-case basis to determine what behavior constitutes sexual harassment. Extreme or severe harassment such as physical abuse or retaliatory employment action for refusal of a sexual advance is well recognized and presents little problem of identification. It is the more pervasive, subtle discrimination which affects the quality of the working environment that is difficult to identify.

According to the EEOC Guidelines the "totality of the circumstances" should be considered to determine if alleged conduct constitutes sexual harassment. The following factors should be considered when making a factual determination of what conduct constitutes sexual harassment.

Contrary to the opinions of several commentators (discussed earlier) these factors are based on the premise that the identification of sexual harassment should be made as a result of an objective assessment. The question to be asked is, "how would the reasonable person in the same or similar circumstances perceive the conduct?" The perception of the victim and the actual intent of the perpetrator should be irrelevant.

Severity of the conduct: as was seen in the survey of federal employees, different types of sexual harassment are perceived as "severe" or "less severe." Physical abuse and terms of employment which are contingent upon the granting of sexual favors are viewed as more severe than visual or verbal harassment. *Number and frequency of encounters:* the number of occasions of sexual harassment and the time span between occasions is relevant. It is generally perceived that persistent sexual harassment is more serious than isolated actions.

Apparent intent of the perpetrator: remember that the actual intent of the perpetrator should be irrelevant. The objective or apparent intent should be determined by asking what reasonable people would have intended had they acted in a similar manner. It should also be considered if the offensive behavior was directed at the victim or merely overheard or seen by the victim. *Relationship of the parties:* from both surveys

---

[45] Sexual Harassment in the Federal Government (Part II): Hearing Before the Subcommittee on Investigations of the House Committee on Post Office and Civil Service 96th Cong., 2nd Sess. 22 (1980).

previously discussed it was learned that superiors are expected to maintain a higher level of conduct. The identical conduct, when displayed by a supervisor, is perceived to be more serious and threatening than when displayed by a coworker.

Provocation of the victim: the victim's behavior and the type of clothing she wears should be considered when deciding what is an "unwelcome" sexual advance. It is doubtful if anyone would determine that a woman could ever be provocative enough to warrant serious physical abuse, but the *Harvard Business Review* study revealed that over three-fourths of the respondents agreed that "Women can often use their sexual attractiveness to their own advantage."[46] Women who wish to avoid visual and verbal harassment should be advised to refrain from wearing skirts slit to the thigh or plunging necklines.

Response of the victim: not only must the victim assume some responsibility for her clothing and behavior, she also must clearly communicate her opinion of offensive behavior. This factor should have limited weight, however, because many women might be afraid to respond honestly. *Apparent effect on the victim:* again, an objective evaluation should be made of the consequences of the offensive behavior. It should be determined if the victim appeared to be physically injured, embarrassed, humiliated, etc. An attempt should be made to assess the seriousness of the injury.

Working environment: the nature of the workplace often determines the appropriateness of the behavior. Reasonable people would expect different behavior from blue-collar coal miners than they would from professionals working in an office. *Public or private situations:* different types of harassment could be more serious depending on whether they were committed in a public or private situation. For example, sexual advances or physical contact would likely be more threatening in a private situation. On the other hand, visual and verbal harassment

_____
[46] Collins, p. 90.

could cause more injury in a public situation.

Men-women ratio in the workplace: it is relevant to consider the number of men and women working together. A woman alone, working with all men, would probably be more vulnerable to sexual harassment.

These factors must be considered in their relationship to each other. Depending upon the circumstances of a particular situation, various factors should be given different weight in consideration. In some situations only one factor may be relevant. Behavior, such as very threatening physical abuse, could constitute sexual harassment regardless of other factors such as frequency of encounters, relationship of the parties, provocation of the victim, or the privacy of the situation. Because of the severity of the conduct the other factors are irrelevant.

However, in cases of visual or verbal abuse, all ten factors may be relevant in making a factual determination of sexual harassment. Visual or verbal harassment may be only slightly irritating when it occurs in one isolated incident. But the same harassment, if repeated frequently and consistently over a period of time, could result in an intimidating, hostile, and offensive working environment.

Conclusion

The judiciary and the Equal Employment Opportunity Commission have agreed that employers have an affirmative duty to maintain a workplace free of sexual harassment. Unfortunately, little direction has been given to those in employee relations who must make the crucial decisions of what specific behaviors actually constitute sexual harassment.

Judicial treatment of sexual harassment under Title VII and in tort actions has illustrated only the most extreme kind of illegal behavior. Definitions offered by the EEOC, other governmental agencies, and commentators are so broad and general that they could conceivably cover a wide spectrum of behaviors. In addition, surveys of executives and federal employees reveal that there are wide variances in perceptions of what conduct constitutes sexual harassment.

In an attempt to aid those required to make factual determinations of sexual harassment, this article suggests ten factors for consideration. The use of these factors should facilitate the necessary decisionmaking and create a new awareness of sexual harassment in the workplace.

Sexual Harassment at Work:
Why It Happens, What to Do About It
By James C. Renick

James C. Renick is Assistant Professor of Public Administration and Social Work at the University of West Florida in Pensacola, Florida.

The intimate violation of women by men is sufficiently pervasive in American society as to be nearly invisible. Contained by internalized and structured forms of power, it has also been nearly inaudible. Women employed in the paid labor force—typically hired "as women," dependent on their income, and lacking job alternatives—are particularly vulnerable to intimate violation in the form of sexual abuse at work.[1] Only recently has this problem of sexual harassment of female workers been given any significant attention. A systematic body of literature on this subject doesn't exist. What does exist, however, are individual complaints by female workers throughout the country. The scant body of literature that has been produced suggests that the relatively powerless position occupied by female workers has contributed to their reluctance in exposing the issue. Finally, however, its impact on women's economic status and work opportunities, not to mention psychic health and self-esteem, is beginning to be explored and documented.

Sexual harassment is defined as any unwanted pressure involving one's sexuality. It includes verbal innuendos and suggestive comments, leering, gestures, unwanted physical contact (touching, pinching, etc.), rape and attempted rape. It is a form of harassment mainly perpetrated by men against women. As in rape and sexual assault, the assertion of power and dominance and the desire to humiliate are often more important than the sexual interaction itself. In addition to being a personal violation, sexual demands in the work place, especially between boss and employee, threaten a woman's economic livelihood and create an atmosphere that is scarcely work-oriented.[2]

Definition and Scope

Sexual harassment may occur as a single encounter or as a series of incidents at work. It may place a sexual condition on employment opportunities as a clearly defined threshold, such as hiring, retention or advancement, or it may occur as a pervasive or continuing condition of the work environment. Complex forms include the persistent innuendos and continuing threat which are never consummated either sexually or economically. The most straightforward approach is: "Put out or get out."

Of the limited number of cases brought to the courts, the types of harassment have varied, but the outcome in most cases has been the same. The first women to complain in the courts that sexual harassment was sex discrimination were all unsuccessful.

Corne and DeVane were two clerical workers at Bausch and Lomb who alleged that the repeated verbal and physical sexual advances, molestation and propositions by their male superior had made their jobs intolerable, forcing them to leave, while women who were sexually compliant received enhanced employment status. Their supervisor's actions, the women alleged, limited them to "the choice of putting up with being manhandled, or being out of work." They argued that the company, by allowing them to be supervised by a man who persistently took unsolicited and unwanted sexual liberties, created sex discriminatory conditions of employment.[3] Dismissing the claim, Judge Frey held that sexual advances are not sex discrimination but "personal" and that the behavior was not "based on sex" because the sexes of the participants could have been reversed.

In another case, Margaret Miller, a black woman, alleged that her white supervisor promised her a better job if she would be sexually "cooperative" and caused her dismissal when she refused. She charged that Bank of America, in policy and practice, permitted men in supervisory positions, in particular her supervisor, to demean women's dignity and that his sexual advances were part of a pattern.[4] The ruling in this case was that the "isolated and unauthorized sex misconduct of one employee to another" could not be considered work place events for which the employer should be held liable.

Dianne Williams, a black public information specialist with the Justice Department, alleged in her complaint that she had had a good working relationship with her immediate supervisor, a black man, until she refused a sexual advance. Thereafter, she asserted that he "engaged in a continuing pattern and practice of harassment and humiliation of her, including . . . unwarranted reprimands, refusal to inform her of matters for the performance of her responsibilities, refusal to consider her proposals and recommendations, and refusal to recognize her as a competent professional in her field."[5] Her supervisor alleged that her poor work performance during this same period led to her dismissal. The administrative tribunal thought the evidence did not establish "any causal relationship" between the rejection of her supervisor's sexual advances, his treatment of her and her termination.[6] Williams appealed.

Exposure of sexual harassment in the services is also becoming more widespread. Army Major General Mary E. Clarke, commander of Fort McClellan, Alabama, in a recent testimony before the House Armed Services Military Personnel Subcommittee, referred to sexual harassment as a serious problem. At the same hearing, Rear Admiral Frances E. McKee, the Navy's Assistant Deputy Chief of Naval Personnel for Human Resource Management, said that a growing public awareness of the problem has helped. And Major General Norma Brown, commander of the Air Force's Technical Training Center at Chanute AFB, Illinois, called sexual harassment in the military "totally intolerable." Representative Marjorie Holt (R-Md.), also speaking at the Congressional hearing, said the key to ending the problem in the military is "educating people from the top down and the bottom up. People must realize this isn't right."[7]

Why Does It Happen?

The sex role stereotyping of women and their status in Western societies have contributed enormously to the lack of concern for the issue of sexual harassment. Many people still believe a woman's place is in the home. Women, it is claimed, are not career-oriented. They are less suited than men to many jobs, they do not stay in jobs, lack education and experience, are absent from work more often than men, are unable to travel, would not be accepted in positions of authority, and are incapable of making decisions based on fact and logic.[8]

In addition to the stereotyping of women, the double sexual standards for men and women in the American culture almost encourage the practice of sexual harassment. Male sex roles encourage men to be strong, aggressive, tough, dominant and competitive. These values, which have come to be considered "male," describe common male behavior in many spheres, including the sexual.[9] On the other hand, powerful social conditioning of women to passivity, gentleness, submissiveness and receptivity to male initiative, particularly in sexual contact, tends effectively to constrain women from expressing sexual aggression (or even assertion).

Adding to the long list of reasons as to why sexual harassment occurs is the economic trap which many working women face daily. Sexual harassment of working women presents a closed system of social predation in which powerlessness builds powerlessness. Feelings are a material reality of it. Working women are defined, and survive by defining themselves, as sexually accessible and economically exploitable. Because they are economically vulnerable, they are always economically at risk. In this perspective, sexual harassment is less "epidemic" than endemic.[10] Such views as, "Women really want unwanted sex," "It is relatively normal for males to seek sexual access to females who are their subordinates,"[11] and "Today's modern world requires that females in business and industry have a little tougher attitude towards life in general,"[12] only add to the frustration women feel in trying to have their complaints recognized.

The Problems Sexual Harassment Creates

Sexual harassment can create social problems, including unemployment, alcoholism and excessive drug use, upon which family disruptions, psychosomatic illness and mental illness follow. The harassed employee tends to take more sick leave and become accident-prone. Absenteeism rises among this group, and work attitudes become increasingly negative.

The effect of harassment on its victims can be devastating. There is a wide variety of reaction, depending on the individual intellect and temperament. The reactions range from extreme indignation and rage to depression and a greatly diminished self-image. Whether the initial reaction was one of depression, diminished self-worth or anger, the results of a study done with patients at the Work Clinic at the University of California Hospital in San Francisco in 1976 showed that the outcome follows some general disability pattern. Some women expressed their reaction by developing vague physical symptoms such as chronic fatigue, loss of strength, various aches, weaknesses and pains. Others reacted with depression and the symptoms of depression, such as sleeplessness and poor motivation. Still others reacted with psychological symptoms: nervousness, hypersensitivity, hostility, memory loss and feelings of victimization.[13]

Women's feelings about their experiences of sexual harassment are a significant part of its social impact. Like women who are raped, sexually harassed women may feel humiliated, degraded, ashamed, embarrassed and cheap, as well as angry. Those who complain, as well as those who don't, express fears that their complaints will be ignored, will not be believed, that they instead will be blamed, that they will be considered "unprofessional" or "asking for it," or will be told this problem is too silly or trivial for a grown woman to worry about, and that they are blowing it all out of proportion.[14]

A general picture of women's reactions to specific sexual harassment incidents from three separate surveys has helped elucidate the issues. The earliest "quasi-systematic" attempt at addressing the issue of sexual harassment was made by *Redbook* magazine in a national survey conducted in January and November of 1976, to which 9,000 women workers replied. Although the survey had some methodology drawbacks (e.g., the respondents were self-selected), the results still proved valuable in gauging the significance of the problem. Nine out of ten women surveyed reported that they had experienced one or more forms of unwanted attention on the job. Also, 75% of the women said they found these unwelcome attentions "embarrassing," "demeaning" or "intimidating."

In the study conducted by the Illinois Task Force on Sexual Harassment and Sangamon State University, of the 1,495 state female employees who replied to the survey, 63% agreed that sexual harassment was a serious problem, and 72% agreed that unwelcome male attentions on the job were offensive. When asked to comment on how they felt about these incidents, 74% reported they felt angry, 56.4% embarrassed and 28.5% felt intimidated. Only 1.5% felt flattered—a clear indication that women do not enjoy these experiences.[15]

Finally, the results of a study researched by the Working Women's United Institute in New York are equally disturbing. This institution provides resources for women who are sexually harassed, acts as a clearing house for information for lawyers and others, presents forums and workshops, and engages in research. Judging from the responses to their study, it is obvious that women neither want such attention nor are flattered by it: 78% of the women surveyed reported feeling "angry," 48% "upset," 23% "frightened," 3% "indifferent," and an additional 27% mentioned feeling "alienated," "alone" and "helpless." They tended to believe the incidents were their fault and that they must have done something individually to elicit or encourage the behavior. Thinking that no one else is subjected to it, they felt individually complicit as well as demeaned. Almost a quarter of the women reported feeling "guilty."[16]

Sexual Harassment as Sex Discrimination

The contours of a legal understanding of the problem of sexual harassment of women are only beginning to emerge. As more cases are brought out and courts become more familiar with the essence of the claim, law on sexual harassment as sex discrimination is developing. Failure to recognize the social context and implications of incidents of sexual harassment has been a major element in those court decisions which have declined to find discrimination. In all cases where the plaintiff alleged discrimination, the courts seemed to think that the incidents were merely "personal" and did not rise to the level of a public problem within the purview of the statute. This view neglects both the negative impact on the women's employment opportunities (two women who brought suit lost their jobs as a result) and the fact that each incident reproduces, with very little personal variation, the unequitable social structure of male supremacy and female subordination which Titles VII and IX seek to eliminate in proscribing sex discrimination as a factor in employment and education.[17]

The relationship of sexuality to gender is the critical link in the argument that sexual harassment is sex discrimination. As a practice, sexual harassment singles out a gender-defined group, women, for special treatment in a way which adversely affects and burdens their status as employees. Sexual harassment limits women in a way men are not limited. It deprives them of opportunities that are available to male employees without sexual conditions. In so doing, it creates two employment standards: one for women that includes sexual requirements and one for men that does not. From preliminary indications, large numbers of working women, regardless of characteristics which distinguish them from each other, report being sexually harassed. Most sexually harassed people are women. These facts indicate that the incidents are something more than "personal" and "unique," and have some connection to the female condition as a whole.[18]

The Law: What Is Being Done?

Sexual harassment, like harassment on the basis of color, race, religion or national origin, has long been recognized by EEOC as a violation of Section 703 of Title VII of the Civil Rights Act of 1964, as amended. However, despite the position taken by the commission, sexual harassment continues to be especially widespread. Because of the continued prevalence of this unlawful practice, the commission has determined that there is a need for guidelines in this area of Title VII law. Therefore, on April 11, 1980, on an interim basis, EEOC amended its guidelines on sex discrimination to add S1604.11 Sexual Harassment.

S1604.11 covers the areas of both unwanted physical and verbal behavior. The commission has taken the position that sexual harassment generates a harmful atmosphere and that the employer has an affirmative duty to maintain a work place free of sexual harassment and intimidation. It sets down in its guidelines three specific criteria that it says constitute unlawful behavior:

1) Submission to the conduct is either an explicit or implicit term or condition of employment.
2) Submission to or rejection of the conduct is used as the basis for employment decisions affecting the person who did the submitting or rejecting.
3) The conduct has the purpose or effect of substantially interfering with an individual's work performance or creating an intimidating, hostile, offensive work environment.[19]

It should also be noted that municipalities and states are also drafting "antisexual harassment" legislation. For example, the State of Florida has bills before the House and Senate which declare discrimination against an individual by an employer for refusal to grant sex favors to be an unlawful employment practice.

Strategies to Prevent Sexual Harassment

Harassment cannot be eliminated, but it can be reduced in frequency, intensity and duration. This can be done by establishing in the work place a culture that exposes, discourages and censures harassment of all kinds. Intervention, either by government or by an employer, should have the effect of attenuating the harassment process and lim-

iting what social support it has. To give women the necessary support to take a stand on the serious problem of sexual harassment, it is essential that as many organizations as possible become involved in bringing the issue to the attention of the public.

For example, the Office of Personnel Management (OPM), the federal personnel agency, has developed a training module on sexual harassment. This module is available to agencies as part of OPM's technical assistance program.

Also, the federal Merit Systems Protection Board, in conjunction with OPM, has initiated a survey of federal workers in an attempt to understand the issues surrounding sexual harassment. According to Alan K. Campbell, the director of OPM:

> It is the policy of the Office of Personnel Management (OPM) that sexual harassment is unacceptable conduct within the workplace and will not be condoned. Personnel Management within the Federal sector shall be implemented free from prohibited personnel practices and consistent with merit system principles.[20]

Professionals from social service agencies throughout the Minneapolis/St. Paul, Minnesota area came together in December, 1978 to form the Coalition Against Sexual Harassment (CASH). According to their first newsletter, "The coalition's goals and purposes include educating the public about sexual harassment, offering consultation about grievance procedures, providing advocacy for adult victims of sexual harassment, gathering data, and sharing information." It would be extremely beneficial if such organizations were formed throughout the country.

In Berkeley, California, a group of female sociology students at the University of California banded together as Women Organized Against Sexual Harassment (WOASH) and waged a campaign against professors who they felt were using the "power of the grade" to elicit sexual favors.

(Despite some misgivings, a Yale graduate student stated that, "A student making a major complaint would expose herself in a way that's more harmful than harassment. The complaint could have a much more profound effect on your future and the focus of your education than the instance of harassment."[21] In a university setting, the effects of sexual harassment on a motivated woman who thinks of herself, and is, a serious worker or student is potentially devastating. Beyond the exclusionary and restrictive results, the feeling that she is not valued for her productivity, accomplishes or promise, but for her woman's body, can cast a pall of resentment and self-doubt over her working or academic career, if it does not drive her out of the pursuit altogether.)[22]

To reduce the incidents of harassment, all supervisory personnel should be trained, if only minimally, to listen to those working under them. Management must be made aware that some individuals and groups are more susceptible to harassment than others. Both supervisor and manager must become aware of their responsibility to treat their workers as individuals and to make work as gratifying as possible for them. Grievance procedures should be established through which the harassed worker could apprise her (or his) supervisor and coworkers of harassment.[23]

Beyond the "Personal"

Far from being simply individual and personal, sexual harassment is integral and crucial to a social context in which women as a group are allocated a disproportionally small share of wealth, power and advantages compared with men as a group. When women work outside the home, they typically occupy jobs that are low on the ladder of financial reward and personal satisfaction, independent of their aspirations, preparations or potential. Often they are shunted to dead-end "women's jobs." In this con-

text, the problem of sexual harassment is revealed both as a manifestation and perpetuation of the socially disadvantaged status of women.

A man in a position of authority, whether a supervisor or a teacher, can use his hierarchically superordinate role to place conditions of sexual compliance on his female subordinate's access to the benefits of her job or her educational program. The necessity of dealing with sexual pressures that are, by virtue of the man's position and actions, bound up with the woman's desired goal (getting a job, doing a job, getting an education) burdens and restricts her access to the means of survival, security and achievement. In a society in which women as a group are at a comparative disadvantage to men, the negative impact that sexual harassment has on the maintenance or improvement of women's positions contributes to the continuation of their socially inferior condition.[24]

The problem of sexual harassment cannot afford to go unresolved. With the changing economic conditions and the decreasing emphasis on sex roles, women not only deserve but expect to be treated as equals in the work place. And as women continue to enter the work force at unprecedented rates, it is imperative that employers reassess their attitudes toward female sexuality and allow women to take their rightful place in the working world, making equal contributions without fear of harassment, exploitation or discrimination.

References

1. Catherine A. MacKinnon, *Sexual Harassment of Working Women* (New Haven, Conn. and London: Yale Press, 1979), p. 1.
2. Definition taken from the survey compiled by the Illinois Task Force on Sexual Harassment, Sangamon State University, March, 1980.
3. MacKinnon, *Sexual Harassment of Working Women*, Supra 1, p. 61.
4. Ibid., Supra 2, p. 62.

5. William V. Bell (Brenson, appellant), No. 76-1833 and William V. Bell, No. 76-1994, U.S. Ct. App. DC. Decided September 19, 1978.

6. On appeal, the Organization of Black Activist Women filed a brief "amicus curiae," which is of special interest, since both the perpetrator and the victim were black.

7. Congressional Subcommittee Hearing reported in *The Navy Times*, February 25, 1980.

8. Review of N.S.W. Government Administration, *Affirmative Action Handbook*, January 1980, pp. 68–74.

9. MacKinnon, *Sexual Harassment of Working Women*, Supra 1, p. 155.

10. Ibid., Supra 1, p. 55.

11. Lionel Tiger, *Men in Groups* (New York: Random House, 1969), p. 271.

12. Quoted in Rina Rosenberg, "A Woman Must Persevere in Battle Against Sexism," *Santa Clara Sun*, August 16, 1975, p. 6.

13. Carroll M. Brodsky. *The Harassed Worker* (Lexington, Mass.: D.C. Heath and Co., 1976), pp. 38–40.

14. MacKinnon, *Sexual Harassment of Working Women*, Supra 1, p. 49.

15. Testimony of Barbara Haler, member of the Illinois Task Force on Sexual Harassment, before the House Judiciary Committee, March 4, 1980.

16. Data collected by the WWUI and reported in Diedre Silverman, "Sexual Harassment: Working Women's Dilemma," *Quest and Feminist Quarterly*, Vol. 3, No. 3 (1976–1977): 15–24.

17. MacKinnon, *Sexual Harassment of Working Women*, Supra 1, pp. 234–235.

18. Ibid., Supra 1, p. 193.

19. "Rules and Regulations," *Federal Register*, Vol. 45, No. 72 (April 11, 1980).

20. Alan K. Campbell, "Policy Statement and Definition on Sexual Harassment," *Women in Action*, Vol. 10, No. 1 (January/February 1980): 2.

21. Quoted by Alice Dembner, "A Case of Sex Discrimination," *Yale Graduate*, Vol. 7, No. 14 (March 6, 1978): 7.

22. MacKinnon, *Sexual Harassment of Working Women*, Supra 1, p. 238.

23. D. Coffee and A. A. McLean, "Mental Health in Industry: Whose Responsibility?" *Journal of Occupational Medicine*, September 1967, pp. 213–214.

24. MacKinnon, *Sexual Harassment of Working Women*, Supra 1, p. 235.

Sexual Harassment
By Jolene Saunders

Jolene Saunders is a free-lance writer who lives in New York. She works for the Ms. *magazine project on campus assault.*

An advertising sales manager twists nervously at a handkerchief in her lap as she listens to her boss at a national magazine explain why she's "not working out." The next day she is fired. This same boss has been sexually harassing her for the past six months.

An assembly-line worker in an urban foundry is let go and told that she will be recalled when work picks up. Three people who were hired after her are not fired. They should have been laid off first according to union "bumping" rights. A year earlier she had reported several sexual-harassment incidents by her supervisor.

A computer-operations supervisor suddenly is assigned to the night shift (11:00 PM to 7:00 AM) in the computer center of a busy Wall Street law firm. The assignment is announced by the managing partner of the firm, who had asked her to sleep with him two weeks earlier.

These stories are based on true incidents, and they are not isolated occurrences. Sexual harassment, like rape and wife beating, took a long time to come out of the closet, and it was only in the early 1970s that women managers and employees began to discuss it openly.

Ironically, harassment claims no longer blaze across newspaper headlines, but not because the problem has died down. On the contrary, it is so commonplace that it no longer is newsworthy. Newspaper columnists such as Art Buchwald have made matters worse by writing sarcastic columns about the issue. In his November 17, 1983, column, he advised job applicants to specify whether they wanted to be verbally harassed on the job and by whom. The superior "could then notify all the males in the office accordingly, and everybody would be spared the consequences."

Defining Harassment

Stopping sexual harassment is difficult because of hazy definitions, inconsistent laws and the highly charged emotions surrounding the subject. Under Title VII of the 1964 Civil Rights Act, employers may not discriminate on the basis of sex, and sexual harassment is a form of sex discrimination. The Equal Employment Opportunity Commission (EEOC), the federal agency charged with enforcing Title VII, clarified its definition of sexual harassment in 1980. The agency adopted the following guidelines: "Unwelcome sexual advances, requests for sexual favors and other verbal and physical conduct of a sexual nature constitute sex harassment when 1) submission to such conduct is made a term or condition of an individual's employment, 2) submission to or rejection of such conduct is used as the basis for employment decisions and 3) such conduct unreasonably interferes with work performance, or creates an intimidating, hostile or offensive working environment."

"Sexual harassment is difficult to prove," says Nadine Taub, LLB, professor of law and director of the Women's Rights Litigation Clinic of Rutgers Law School in Newark, New Jersey. "It is a lot like rape, because many harassment incidents happen without other witnesses present." Interpreting the EEOC definition also is problematic. "To a certain extent, some things can be sexually harassing in some situations and not in others," explains Karen Sauvigne, executive director and cofounder of the Working Women's Institute, a New York–based consulting firm that helps corporations solve sexual-harassment problems. For example, if a supervisor repeatedly asks an employee for a date, this might be considered harassment, while in a nonworking situation, persistent interest might be casually overlooked.

The Real Story

Despite legal prohibitions, the problem of sexual harassment is widespread. Studies show that nearly half of all working women have been harassed at some point, with an overwhelming incidence of sexual harassment in formerly all-male workplaces such as construction companies and the armed forces. A 1982 report in the military weekly, *Army Times,* said that three out of four women soldiers surveyed had been sexually harassed during the preceding 12 months. The army added a course soon after on preventing sexual harassment to its basic training, to sensitize all soldiers to this problem.

Another 1982 study conducted by the US government, this time to measure the success of affirmative-action hiring policies at four government-financed construction projects, found that nearly all women respondents had been sexually harassed. Incidents ranged from practical jokes to one case of rape. Most of these women, including the rape victim, did not file complaints for fear that they might wind up losing their jobs.

The editors of the *Harvard Business Review* and *Redbook* magazine surveyed 7,408 *HBR* subscribers in 1981 (almost 25 percent responded in the United States) on the issue of sexual harassment. Some of the most interesting findings: Sexual harassment is seen as an issue of power; men and women generally agree in theory on what sexual harassment is but disagree on how often it occurs, and most respondents view sexual harassment as a serious matter and favor company policies against it. Yet few companies have set up their own policies. (For example, only 29 percent of the *HBR* respondents work in companies where top executives have issued statements to employees disapproving of sexual misconduct, but 73 percent of the respondents favor such corporate statements.)

Studies show also that sexual harassment takes a toll on employers. According to a two-year study of federal employees conducted by the US Merit Systems Protection Board (MSPB), 42 percent of the 694,000 women questioned, and 15 percent of the 1,168,000 men said they had been sexually harassed. The MSPB estimated that the cost to employers in terms of morale, productivity, lost time and turnover was $189 million.

Corporate Response

Legal pressures aside, more and more employers are realizing that harassment is not just a personal problem between two employees, it is a personnel problem that can affect the entire company. "Employers have an interest in maintaining a working environment that is free from sexual harassment," explains Sauvigne of WWI (Working Women's Institute, Ed.). "As the US Merit Systems Protection Board demonstrated, it costs companies money to ignore sexual harassment."

Social pressures from inside and outside corporations are forcing management to take action. "I don't see a backsliding in terms of corporate or institutional policies regarding sexual harassment," Sauvigne says. "Increasingly the employer, and society as a whole, is recognizing that the use of sexual comments, innuendos, sexual propositions or unwanted touching is something that causes stress for workers and is *not* appropriate for male or female workers to be doing."

In a defensive move, spurred as much by attempts to curb losses of productivity and money as by a desire to comply with the law, many employers now are clamping down on illegal behavior. In 1982, Bell Laboratories declared sexual harassment its main affirmative-action issue. "Bell Labs admits sexual harassment exists and is willing to try to do something about it," says Mel Robin, a member of Bell's technical staff and co-chairperson of an employee group that recommended WWI to conduct departmental training sessions. "I'm proud of Bell Labs. Other companies are not doing anything in terms of training sessions because they are hoping that women will think the problem is their fault and not take action.''

WWI provides trainees with information about self-help and coping strategies, reaffirming that the company policy as well as federal guidelines prohibit sexual harassment in the workplace. Trainees also participate in workshop exercises such as roleplaying to encourage communication. ''It is particularly difficult for men and women to discuss sexual harassment, because we don't have the skills. We're not taught to be able to speak about it or hear about it in nondefensive ways,'' says Sauvigne. ''Men need to learn to hear 'I don't like it when you do that' without it meaning 'You're a bad person' or 'I don't like you.' And women need to learn to be able to say it.''

In training sessions that involve management, WWI discusses appropriate corrective action and the extent of supervisory responsibility under the EEOC guidelines. These guidelines explain how the EEOC will handle discrimination cases. Although they are not statutes, the guidelines are regulations that the courts defer to. They place liability on employers for the actions of supervisors and, less stringently, for acts committed by colleagues and other employees. Employers also are responsible for developing programs to prevent sexual misconduct in the workplace. ''Corporate programs are important,'' explains Rutgers' Taub, ''because they decrease the number of employee claims. However, once an employee starts litigation, an in-house program will not decrease employer liability.''

''What WWI is trying to do,'' says Sauvigne, ''is build the responses inside the institution so that the harassment stops before someone loses a job. In a few cases (as at Bell Labs) the impetus for bringing the institute in is that some kind of study has been done and it has been demonstrated that sexual harassment is a problem for the company. When a company finds that out, it

shouldn't be shocked. It's a problem everywhere.''

Corporate managers are issuing guidelines and warnings to their employees, and several companies have come up with their own solutions. One large New York brokerage firm recently warned its 10,000 employees that sexual harassment wouldn't be tolerated. It announced that complaints should be reported immediately to the employee-relations department, where cases would receive confidential attention. A memo posted in a New York law firm concedes that ''differing personal codes of sexual behavior make defining sexual harassment difficult.'' But US law forbids ''petting, pinching, hugging, kissing, fondling or brushing up against'' someone, among other things. Violators, the memo adds, may be fired.

Employee Tactics

In addition to a strong company policy, there are actions that employees can take on their own. WWI has issued guidelines for employees to follow if they feel they are being sexually harassed (see address below). Here are the most important points:

- Trust your instincts.
- Seek advice and counsel from friends and co-workers.
- Don't ignore the harassment.
- Assess your options: Keep a log or diary in a secure place, not in your desk. Put your complaint in writing. Talk to the ombudsperson, or to the affirmative-action or EEO office. Make a formal complaint and follow it up the hierarchy. Find out if other people (past or present employees) in your area have been harassed. If they have, you'll get support and credibility.

Another successful tactic is the direct letter to the harasser. According to Mary Rowe, PhD, a labor economist at the Massachusetts Institute of Technology who has worked on sexual harassment for the past 12 years, ''This type of letter is the single most effective way to stop harassment.'' Below is an example of Rowe's letter.

Adapt it to suit your own needs, and use the last paragraph to say what you want to happen. Keep a copy of the letter for your files.

Dear _____,

On December 15, 1983, when I met you to discuss my marketing project, you asked me to come to your apartment that evening and said it would help the success of my project. Several times in the past few months when I talked to you in your office, you put your arm around me and rubbed my back. Once you tried to fondle my breast. Last week at an office party, you asked me to go to bed with you. I do not believe you can judge my job performance fairly under these circumstances.

I want our relationship to be purely professional from now on.

Rowe reports: "The typical reaction from the harasser was no reaction. The harassment just stopped."

Several corporations have set up formal grievance procedures for their employees, either through a union contract or an independent company policy. These procedures are substantially quicker and cheaper for both parties than filing a lawsuit. The employer and her company can avoid unwanted publicity and the employee is more likely to stay in her job. Almost all employer policies and union contracts forbid sex discrimination in employment. But be careful: There are short time limits (depending on the state) for filing grievances, and the complainants must bring the evidence—usually an upsetting experience.

A Day in Court

Litigation and the preliminary EEOC complaint are the last resorts for many sexual-harassment victims. After trying to resolve a situation within a company, an employee might want to try outside resources. Some women prefer to file complaints outside the company from the beginning, since it often is more private. According to Taub, "The litigation process is emotionally draining, but the resolution

can be much more satisfying than in-house arbitration."

For those who go outside their company, the first step is filing a discrimination complaint at the EEOC or a state or city human-rights agency (see "For More Information"). You cannot file a court case without going through this step, which is designed to avoid unnecessary court cases. Complaints to the EEOC must be filed within 180 days of the date you were sexually harassed. These time constraints are annoying, but they are the kind of details that can cause you to lose your case. At the EEOC a counselor will help the complainant file a claim—the claim will be evaluated to make sure it fits the technical requirements of Title VII and the agency. An EEOC representative will send a notice to the employer (usually within ten days after the charge is made) stating that a claim has been filed and explaining the illegality of any retaliatory measures taken against you for making a claim. The EEOC will investigate the claim and attempt to mediate a solution in a multistage process, working directly with the complainant and her employer.

Generally (again depending on the state), if a claim filed with the EEOC is not settled to the complainant's satisfaction within 180 days, you may request a right-to-sue letter and then can file suit under Title VII in the federal courts. (A right-to-sue letter can be requested at three stages in the EEOC process.) You have exactly 90 days to file the lawsuit, and it's crucial to have a lawyer ready to go on your case: Consult with an attorney specializing in employment-discrimination law before you start proceedings. Litigation can be frustrating, time-consuming and expensive. On the other hand, a lawsuit can cost the employer time, money, bad publicity, embarrassment and maybe a negative judgment.

Bundy v. *Jackson* is the classic court case in sexual harassment. In 1972, Sandra Bundy was a vocational-rehabilitation specialist with the District of Columbia Department of Corrections. She was propositioned by Jackson, who subsequently was promoted to director of the agency. In 1974, Bundy was sexually intimidated by two other supervisors. In April 1975, after being passed over for a promotion for poor work performance, she filed a complaint with the EEOC and a complaint with her department—but nothing happened.

Bundy was promoted in 1976 and was eligible for another promotion in July 1977. The judicial climate had become more favorable, so she decided to try again. She filed another complaint in District Court in August 1977. The court ruled against her because it concluded that sexual harassment itself didn't constitute discrimination under Title VII. The District of Columbia Circuit US Court of Appeals reversed the ruling in 1981. On the basis of an earlier case, *Rogers* v. *EEOC*, the court ruled that there was a Title VII violation in the Bundy case because the employer had "created or condoned a substantially discriminatory work environment, regardless of whether complaining employees lost any tangible job benefits as a result of the discrimination."

Bundy's case illustrates the way a sexual-harassment case can drag on. "Corporate supervisors and employees can avoid litigation," says Sauvigne of WWI, "if they do something about sexual harassment *before* it escalates. If everyone is scared of the problem, they'll bury their heads and someone will end up getting a raw deal."

For More Information

Alliance Against Sexual Coercion, Box 1, Cambridge, MA 02139; or call: 617-547-1176.

9 to 5, the National Association of Working Women, 1224 Huron Road, Cleveland OH 44115; or call: 216-566-9308.

National Organization for Women; check your phone book for local chapter address and telephone number.

Working Women's Institute; write: 593 Park Avenue, New York, NY 10021; or call: 212-838-4420.

File sexual-harassment complaints at the following offices:

Equal Employment Opportunity Commission (EEOC); check your phone book under US Government Offices for your local office.

State human-rights agency; check the White Pages of your phone book under State Government Offices. Look under City Government Offices for telephone and address of your city's human-rights agency.

For further reading:

Sexual Harassment on the Job, by Constance Backhouse and Leah Cohen (Prentice-Hall, $5.95 paper).

Sexual Harassment of Working Women, by Catherine A. MacKinnon (Yale University Press, $6.95 paper).

How to Deal with Sexual Harassment, by David J. Miramontes (Network Communications Inc.). Write: Network Communications, PO Box 2398, San Diego, CA 92126.

Note

[1] I am indebted to Laurence Behrens and Leonard J. Rosen for this categorization of writing from sources, as found in their textbook *Writing and Reading Across the Curriculum,* 2nd ed., Boston: Little, Brown and Company, 1985.

CHAPTER 5

Planning, Writing, and Presenting Your Research Paper

■ INTRODUCTION

It is through the process of actually writing your research paper that you will verify for yourself, and eventually for your readers, the answer to your starting question. You need to present that answer in the best possible fashion, using an appropriate research format and correct writing style. To handle in a reasonable way the large body of material you have accrued, you must approach the task systematically.

■ PLANNING YOUR RESEARCH PAPER

After you have completed the primary research, library research, and preliminary writing on your topic, you are ready to begin planning the actual research paper. There are two important components that you need to consider as you begin to plan: rhetorical situation and organization.

Rhetorical Situation

The context in which you are writing an assignment is called the *rhetorical situation*. The term *rhetoric* refers to written or spoken communication that seeks to inform someone of something or to convince someone of a particular opinion or point of view. For any writing assignment, you need to analyze the components of the rhetorical situation—(1) the writer's purpose, (2) the writer's persona, (3) the potential reader or audience, and (4) the subject matter.

Purpose

When preparing to write, a writer must decide on the actual purpose of the piece. What is the goal that should be accomplished? Many times the goal or purpose will be implicit in the writing assignment itself. For example, for a newspaper reporter, the goal is to present the facts in an objective manner, interpreting events for newspaper readers. For your research paper assignment, you need to determine your purpose or goal and define it carefully. The purpose does not have to be grandiose or profound —it may simply be to convince your readers that you have a fine grasp on the topic and are making some important points, or to inform your readers of the current state of knowledge in a particular field.

Persona

You also need to decide just how to present yourself as a writer to those who will read your work. Do you want to sound objective and fair, heated and passionate, or sincere and persuasive? The term *persona* is used to describe the identity that the speaker or writer adopts. As you know, we all play many roles, depending on the situations in which we find ourselves: with our parents, we may be quiet and reserved; with our peers, outgoing and comical, and so on. Similarly, you can be flexible about how you portray yourself in your writing, changing your persona with your purpose and audience. First, establish your credibility by being careful and thorough in your research and by showing that you have done your homework and understand what you are writing about. Furthermore, prepare your finished product with care and attention to detail. If you do not, your readers will assume that you are sloppy and careless and will largely discount anything you have to say. Many job applicants never even make it to the interview stage because their letters of application convey the subliminal message "here is a person who is careless and inconsiderate of others."

Audience

Identifying those who may be reading your writing will help you to make decisions about what to include or not include in your research paper. Those who are the most likely to read your writing make up your *audience*. For example, a newspaper reporter must assume that his or her readers were not present at the event being covered; thus he or she must take care to reconstruct details for the readers. Furthermore, for a local newspaper, a reporter can assume that the readers reflect the general population of the region.

In the case of a college research paper, the primary audience will be the instructor of the course. You should assume that the instructor is knowledgeable about the subject, reasonably intelligent, and particularly interested in the accuracy of the research. Prior to each writing task, think about the characteristics of the particular readers you want to reach. As

Snoopy discovers in the accompanying cartoon, knowing your audience and its likes and dislikes is all important (and difficult).

© 1983 United Feature Syndicate, Inc. Reprinted by permission.

Take time before writing to consider carefully who will read your research paper. It will make a difference to you, both in how you approach your topic (Are my readers novices or experts in the field?) and in the tone you adopt (Are my readers likely to agree with me or must I win them over to my point of view?). If your instructor has made no stipulations about the intended audience for your research paper, it is a good idea to discuss the issue of audience with him or her.

Subject Matter

The most important component of the rhetorical situation, however, is the subject matter. Though no piece of writing exists in isolation (hence the need for analyzing the purpose, persona, and audience), the content that you are presenting to your audience will be the core of any piece you are writing. You must decide from the mass of material you discover in your research what to include in your written presentation. These decisions will be based on your starting question, your analysis and evaluation of your sources, and your thesis statement. Knowing what your ultimate goal is, how you wish to sound, and who your readers are will help you decide what source materials to use.

Organization

Once you have gathered and evaluated source materials on your topic, completed your preliminary writing assignments, and analyzed the rhetorical situation, you can begin to organize your source material. During the planning stages, you need to decide how you will give pattern and order to your research paper. The importance of planning cannot be overemphasized. Readers will use your skeletal plan, which should appear in some form in the written research paper, to reconstruct your meaning. Many recent investigations into the reading process have shown that readers reconstruct meaning in writing by using organizational plans—that is, explicit directional signals left by the writer in his or her work. Remember, the longer the research paper the more you need to plan explicitly.

First, find a controlling pattern for your research paper. Your thesis is a good place to look for a controlling pattern. Ask yourself what organizational plan it suggests. Perhaps your thesis implies that a particular result has a specific cause (this would be a cause-and-effect organizational pattern), or perhaps your thesis implies a relationship between two similar or dissimilar ideas or events (a compare-and-contrast organizational pattern). Other organizational patterns are classification and definition, question and answer, problem and solution, narration and description, and process analysis.

Organizational Patterns

1. *Cause and effect.* Many research projects and/or reports seek to link phenomena through cause-and-effect relationships. For example, from a chemical experiment: "The cause of the chemical change was the new substance introduced into the compound; the effect of the experiment was the change in chemical structure." From political science: "The cause of the incumbent's unsuccessful ad campaign was the negative image projected in his TV advertisements; the effect of the ad campaign was to unseat the incumbent."

2. *Compare and contrast.* Many research projects seek to compare or contrast two or more ideas, issues, or events. In comparing, we look for likeness; in contrasting, for difference. For example, from history: "The events surrounding World War I and World War II are compared and contrasted in an effort to understand how they were alike and different." From psychology: "The case histories of two psychotic individuals are studied to find common threads."

3. *Classification and definition.* To make sense of our world, we classify and define ideas, issues, and events by their characteristic parts. When we define something, we describe what it is and perhaps what it is not. For example, from sociology: "A ghetto is defined as a section of an urban area heavily populated by a particular minority group. A slum is not the same as a ghetto because a slum may contain a mixture of minority groups, whereas a ghetto (which can be a slum) contains one predominant minority group."

4. *Question and answer.* In this pattern, a specific question is raised and probable answers to the question are presented. The question-and-answer pattern can exist by itself or as a part of another pattern, perhaps cause and effect—for example, "What caused the Vietnam War?" From literature: "What are the major themes in Shakespeare's *Hamlet*?" (In this case, answers would be taken from the text itself.)

5. *Problem and solution.* In this pattern, a particular problem is identified and solutions to the problem are posed. For example, from

business: "The productivity of automobile workers in the United States has fallen considerably in the past two years." The researcher looks at the problem and proposes solutions to help raise productivity levels: "Solutions might include pay incentives, improved work environment, and exercise facilities for employees."

6. *Narration and description.* Sometimes a narrative (story) or a description of a particular thing or event is included in a research paper. For example, from astronomy: "A new star is located in our galaxy. It is described in detail with reference to its size, shape, characteristics, location, and so on. Also, a narrative is written to account for its probable origin and future development (based on the description)."

7. *Process analysis.* Often, a particular process will be important in a research paper. Analysis of the process by which nuclear fission occurs is an example of a process analysis in physics. An example from political science would be the analysis of the election process in a democratic system.

The patterns described here are meant only to suggest possible ways of planning and organizing a research paper. Any project will necessarily combine several of these patterns, perhaps using one main pattern as an overall guide. As humans, we have standard ways of making sense of our environments. The patterns described above reflect our habitual ways of organizing experience. Our readers will be looking for familiar plans in our writing, so the more explicitly we signal our plans, the more likely it is that the readers will understand what we have to say.

One final note about planning: write your plans in your research notebook, but be sure to keep them flexible. In the actual process of writing your first draft, you may be led to new insights and discoveries. Do not cut off the discovery function of writing by rigidly sticking to a particular plan. Rather, be open to changing your plan to accommodate any new insight you might have along the way. When an architect is planning a building, he or she makes and discards several blueprints as the planning proceeds. Use your plans as blueprints—as guides only—not finished buildings encased in concrete.

EXERCISES

1. For one of the following writing assignments, write a thesis statement, informal outline, and one-paragraph summary of contents. Pay explicit attention to rhetorical context and to organization.
   A. a brochure on making the transition from high school to college written to an audience of high school students
   B. an editorial on academic cheating for the college newspaper
   C. a proposal for improving the food in the dorm cafeteria written to the coordinator of food services

2. Analyze the organizational patterns of the following student paragraphs. Identify the pattern that seems to dominate each paragraph and any other supporting patterns.

   A. When the rock star stepped on stage, he flashed a sexy smile at all the girls in the front row. He pranced to the music of their frantic screams, the muscles rippling on his bare torso. Slowly, excruciatingly, his left hand lifted the mike to his lips, his throat rumbling a low-pitched love phrase. He laughed as the girls fainted, exulting in his wild power over the female sex. Once again, he knew he was a god.

   B. The student who enrolls in a premedical program can look forward to a grueling four years. The primary reason for the tough course of study is that a premed student must be well versed in both sciences and liberal arts. In addition to obtaining a degree in a particular field of study—for example, psychology—the premed student must fulfill the medical school's prerequisite courses: chemistry (four semesters), physics (two semesters), biology (four semesters), and calculus (one semester). As well, the student must maintain a 3.5 grade point average to be considered by a medical school.

   C. In Israel the cost of gasoline has gone to more than $3 a litre. High prices for fuel also pervade Europe and the Orient. But in places like Ecuador, the Arabian countries, and the United States, prices are less than half what they are in Israel. This difference in prices is not because Israel, Europe, and the Orient are incapable of marketing gasoline economically. Rather, places like Ecuador and the United States are capable of providing themselves with gasoline through their own transport systems while Israel, Europe, and the Orient are not. The price of commodities like gasoline, which require special transport, will continue to rise as transportation costs rise.

■ OUTLINING AND DRAFTING YOUR RESEARCH PAPER

Constructing an Outline

Once you have written a thesis statement and decided on a general organizational plan, you are ready to construct a specific outline for your research paper. First, reread your notecards and/or research notebook, keeping your thesis in mind. Set aside any information that is not directly relevant to your thesis. Then, sort your notes or notecards into related categories of information. Your organizational plan will give you the skeleton of your outline. For example, if you decide on a cause-and-effect pattern, you will probably need to discuss causes first, followed by effects. It is important to "flesh out" that skeleton by incorporating major points and subpoints into an outline. You need not be overly concerned about formal outline structure, unless your teacher stipulates a particular outline format. An outline should be a guide to you when you write, and not a constraint that confines and limits your thinking. Therefore, you may change your outline several times as you make new discoveries while writing. Here is an example of an informal outline, drawn from Randy Elder's project on computer crime:

Title: An Intelligent Crime

Thesis: Although crime by computer has made a nice profit for many, these crimes can be eliminated if owners and managers of computer centers and systems recognize the problem and take steps to prevent these crimes.

Introduction:
  Define computer crime
  List the types of computer crimes
  Define the role of the computer in each crime

History:
  Describe the origin of computer crime, with examples

Types:
  Sabotage
  Data Diddling
  Wiretapping
  Piggybacking and Impersonation

General Security Measures

Conclusion:
  Computer systems can be made secure

Drafting Your Paper

After you have completed your outline, you are ready to write the first draft of your research paper. Remind yourself of your general understanding of the topic, of your starting question, and of the answer to that question as stated in your thesis sentence. When writing your first draft, follow your outline and use concrete and simple language to explain your research conclusions.

Do not be overly concerned at this time about mechanics, usage, and spelling, but concentrate on communicating information and presenting that information in an orderly way. If you have prepared sufficiently, the actual writing of the paper will be an important means of verifying for yourself the insights you have gained through your research.

As you are writing the first draft, it is important to pay attention to which material you have taken from which sources. Again, do not be concerned at this time about the formal details of documentation, which will be dealt with later, but do mark in the draft any ideas or words taken from your sources. Remember to place any word, phrase, or sentence you copy directly from a source in quotation marks and to note down the author and page reference for the quotation. Similarly, you must acknowledge paraphrases and restatements of ideas taken from a source even though you have cast them into your own words.

You need not document "common knowledge" on your topic. This term refers to knowledge that is generally known or accepted by educated people. If you can find information readily in general reference works such as encyclopedias or in the popular media (television, radio, newspapers, or magazines), that data is probably common knowledge and need not be documented. For example, it was not necessary for Randy to document the fact that computer crime is widespread, since the prevalence of computer-related crimes is well known. In general, facts and historical dates need not be documented. However, it is better to overdocument than to underdocument and be accused of plagiarizing. When in doubt, document.

■ REVISING YOUR RESEARCH PAPER

There is still important work to be done on your paper once you have completed a rough draft. You must revise the paper to make the most effective possible presentation of the research. Your readers will expect you to be clear and correct in your presentation so that they will not be distracted by confusing language or incorrect punctuation. Read your rough draft several times, each time paying attention to a different aspect of the paper for possible revision and correction. The first time you read the rough draft, pay attention to the overall structure and style of the paper; the second time check grammar and punctuation; the third time, make sure source materials (paraphrases and quotes from sources) are incorporated smoothly into the text. Finally, consider formal details such as conventions of documentation, format, and presentation. After your paper has been typed, proofread it several times to catch and correct all typographical errors.

Revising for Structure and Style

The first time you read your draft, pay attention to the organizational structure and overall style of the paper. At this point, decide if you need to make any major changes in the order of the ideas or if you should alter the tone. A helpful acronym to keep in mind as you revise for such large issues is *EARS*. Your revising EARS include the following: *E*, eliminate; *A*, add; *R*, rearrange; and *S*, substitute.

Do not be afraid to *eliminate* unnecessary material in your paper. Your teacher will prefer a paper that is tightly focused to one padded with irrelevant details. Conversely, if you discover a section of your paper that seems thin, do not hesitate to *add* more information: more evidence to support an idea, more explanation to clarify an idea, and so on. Be sure that the major sections of the paper are arranged in a logical order. If there seems to be any confusion, *rearrange* major sections. Finally, if you find an example or a piece of evidence that does not seem persuasive in the context of the paper, *substitute* a new example for the one you currently have. Remember, your rough draft is exactly that—rough. It is important for you to read it critically now so that you can improve the overall presentation of your ideas. Asking yourself these questions can help you to improve the structure and style of your paper:

1. Is my introduction engaging and interesting? Does it make the reader want to read on?
2. Is my thesis clearly stated early in the paper so that the reader knows what to expect?
3. Is the organizational pattern of the paper clearly marked for the reader by subheadings and/or directional signals?
4. Are the various sections of the paper linked by good transitional words and phrases?
5. Do the sections of the paper appear in a logical order or do I need to rearrange the parts?
6. Is each section of the paper supported with sufficient data and evidence from the sources and from my primary research?
7. Is my conclusion adequate? Does it highlight the answer to the starting question that motivated the research?
8. Is my language concrete and clear? Are there unnecessary words or phrases that I could cut out?
9. Is my tone objective? Do I sound interested and concerned about the subject but not overly emotional?

Rework any troublesome aspects of the paper. If a particular section of the paper lacks sufficient evidence, go back to the library for some appropriate supporting material. If you are unsure about the tone of your paper or the clarity of the language, have a friend or classmate read through the draft as well. Ask that person to answer the above questions and to tell you where he or she was confused or unsure about your ideas. An outside reading of your work can sometimes provide the distance needed for an objective evaluation.

Improving Paragraphs

It is important to look first at the overall structure of your paper. Then, begin to narrow the scope of your revising to individual paragraphs. Check to be sure that each paragraph has a single major focus and that the ideas within the paragraph are all related to that focus. Focusing your paragraphs in this way will be a great aid to your reader. Where this is done, a new paragraph will indicate a change to a new idea or focus. Often, the first sentence of each paragraph serves as a transitional sentence, bridging the gap between the ideas in the two separate paragraphs. This is the time to check for transitions between paragraphs as well as paragraph focus.

Improving Sentences

In continuing to narrow the scope of your revising, look at individual sentences within your paper. Revise any sentences that seem awkward or confusing. In general, the more simply and directly you state your ideas, the better. Do not use overly complex sentence structures—they will only confuse your reader. Any very long sentences may need to be broken down into two shorter sentences. On the other hand, a series of short, choppy sentences may be more effective as a single long sentence. Your teacher can help you decide how best to revise your sentence style.

Improving Words

Next, look at individual words in your paper with an eye toward spotting confusing vocabulary or unnecessary jargon. Define any terms that might be unfamiliar to a general reader and replace any jargon specific to a field or discipline with more common words.

The following passage from a student paper shows how the writer revised for structure and style:

Sexual harassment not only affects the individual but also has a tremendous effect on the organization in which it occurs. [Employers are beginning to recognize ~~SH~~ *this problem* because it costs them ~~money and causes stressful situations in the working environment~~ in terms of morale, productivity, and lost time.] ~~Business org. need to admit that SH is a problem & then attempt to do something about it.~~ If harassment keeps going on w/out anything being done about it, there will be a lack of trust between the employees and the employer.

move to end

See the final version of this paragraph on page 253.

Revising for Grammar, Punctuation, and Spelling

Once you have revised the overall structure and style of your paper, you are ready to read the paper again, this time with an eye to grammar, punctuation, and spelling. It is important to present your ideas clearly, but it is equally important to present your ideas correctly. A reader will discount you as either ignorant or careless if your work is full of grammatical errors. As you read your paper again, ask yourself the following questions:

1. Is the grammar of each sentence correct? Does each sentence contain subjects and predicates?
2. Do subjects and verbs agree?
3. Are pronouns clear and unambiguous in their reference?
4. Is the punctuation correct? Have I used too many or too few commas?
5. Are there any words that I need to look up in the dictionary, either for meaning or for spelling?
6. Have I used the active rather than the passive voice?

It would be helpful for you to refer to a recent grammar and usage handbook for questions of English grammar, punctuation, and syntax. (For information on punctuating direct quotes, see the section below on incorporating quoted material.) Also, use a dictionary to check the meaning and spelling of individual words. Take the time now to check carefully for such problems in your writing. As always, errors in grammar, punctuation, syntax, and spelling detract from your message and make a negative impression on your reader. A paper full of grammatical or spelling errors signals the reader that the authority of the writer, and hence the authority of the research, is questionable. The following passage from a student paper shows revisions made to correct grammar, punctuation, and spelling:

He also noted that ~~these~~ *sexual harassment* victi~~ons~~ *ms* often ~~felt~~ *feared that* their complaints would go unheard, and they would be blamed for wh*a*t happen*e*d, or they would be considered unprofessional. In addition, Renick found that SHed women had many of the same feelings as ~~those~~ *woman* who had been raped. These ~~feelings~~ *feeling* included humiliated, cheap, embarrassed, and angry.

For the final version of this paragraph, see pages 255–256.

Revising with a Word Processor

A new tool is now available to writers—the word processor. If you have access to a word processor, you may find that it helps you to revise your paper. Many writers who use word processors outline their work on paper before writing a rough draft. Some writers type their rough draft directly into the word processor, and others write rough drafts on paper and then type them into the word processor for revising. In any case, it is at the revising stage that the word processor is especially useful. It makes the act of changing your paper easier, since it allows you to eliminate, add, rearrange and substitute material, altering individual words, sentences, paragraphs, and even whole sections of the paper without having to re-copy or retype.

A word processor can also help you to proofread your paper and to check for selected stylistic or grammatical problems. There are software programs available that will check for spelling, style (e.g., excessive use of the *to be* verbs, excessive use of prepositions), and vague words or jargon. Software to help students write better and more easily is being continually developed and improved. Again, if you have access to word processing, you may want to investigate software designed to help you improve your writing.

Incorporating Reference Materials

Earlier, in the section on writing the rough draft, I suggested that you should not worry about the smooth incorporation of quoted material until you began revising your paper. We have now reached the stage at which you should look at all of the source material in your paper to be sure that you have incorporated it smoothly and appropriately into the flow of your ideas. Your source material should be primarily in the form of paraphrases and summaries. Though they are in your own words, both paraphrases and summaries still require documentation (identification of the source either through in-text citations or footnotes or endnotes). Putting source material into your own words will greatly improve the "flow" of your paper, because the style will be your style and thus consistent throughout. You should use direct quotation *very* sparingly. It is extremely distracting to read strings of direct quotes, because excessive quotation creates a choppy, disjointed style. The better alternative is to incorporate para-phrases and summaries of source material into your own ideas both gram-matically and logically. At this time, check your paper to be sure you have documented all source material accurately and fairly. By following the documentation style outlined in one of the following chapters (Chapters 6, 7, 8, or 9), you will be able to produce a paper that is correctly and accu-rately documented for your chosen academic discipline. Mainly, remem-ber to document both completely and consistently, staying with one par-ticular documentation style.

Incorporating Direct Quotes

At times you may want to use direct quotes in addition to paraphrases and summaries. To incorporate direct quotes smoothly, observe the following principles:

1. When your quotations are four lines in length or less, surround them with quotation marks and incorporate them into your text. When your quotations are longer than four lines, set them off from the rest of the text by indenting five spaces from the left and right margins and triple-spacing above and below them. You do not need to use quotation marks with such block quotes. (Note: In some disciplines, block quotes are customarily indented ten spaces from the left margin only.)

2. Introduce quotes using a verb tense that is consistent with the tense of the quote. (A woman of twenty admitted, "I really could not see how thin I was.")

3. Change a capital letter to a lower-case letter (or vice versa) within the quote if necessary. (She pours her time and attention into her children, whining at them to "eat more, drink more, sleep more.")

4. Use brackets for explanations or interpretations not in the original quote. ("Evidence reveals that boys are higher on conduct disorder [behavior directed toward the environment] than girls.")

5. Use ellipses (three spaced dots) to indicate that material has been omitted from the quote. It is not necessary to use ellipses for material omitted before the quote begins. ("Fifteen to twenty percent of anorexia victims die of direct starvation or related illnesses . . . [which] their weak, immuneless bodies cannot combat.")

6. Punctuate a direct quote as the original was punctuated. However, change the end punctuation to fit the context. (For example, a quotation that ends with a period may require a comma instead of the period when it is integrated into your own sentence.)

7. A period, or a comma if the sentence continues after the quote, goes inside the quotation marks. (Though Cathy tries to disguise "her innate evil nature, it reveals itself at the slightest loss of control, as when she has a little alcohol.")

8. If an ellipsis occurs at the end of the quoted material, add a period before the dots. (Cathy is "more than Woman, who not only succumbs to the Serpent, but becomes the serpent itself . . . as she triumphs over her victims. . . .")

9. Place question marks and exclamation points outside the quotation marks if the entire sentence is a question or an exclamation. (Has Sara read the article "Alienation in *East of Eden*"?)

10. Place question marks and exclamation points inside the quotation marks if only the quote itself is a question or exclamation. (Mary attended the lecture entitled "Is Cathy Really Eve?")

11. Use a colon to introduce a quote if the introductory material prior

to the quote is long or if the quote itself is more than a sentence or two long.

12. Use a comma to introduce a short quote. (Steinbeck explains, "If Cathy were simply a monster, that would not bring her in the story.")

■ CONSIDERING FORMAL DETAILS

Always type research papers or have them typed for you. Use a standard type face and a fresh typewriter ribbon. The typing paper should be a standard weight and size (8½ × 11 inches), not erasable (it smudges), and not onionskin (it tears). If you do not have a self-correcting typewriter or a word processor, use liquid paper or correction tape to correct errors.

Spacing

Use only one side of the paper and double space all the way through, even for long quotes that are indented in the text. Leave four blank lines between major sections, three between heading and section, and three above and below indented, long quotes (more than four lines of text). Also, double space the endnote page (if used) and references page.

Margins

Use a margin 1 to 1.5 inches wide on all sides of each sheet. Use a typing guide (a sheet of paper that goes behind the sheet you are typing on and whose dark ruled lines show through), set the margins on your typewriter, or mark each sheet with a pencil dot 1 inch from the bottom so you will know when to stop typing on a page. If you are typing footnotes at the bottom of the page, plan your bottom margins very carefully to allow room for the notes.

Title

Ask your instructor if you need a title page. If the answer is yes, find out what information should appear there. Generally, title pages contain three kinds of identifying information: the title of the paper, author identification, and course identification (including date). If you do not need a separate title page, put your name, date, assignment name, and any other identifying information on the upper right-hand corner of the first page. Center the title on the first page three lines below the identifying information or, if you use a separate title page, one inch from the top of the page. The title should not be underlined, surrounded by quotation marks, or typed in capital letters. Leave three lines between your title and the beginning of the text.

Numbering

Number each page starting with page 2. Place the numbers in the upper right-hand corners or centered at the bottom of the pages. You need not number the endnote page and the references page. Rather, identify them with the appropriate heading centered one inch from the top of the page and followed by three blank lines.

Indentation

Use uniform indentation for all paragraphs (five spaces is standard). Indent long quotes (more than four lines long) five spaces from both right and left margins or ten spaces from the left margin only. Indent the second line of a reference-list entry five spaces. Leave two spaces between each sentence and after a colon or semicolon. Divide words at the end of lines according to standard rules. Use your dictionary if you are unsure of where to divide a word.

The Endnote Page

If your paper will have endnotes, type them on a separate page immediately after the text of your paper (and before the references page). Center the title, "Notes" or "Endnotes," one inch from the top of the page, and type it in capital and lower-case letters (not all capitals). Do not use quotation marks or underlining. Leave three blank lines between the title and the first line of your notes. Type the notes in consecutive order based on their appearance in the text. Indent the first line of the note five spaces from the left margin, type the superscript number, and leave a space before beginning the note. For any run-over lines of each note, return to the left margin. See Chapter 8 for the specific format of endnotes.

References Page

Center the title "References," "Works Cited," or "Bibliography" and type it one inch from the top of the page in capital and lower-case letters (not all capitals). Do not use quotation marks or underlining. Leave three blank lines between the title and the first line of your references. The references themselves should be typed, double spaced, and listed in alphabetical order by the author's last name (or the title if the author is not known). (Note: In the number system, references are listed consecutively as they appear in the text.) To make the alphabetical list, sort the bibliography cards (on which you have recorded the sources actually used in your research paper) into alphabetical order and transcribe the information in the proper form from the cards to your list. For the specific form references, see the appropriate chapter for your discipline (Chapters 6, 7, 8, or 9). The references page follows the last page of your paper or the endnote page (if included) and need not be numbered.

Proofreading

Once your paper has been typed to your teacher's specifications (or in accordance with the format described above), you will need to proofread carefully for any typographical errors. Your teacher will probably not object to your making corrections on the paper, preferring that you correct any errors, even though this may necessitate some handwriting on the typed page, rather than leaving them uncorrected. One helpful way to proofread for typing errors is to begin at the bottom of the page and read up one line at a time. In this way, you keep yourself from reading for meaning and look only at the "form" of the words. You can spot errors more easily when you are not actually reading the paper. Keep your dictionary handy and refer to it whenever you have any doubt about the spelling of a word. Use your grammar and usage handbook to double check any last-minute questions about grammar and punctuation. If you have a word processor, run your paper through an automatic proofreader. It is impossible to overstress the importance of careful proofreading. Even if the paper was typed for you by a professional typist, you will probably find errors when proofreading. Since you are the paper's author, any errors are your responsibility, not the typist's. It is a good idea to save all early drafts of your paper even after the paper has been typed. Early drafts serve as a record of your thinking and your work on the paper. If you have taken care at every stage of the revision process, your paper will be one you can be justifiably proud of.

■ WRITING AN ABSTRACT

You may be required to write an abstract of your research paper in some cases. An *abstract* is a very short summary of your paper, usually one-tenth to one-twentieth the length of the whole (as compared to a summary paper, which is generally one-third the length of the source). The purpose of an abstract is to condense the essence of the paper. Thus, the reader must be able to understand the essence of the paper from reading the abstract itself without actually reading the paper. Your abstract should cover the purpose of your paper as well as the major topics discussed in it.

To write an abstract, begin by reading through your paper again, underlining important points just as you would when reading any source. Identify and underline the subject, purpose, thesis, and essential content of your paper. If you have clearly organized and focused your paper, important points should occur at the beginning of paragraphs or major sections. Do not underline background material, definitions or descriptions of terms or ideas, supporting examples, references to sources, or information not explicitly related to the thesis.

After underlining the important ideas, list those underlined sentences just as you would if you were writing a summary. Condense and combine sentences if possible to incorporate the information in a few compact sentences. Revise your abstract to make it complete and grammatically correct, checking to be sure you have used complete sentences rather than sentence fragments. The information in your abstract will necessarily be densely packed, but it should still be readable and understandable.

For an example of an abstract (often called a synopsis in business writing), see the paper on sexual harassment in Chapter 9.

PART TWO

Model Research Projects

CHAPTER 6

Writing a Research Paper in Science and Technology

■ INTRODUCTION

As discussed in Chapter 1, sciences in general attempt to explain phenomena in the natural and physical world. Since scientists rely on current technology as tools to help them in their work, technology itself has become a branch of science. Scientific researchers must have knowledge of the current research being conducted by others in their fields. They must also have knowledge of the technologies needed to conduct that research. Though the experimental method is at the heart of scientific research, library research is also important. It is in the scientific journals and reviews that scientists report their findings for scrutiny and replication by other researchers. You need to become familiar with the library tools used by scientists so you can gain access to the current thinking in their fields.

The scientific research paper, often called a review, reports the state of knowledge on a particular defined scientific topic. In the review, you summarize for your readers the present situation in an ongoing field of research. Your contribution, then, will be in the way you organize and present the complex information, thus making it easily accessible to the reader. In the scientific review paper, you do not interpret the data or argue a particular position (as you often do in research papers in the social sciences and humanities). Rather, you present the facts through paraphrase and summary as objectively as you can. Several library research principles and skills will be important for you as you investigate the topic you have chosen to review. These include

1. A familiarity with library research tools, including bibliographies and indexes used in science and technology.

2. The ability to understand and evaluate data from a variety of sources.
3. The ability to paraphrase and summarize information in your own words.
4. The ability to synthesize the information gathered into an organized presentation of the data.
5. The ability to employ the formal conventions of scientific review papers.

■ A GUIDE TO THE SCIENTIFIC RESEARCH PROCESS

To begin your review paper, first determine a topic and narrow it to a manageable, researchable size. If you are taking a science course now, your textbook is a good place to begin looking for research ideas. Check the table of contents in your textbook and in any references that may be listed. Another source of ideas is current scientific journals. Randy Elder, whose research serves as the model for this chapter, became interested in the subject of computer crime when he read an article about it in *Discover* magazine. As a computer science major, he was already interested in both science and technology. Be sure you select a topic that will hold your interest and attention, preferably a topic that you already know something about, so that you will be an informed and objective reporter in your review.

Preparation

You will need to gather the necessary materials for your research project—notecards and a notebook; then make a time schedule that will give you several weeks to conduct your library research and several weeks to write a draft and final copy of your review paper. If you foresee that your research project will contain primary research data, make sure you allow yourself sufficient time to gather that data. Careful planning at the outset of such a major project will ensure that you have enough time to carry out the research necessary to write an informed review.

Developing a Search Strategy

Randy had formulated some general impressions about the uses and abuses of computer technology through his own experience and through reading. He wanted to discover the current thinking in computer science on the kinds of crimes committed with computers and on how to prevent those crimes. His library search, then, began with a look at general background sources on computers and moved to more specific works on computer crime. The following is an outline of Randy's search strategy (your particular search may differ somewhat from this outline):

Randy's Search Strategy

1. Look up computer crime in encyclopedias and dictionaries for general information.
2. Look up reviews already done on computer crime.
3. Use subject indexes and citation indexes for access to science and technology journals.
4. Use the card catalog to find books on computer crime and to locate materials.

Many students begin their research at the card catalog; however, you may find it more profitable to begin with the general sources in the reference area of your library. In a scientific review, it is important to obtain the most current library information. Since books take years to write and sometimes years to produce, even the most recent editions of books can contain information that is three or four years old. The most recent information is probably in journals, which generally publish papers one or two years after the studies are conducted and written up. Since the reference area of your library contains the tools that give you access to a variety of materials, it is a good idea to begin your search there. To illustrate the use of a library search strategy in the sciences and technology, I will lead you through the search steps above using Randy's research on computer crime as a model for your own search.

EXERCISE

Outline your own search strategy, beginning with general and working to specific sources. Draw up a research time schedule.

Search 1

By reading general information about your topic, you can put it into a context and start focusing your search—narrowing your topic to a manageable size. Also, in reading general and specialized encyclopedias and dictionaries, you will learn what is considered common knowledge on the topic. Depending on your particular topic, you will be reading general encyclopedias, such as the *Britannica*, and specialized encyclopedias, such as the *McGraw-Hill Encyclopedia of Science and Technology*. The sources commonly used in the sciences are listed in Chapter 3. Randy used the following background sources, which he listed in his research notebook as the beginning of his working bibliography:

> *McGraw-Hill Encyclopedia of Science and Technology*, 5th ed. New York: McGraw-Hill, 1980.
>
> *Van Nostrand's Scientific Encyclopedia*, 15th ed. New York: Van Nostrand Reinhold, 1976.

The Encyclopedia of Computer Science and Engineering. Anthony Ralston, ed. New York: Van Nostrand Reinhold, 1983.

At the end of each general source, such as the encyclopedias mentioned above, you will usually find a list of bibliographic citations and references. This reference list can be an important place to locate "key sources" and reports written about your topic. List any promising references on your working bibliography, because later they may lead you to valuable information. It is not necessary for you to look up each entry on your working bibliography at this time. In the specialized encyclopedia, *Encyclopedia of Computer Science and Engineering*, Randy found and listed the following references:

1976 Parker, D. B. *Crime by Computer*. New York: Charles Scribner's Sons.

1979 Hsian D., Kerr, D. S., and Madrich, S. *Computer Security*. New York: Academic Press.

EXERCISE

Find and read background sources relevant to your topic to obtain general information. See Chapter 3 for a list of general sources and a list of sources specific to sciences and technology.

Focusing Your Search

After you have read several background sources about your topic, you are ready to narrow the topic for your review. Randy, for example, decided to report on what computer crime is and how it can be prevented. This meant that he could focus on articles and books that dealt specifically with the nature and prevention of computer crimes. He developed a starting question to guide his research: "What is computer crime and how can it be prevented?" Without such a focus, he might have wandered aimlessly through the material about computers with no clear direction to the research.

EXERCISE

Define for yourself just what topic you are trying to review and what specifically within that topic you will cover in your review paper. Then write a starting question that you intend to investigate in your research.

Search 2

For many scientific review papers, reviews and reports of research that have already been written on the topic are useful. It is customary for scientists to publish reviews of current scientific studies periodically to help other scientists keep abreast of the field. Even though you are writing a scientific review yourself, it will be helpful to see what others have to say on the subject before you begin. You may need to update somewhat any review or report you find by reading the most current sources in the field.

Reviews of research and research reports can also provide you with reference lists from which to build your working bibliography. Generally, scientific disciplines publish annual reviews in a particular journal within the field. In the card catalog, look up the field, for example chemistry, and find the annual review journal. If your library carries the *Index to Scientific Reviews*, you can locate relevant reviews there as well. If you have difficulty finding reviews from a particular field, do not hesitate to ask your reference librarian for assistance.

Another useful tool for finding current articles and reviews is the *Current Contents* journal, which indexes articles and reviews by discipline. The following are some examples of *Current Contents* journals relevant in the sciences:

Current Contents: Physical, Chemical, Earth Sciences

Current Contents: Engineering and Technology

Current Contents: Agriculture, Biology, and Environmental Sciences

The *Current Contents* journals are particularly useful because they allow easy and quick access to current articles and reviews written on a particular subject. *Current Contents* publish weekly issues, which include the tables of contents from the latest journals in a particular discipline. The journals are indexed by key title words and by authors. By looking up *security* in the title-word index of several volumes of *Current Contents: Engineering and Technology*, Randy discovered the following recent articles, which he listed on his working bibliography:

"Security and Secrets." *Datamation*, Vol 20, No 2, Feb. 1984

R. E. Johnston. "How to Select and Implement a Data Security Product." *Infosystems*, Vol 31, No 3, March 1984

Depending on your particular scientific topic, you may need to use biographies of researchers as well as reviews of research. Two important scientific biographies you may want to refer to are

American Men and Women of Science, 13th ed. J. Cattell, ed. New York: Bowker, 1976 (for living scientists).

Dictionary of Scientific Biography. New York: Scribner's, 1970–1981 (for scientists no longer living).

EXERCISE

Locate and read reviews of research available on your topic. Use biographies if you are reviewing an important person. See Chapter 3 for a list of sources used in the sciences and technology.

Search 3

Once you have gathered a substantial amount of information on your subject and have noted several key references, you are in a position to expand your bibliography by gathering the names of additional researchers not listed in the works you have used so far. Supplying such information is the principal function of the *subject indexes* and *citation indexes*.

The subject indexes, such as *General Science Index* or *Applied Science and Technology Index*, list articles published in a given year by subject and author. By using these indexes, you can search for citations to journal articles written on your topic. You should usually start with the most recent volume of the index and work your way back, looking up your topic in several volumes of the index. For example, in the *Applied Science and Technology Index*, Randy looked up *computer security* and found a cross-reference that told him to see *Electronic Data Processing—Security Measures*. Upon looking up this heading, he found the following source:

S. Walsh. "Software Security." *Data Process* 25: 9–10, April 1983

The second type of index you will need to use in your library search is the citation index. Through the use of the citation index, you can begin with a particular researcher's name and work your way forward to other researchers who have listed (cited) that researcher in their subsequent work. Citation indexes are relatively comprehensive listings of such citations. The key sources listed in other reference works are the cited sources in the citation index. Typically, you will know the names of key researchers on your topic after a thorough search of the encyclopedias and reviews of research. Then you can follow up by searching each volume of the citation index for citations to these key sources that have appeared since the original publication of the key source. In this fashion, you will quickly build your working bibliography.

The most important citation index for the sciences is the *Science Citation Index*. Randy, for example, knew that D. B. Parker was a major researcher on computer crime, because one of the books he had written was cited in a specialized encyclopedia. Randy looked up the name of the key source, D. B. Parker, in the most recent citation volume of the *Science Citation Index*. He found D. B. Parker's 1976 book, *Crime by Computer*, listed as a cited source (meaning that authors had used his work in subsequent research). Under Parker's name were listed the researchers who had used his work as a basis for their own (that is, the citing sources). Randy added the following source to his working bibliography as found in the citation index:

Crane, H. D. IEEE System M 13 329 83

Listed first is the name of the author who cited Parker's work; then comes the abbreviated title of the journal, followed by publication data—

volume number, page number, year. To find the full title of the journal, you must look at the abbreviations list at the front of the *source* volume. In this case, the abbreviation refers to *Industrial and Electrical Engineering Transactions on Systems Management.*

It may take you some time to become familiar with how the citation indexes work, but doing so will be well worth the effort. These indexes are a major tool in the sciences. When using the citation index, you may find that the complete title of the citing source is omitted, so it may be difficult to know if the article will turn out to be relevant to your search or not. By looking up the author's name in the *source* index for the same year, you may find a more complete listing. You should review each article later to determine its importance to your search.

EXERCISE

Use subject and citation indexes to find titles of articles related to your topic. For a complete list of indexes in the sciences and technology, see Chapter 3.

Search 4

At this point in your search you will want to use the card catalog. First, use the card catalog to help you track down the sources you have already located in your library search. Second, use the card catalog for its cross-referencing function: using the subject listing to locate additional titles on the same or related topics. (For information on using the card catalog, see Chapter 4.) By looking up *computer crime* in the subject card catalog, Randy found the following important books on his topic:

> Martin, J. D. *Security, Accuracy, and Privacy in Computer Systems.* Prentice-Hall, Englewood Cliffs, New Jersey, 1973.
>
> Parker, D. B. *Fighting Computer Crime.* Charles Scribner's Sons, New York, 1983.
>
> Tassel, D. V. *Computer Security Management.* Prentice-Hall, Englewood Cliffs, New Jersey, 1972.

EXERCISE

Use the card catalog's subject listing to find additional books and materials on your topic. Use the *Library of Congress Subject Heading (LCSH)* list to find the headings under which sources for your topic are cataloged.

Evaluation

Once you have located a book or an article, immediately evaluate it for its relevance or usefulness in your search. It is not unusual for a book or article with a very promising title to turn out to be something totally different from what you expected to find. Or you may discover a controversy in the field that you were not aware of prior to your search. As you review your sources, continually sort through and discard any that are not relevant. If, after an initial screening, a book looks as though it could be useful to you, check the book out at the circulation desk. In the case of articles, either photocopy them for later use or take notes from them in the library, since they are generally "noncirculating materials" and cannot be checked out.

EXERCISE

In your research notebook, evaluate each article and book to be used in your research paper. Follow the source evaluation guidelines in Chapter 4.

Taking Notes

As you begin to take notes on the sources, remember to record complete bibliographic information so that you will not need to look up a particular source again. For each source on your working bibliography that you locate in the library, make a bibliography card. On the bibliography card, write the complete library call number in the upper left-hand corner and the control number of the source in the upper right-hand corner. Enter complete bibliographical information on the card: author, title, and publication data (see "Documentation in Science and Technology," below, for examples of science citations). If you are using notecards, write the corresponding control number in the upper right-hand corner of the card and title the card. If you are taking notes in your research notebook, take care to identify each source. Put into quotation marks any information taken directly from the source, and at the end of the note itself mark down the exact page number on which you found the material and whether you paraphrased or quoted the author. Taking care at this stage will benefit you when you get to the actual writing stage.

Search 5

If your scientific research project includes any primary research, you will want to conduct it before beginning to write your research paper. For scientific reviews, however, you will probably not be incorporating any primary research data.

■ ORGANIZING AND WRITING THE SCIENTIFIC REVIEW PAPER

A major task in writing a scientific review is organizing the material you have gathered. It is your job to make sense of the information you found in your library search. Remember, you are trying to make the information accessible to your readers as well as objective and comprehensive. When Randy narrowed his topic, he decided to review the nature of computer crime and the ways of preventing it. After completing his library search, Randy was able to propose an answer to his starting question in the form of a thesis statement: "Although crime by computer has made a nice profit for many, these crimes can be eliminated if owners and managers of computer centers and systems recognize the problem and take steps to prevent these crimes." This thesis statement provided for Randy an overall organizational plan—that is, defining computer crime and describing ways to prevent it. For each of the major types of computer crime, then, he decided to define the crime, give some examples, and indicate how it could be prevented. The main body of the review would be information on particular types of crimes and their prevention. He decided to introduce the review with a brief history of computer-related crimes and conclude with a section on general security measures needed to prevent computer crimes. This organizational plan made the information easily available to the reader. He divided each subsection with descriptive headings to further help the reader discern his organizational plan. Scientific reviews often are subdivided in this way to allow the reader easy access to the information.

EXERCISE

Write a thesis statement and sketch a preliminary organizational plan for your research paper. Refer to Chapter 5 for help with organization.

Arranging the Materials

Once Randy had decided on the thesis statement and organizational plan, he sorted his notecards by their titles to fit the subtopics in his plan (types of crimes and methods of prevention). He set aside any information that did not seem to fit into the paper, such as information he had gathered on the history of computers in general. This material was not relevant to his particular thesis statement. To make a unified, coherent presentation of your research, you must discard any information that is irrelevant. With his preliminary plan set, Randy wrote a more detailed outline to guide him in writing the paper:

```
                    Informal Outline


        Title: An Intelligent Crime

        Thesis: Although crime by computer has made a nice profit for

        many, these crimes can be eliminated if owners and managers of
```

computer centers and systems recognize the problem and take
steps to prevent these crimes.

Introduction
> Define computer crime
>
> List the types of computer crimes
>
> Define the role of the computer in each crime

History
> Describe the origin of computer crime and give
> examples

Types of Computer Crime and Their Prevention
> Sabotage
>
> Data Diddling
>
> Wiretapping
>
> Piggybacking and Impersonation

General Security Measures

EXERCISE

Sort your notecards by their titles, or number related ideas in your research notebook. Write an informal outline of your research paper, using
your thesis statement and organizational plan as a guide. Begin writing the
first draft of your research paper. (See Chapter 5 for additional guidance.)

Writing the First Draft

After you have completed your outline, you are ready to write the first
draft of your research paper. Remember, you are writing in order to review
for your readers the current state of thinking on a particular scientific
topic. Remind yourself at this time of the general understanding you had
of your topic and of your answer to the question you posed as you began
researching. When writing your first draft, use concrete and simple language to explain as objectively as you can the current thinking on your
topic. Your outline will guide the writing of this first draft. Any word,
phrase, or sentence you copy directly from a source must be placed in
quotation marks, followed by the last name of the author, the date the
source was published, and the page number (in parentheses):

> Data diddling is the "simplest, safest, and most common method used in com-
> puter-related crime" (Parker, 1983, p. 71).

(Note: In the number system, sources are identified by a superscript number or a number in parentheses immediately following the sources instead of the author's name, date, and page number in parentheses. See "The Number System," below.)

Similarly, paraphrases and restatements of ideas taken from a source should be given documentation even though you have recast them in your own words:

> The first computer-related act that resulted in prosecution was in 1964 (Martin, 1973).

Remember: you do not need to document common knowledge on your topic.

For general information on planning, writing, and revising your scientific review paper, refer to Chapter 5. Use the following information on documentation in the sciences and technology to cite sources in the correct form. The sample review paper at the end of this chapter serves as a model of a scientific review conducted on a limited, accessible technological topic.

■ DOCUMENTATION IN SCIENCE AND TECHNOLOGY

There is no uniform system of citation in the sciences and technology, but some general principles apply to most scientific disciplines. The sciences use in-text citation and list the works cited at the end of the text. The recency of the source is important, so the year of publication is stressed in the citation. Entire works rather than specific pages are generally cited, and direct quotes are seldom used.

Internal Citation

In the sciences, authors are cited within the text itself by means of either the author/year system or the number system.

The Author/Year System

The author/year system is widely used in the sciences and has been adopted (with variations) by the social sciences. It is a fairly easy system for the reader to use. The following principles should be observed:

1. When an author's work in general is cited, the source material is followed by the last name of the author and the date of the source article in parentheses:

Data diddling is a common type of crime (Parker, 1983).

2. If the source material is paraphrased or directly quoted, the page number should be included:

Data diddling is the "most common method used in computer-related crime" (Parker, 1983, p. 71).

3. If the author's name is used in introducing the source material, only the date is necessary:

According to Parker (1983), data diddling is the most common type of computer crime.

4. Multiple sources may be cited:

Recent research (Parker, 1983; Milleen, 1981; Browne, 1983) indicates that computer crime is on the rise.

The Number System

The number system is also used in the sciences. Here a number is assigned to each source listed on the bibliography (references-cited) page. To cite the source within the text, then, one simply lists the number of that source, either in parentheses or as a raised superscript:

The security officer heads security around the computer center (3).

The security officer heads security around the computer center.[3]

You may cite multiple sources easily with this system:

Recent studies (3,5,8) show that computers are increasingly used to commit crimes.

Recent studies[3,5,8] show that computers are increasingly used to commit crimes.

Content Notes

Some scientific papers might require notes that explain something about the text itself rather than refer to a particular source being cited. These content notes are listed either as footnotes or endnotes rather than internal citations. For the proper form of footnotes and endnotes, see Chapter 8.

The Reference List

The reference list, found at the end of your research paper, contains all the sources actually used in the paper. The title of this page is "References" or "Works Cited." The purpose of the reference list is to help readers find the materials you used in writing your paper. Therefore, you must give complete, accurate information here. The following principles are generally accepted for the reference list in the sciences and technology:

1. On the references or works-cited page, references are arranged in alphabetical order and may be numbered. (Note: The numbering system may proceed consecutively—that is, in the order in which the sources appear in the text.)
2. Authors are listed by surnames and initials.
3. Generally the first word only of a title is capitalized, the title of an article is not enclosed in quotation marks, and the title of a book is not underlined. (Note: Some disciplines, including computer science, use quotation marks and underlining.)
4. Names of journals are often abbreviated.
5. The volume and page number system often resembles that found in the indexes (for example, 19: 330–360). Sometimes the volume number is in boldface type, indicated by a wavy line in manuscript: **16,** or 16.
6. The year of publication appears either immediately after the author's name or at the close of an entry:

Book: Tassel, D. V. 1972. Computer security management. Englewood Cliffs, N.J.: Prentice-Hall.

Article: Milleen, J. K. 1981. Verifying security. ACM Computing Surveys **16:**-350–354.

7. If the same author has published two or more works in the same year, indicate this with a lower-case a and b: 1984a, 1984b.
8. Author/year system: The first word of the entry is typed at the left margin. Subsequent lines of the same entry are indented five spaces. Generally, the entire reference list is double spaced.

   Number system: The numbers are typed at the left margin. The first line of each entry is typed two spaces after the number. Subsequent lines are even with the first line. (See the reference list at the end of the sample paper in this chapter.)

If you are writing a paper for a specific discipline, it is important for you to find out which documentation form your instructor prefers. Some style guides that will help you are

Council of Biology Editors Style Manual, 4th ed. Council of Biology Editors, 1978.

Style Manual for Physics. New York: American Institute of Physics, 1973.

Writing Guide for Chemists, by W. J. Gensler and K. D. Gensler. New York: McGraw-Hill, 1968.

The model references in the accompanying table are based on the form used in many science journals. They follow the style outlined in the *Council of Biology Editors Style Manual*. For further examples, refer to one of the manuals listed above. The sample paper at the end of the chapter uses the number system and the reference list form (slightly different from the model references below) common in engineering and technology.

MODEL REFERENCES: NATURAL AND PHYSICAL SCIENCE

Type of Reference	Example
BOOKS	
1. One author	1. Campbell, R. C. Statistics for biologists. 2d ed. London and New York: Cambridge Univ. Press; 1974.
2. Two or more authors	2. Snedecor, G. W.; Cochran, W. G. Statistical methods. 6th ed. Ames, IA: The Iowa State Univ. Press; 1967.
3. Two or more books by the same author	3. Parker, D. B. Crime and computer security. Encyclopedia of computer engineering. New York: Van Nostrand Reinhold; 1983a.
	Parker, D. B. Fighting computer crime. New York: Scribner's; 1983b.
	(Note: In number system, omit the a and b.)
4. Book with an editor	4. Buchanan, R. E.; Gibbons, N. E., editors. Bergey's manual of determinative bacteriology. 8th ed. Baltimore: Williams and Wilkins; 1974.
5. Section, selective pages, or a chapter in a book	5. Jones, J. B.; Beck, J. F. Asymmetrical syntheses and resolutions using enzymes. Jones, J. B.; Sih, C. J.; Perlman, D. eds. Applications of biochemical systems in organic chemistry. New York: Wiley; 1976: 107–401.

6. Book with a
   corporate author

6. American Society for Testing and
   Materials. Standard for metric
   practice, ANSI/ASTME 380–76.
   Philadelphia: American Society for
   Testing and Materials; 1976.

7. Work known by
   title

7. American men and women of science.
   13th ed. Jacques Cattell Press, ed.
   New York: Bowker; 1976. 6 vol.

8. All volumes in a
   multivolume work

8. Colowick, S. P.; Kaplan, N. O. Methods
   in enzymology. New York: Academic
   Press; 1955–1963. 6 vol.

ARTICLES

1. Journal article
   (one author)

1. Solokov, R. Endangered pisces: The
   Great Lakes whitefish is exploited by
   both lampreys and humans. Nat. Hist.
   90:92–96; 1981.

2. Journal article
   (two or more
   authors)

2. Berry, D. J.; Chang, T. Y. Further
   characterization of a Chinese hamster
   ovary cell mutant defective.
   Biochemistry 21:573–580; 1982.

3. Article on
   noncontinuous
   pages

3. Balack, J. A.; Dobbins, W. O. III.
   Maldigestion and malabsorption:
   making up for lost nutrients.
   Geriatrics 29:157–160, 163–167; 1974.

4. Article with no
   identified author

4. Anonymous. Frustrated hamsters run on
   their wheels. N. Sci. 91:407; 1981.

5. Newspaper article
   (signed)

5. Shaffer, R. A. Advances in chemistry
   are starting to unlock the mysteries
   in the brain. The Wall Street Journal.
   1977 Aug. 12; 1 (Col 1), 10 (col 1).

6. Newspaper article
   (unsigned)

6. Puffin, a rare seabird returns where
   many were killed. The New York Times.
   1977 Sept. 6; Sect. C: 28.

TECHNICAL REPORTS

1. Individual author	1. Brill, R. C. The TAXIR primer. Occasional paper—Institute of Arctic and Alpine Research. 1971; 71 p. Available from: Univ. of Colorado, Boulder, CO.
2. Corporate author	2. World Health Organization. WHO Expert Committee on Filariasis: 3d report. WHO Tech Rep. Ser 542; 1974. 54 p.

OTHER SOURCES

1. Motion picture	1. Rapid frozen section techniques [Motion Picture]. U.S. Public Health Service. Washington DC: National Medical Audiovisual Center and National Audiovisual Center; 1966. 6 min.; sd; color; super 8 mm; loop film in cartridge; magnetic sound track.
2. Dissertation or thesis (unpublished)	2. Dotson, R. D. Transients in a cochlear model. Stanford, CA: Stanford Univ.; 1974. 219p. Dissertation.
3. Letters	3. Darwin, C. [Letters to Sir J. Hooker]. Located at: Archives, Royal Botanical Gardens, Kew, England.
4. Unpublished paper	4. Lewis, F. M.; Ablow, C. M. Pyrogas from biomass. Paper presented to conference on capturing the sun through bioconversion. Washington DC; 1976. Available from Stanford Research Institute, Menlo Park, CA.

EXERCISES AND RESEARCH PROJECT

Complete the exercises outlined in this chapter as you research a limited scientific or technological topic and write a scientific review paper. The three exercises below will give you additional practice using skills associated with science research projects.

1. For each entry on your reference list, write a three- or four-sentence annotation that describes the content of that source.
2. Write a "review of the literature" report that summarizes in three to four pages the major ideas found in your sources. Often a literature review, which lists and comments on the works done to date in a particular area of scientific investigation, will be a component of a larger scientific paper. The review of the literature will proceed in chronological order based on the publication date of the source and thus will differ from the scientific review paper, which may be organized around concepts or other categories.
3. When you have finished writing your paper, write an abstract (approximately 100 words long) of your paper in which you summarize the major points in your review (see Chapter 5 for a discussion of how to write abstracts).

```
SAMPLE REVIEW PAPER: SCIENCE AND TECHNOLOGY FORMAT
            (Optional title page)
```

```
                 An Intelligent Crime


                         by

                    Randy Elder




              Computer Science 2304-001
                     Dr. Mackie
                   May 15, 1984
```

Title page includes title, student identification, course identification

[1 inch]

An Intelligent Crime

[3 lines]

First note number refers to first source on work cited page in number system

Students' categories

A computer crime is one committed with the use of a computer or computer-related object. The different types of computer crime include sabotage, impersonation, piggybacking, data-diddling, and wiretapping (1). Although these are not the only types used, they are used to commit the majority of computer crimes. To commit these crimes, the computer plays four roles: (a) object--computer is destroyed, and possibly the computer center and data are destroyed; (b) subject--computer is site of crime and is manipulated to commit a crime; (c) instrument--computer is used as a tool to create the crime; and (d) symbol--computer is a symbol of intimidation or deception; false advertising of nonexistent services.

The first computer-related act resulting in prosecution was in 1964 (1). A Texas programmer stole $5 million worth of programs from his employer. The first federal case involving a computer was U.S. v. Bennett in 1966. A banker changed the bank's program to make the computer ignore his checking account when looking for overdrafts. Another crime was in New York City when a bank teller transferred $1.5 million to his personal account. One other computer-related crime was when an engineering student was able to gain access to the supply system of the telephone company and steal 1 million worth of equipment. These are just a few of the many crimes that have been committed using computers or computer-related

2

objects. Although crime by computer has made a nice profit for many, these crimes can be eliminated if the owners and managers of computer centers and systems recognize the problem and take steps to prevent these crimes.

[4 lines]

Thesis statement

Sabotage. This form of computer crime can be done logically as well as physically. Physical acts can be done by anyone who can get close enough to the computer system. Examples are the computer being shot at, burned or blown up, stabbed with screwdrivers, or even being attacked by the heel of a woman's shoe. The computer is not the only target; often it is the data itself. The data is usually stored on diskettes or tapes. These tapes and diskettes can easily be destroyed or the data on them erased by contamination from a substance or strong magnetic field. Logical sabotage can also be very harmful to a computer center. A programmer could modify a program so that it would give wrong answers even though they looked right. Someone could change the data so that the output, usually a printout, would be wrong or misleading.

Subheadings help organize review

"The computer has occasionally been a target for antiestablishment rebels, antiwar protestors, and rampaging students. This has resulted in a number of serious sabotage attacks on computer centers" (1, p 5). A group called Students for a Democratic Society destroyed 1000 magnetic tapes at Dow Chemical. It cost the company approximately $100,000. In another incident students at Sir

Refers to page 5 of source 1. Direct quotes and paraphrases need page reference.

3

George Williams University set fire to the computer center, causing $2 million damage to computer equipment. They also threw out the window all magnetic tapes, diskettes, programs, and cards.

All the above incidents could have been prevented if the owners and managers of the computer centers had taken precautions. The main precaution should be physical access controls, such as fences, guards, electronic surveillance equipment, alarms, and electronically locked doors. Another security measure is a mantrap, which allows only one person to enter at a time (1). After passing through the first door by using an electronic badge or key, a person would be required to stand on a scale to measure his weight, making sure that he was not carrying something or determining if an unauthorized person was in the mantrap. If he passes all the tests, he is allowed to enter through a second door. A security guard would monitor the mantrap and let people in the second door. Other safeguards include keeping the computer center on a low profile to discourage outside attention, protecting tape/disk storage, and supervising the workers in the center to make sure that employees are doing only their jobs and not something else.

Wiretapping. There are two kinds of wiretapping, active and passive. In active wiretapping the intruder sends data on a telephone or other communication line. In passive wiretapping

Each section describes the crime, gives examples, provides solutions

4

the intruder listens to data given on a line. The
only tools needed are a terminal and a modem, which
enables computer signals to be carried over
telephone lines. After a few days of practicing, a
person is able to reach out and touch someone else's
data base. After experimenting with his new
knowledge, a potential intruder will try to break
into confidential computer files. He must first log
on--get the computer to recognize him as a legitimate
user--by giving an identification name or number and
then a personal password. After successfully being
logged on, the intruder is able to look at some if not
all of the files in the computer's memory.

Most cases are not even detected, because
wiretapping is hard to detect if there are no
protective devices. One incident was discovered in
Japan. The chief technical engineer at Nippon
Telegraph and Telephone Public Corporation was
responsible for maintaining and testing a telephone
line that was used to transmit cash card account
information to and from a bank. He tapped this line
and, using home-made equipment, was able to transfer
money to his personal account. In three years he had
made over $520,000 before he was caught (1).

Protecting against wiretappers is easy if
computer center managers just realize that something
needs to be done. The best protection is
encryption. When information is sent from the
computer, encryption scrambles the data so that if
someone intercepts it, all they get is
gobbledygook. The only way a person could get the

Defines term "log-on"

5

information would be through a deciphering device,
but it is impossible to decipher the data unless you
are an authorized user.   Other safeguards include
having the passwords contain at least four
characters (letters, numbers, symbols) with no
meaning to the owner.   The computer should also
record every attempt to enter it and should wait five
seconds after every wrong try at the ID or password
and hang up after three wrong guesses.   An extreme
measure would be for the computer to trace a call
after several unsuccessful attempts and then the
police could take over.   Passwords should be changed
every six months or more frequently if the user
suspects his password has been discovered (2).

Refers to second source

Data—diddling.   Data—diddling is the
"simplest, safest, and most common method used in
computer—related crime" (3, p 71).   It involves
changing data before or during its input or output
from a computer.   This crime can be committed by
anyone who has access to the processes of creating,
recording, transporting, encoding, examining,
checking, converting, or transforming data.   Almost
anyone could commit this crime because it is the
easiest and simplest.   The more original the crime,
the better the chance that it will go undetected and
the criminal will get away with a very good profit.
       A good example of this crime was a person
substituting his bank depositor slips among the
slips at the bank desk (4).   All during the day

Gives specific examples

6

people were using his deposit slips to make their deposits.   The next day the man closed his account, which had mushroomed to over $50,000, and he has never been seen since.   Another case involved a programmer with a bad credit rating who was given an assignment to write a check–handling program for the bank that handled his account.   While writing this program, he programmed the computer to ignore his account if there were insufficient funds.   It worked until the computer system broke down and a check of his bounced, revealing the scheme.   In another incident an alert programmer noticed that in calculating interest, the computer rounded the figure to the nearest cent and truncated the rest (2.666667 would become 2.67, and .003333 would go to the bank).   This programmer took the truncated part and transferred it to his account.   In a short while it had accumulated a sizeable profit.   It worked until bank auditors noticed he was withdrawing large sums without depositing much.   One last case involved three employees of a securities firm who used the computer as a scapegoat while embezzling more than $500,000 over a period of several years.   The trio took a little from several customers' accounts and when the customer complained, they said that it was the "dumb" computer's fault.   They were eventually caught:

[3 lines]

Protection against data–diddling requires extensive safeguards. . . .   A computer

Ellipses dots indicate omitted material

is the ideal detection device to discover
deviations from normal transaction
activities by analyzing input data in a
range of statistical ways, from simple to
sophisticated (4, p 74).

[3 lines]

Other safeguards include program testing: no
user is allowed to use a program that he wrote
himself, and the operator will not be allowed to know
the function of the program that is being
run.   Diskettes/tapes should be labeled with
alphanumeric labels, nothing that would indicate the
function of the program.   The specifications of
programs should be approved by a group, and the
program should be inspected to make sure that it does
only what it is supposed to do.   Testing of a program
should be done by a group, excluding the
programmer.   When modifications are made to a
program, a record should be kept of who authorized
the modification and who did the programming. Programs
should be done by several different programmers,
especially if they are for sensitive data. Audits should
be given at regular intervals with surprise audits
periodically (5).

Piggybacking and Impersonation.   This type of
crime can be committed in two ways, physically and
electronically.   Physical piggybacking is used by an
unauthorized person to get into a computer
center.   A piggybacker, with his hands full of

Long quotes set off from text by indenting five spaces from right and left margins. No quotation marks needed.

computer—related objects, would wait outside the
entrance to the computer center until an authorized
user went in. When the authorized user opened the
door with his key or electronic badge, the
piggybacker would walk in with him. Electronic
piggybacking can be done by placing a hidden terminal
on the same circuit as a legitimate terminal. The
hidden terminal can be used anytime that the
legitimate terminal is not being used. Another
example of electronic piggybacking is when an
authorized user does not log off properly and leaves
the terminal as though the user is active. Besides
piggybacking, computer criminals use
impersonation. "Impersonation is the process of one
person assuming the identity of another" (4, p
96). There are several ways this can be done. A
person when logging on can use someone else's ID and
password, or someone else's ID card or key to gain
entry into the computer center.

　　　An example of an impersonation involved a young
man who posed as a magazine writer. He called the
telephone company saying that he wanted to write an
article on the computer system of the telephone
company. He was given a detailed tour of the center
and explanations of the application systems, and by
using the knowledge he was able to steal $1 million
worth of telephone equipment from the company. In
another case a person stole several credit cards that
required a personal ID to withdraw money from an
automatic teller. This person then called the
owners of the cards and said he was from the bank and
needed the ID number to protect the owner. The

9

owners gave out their personal ID numbers, and the
criminal withdrew the maximum from the automatic
teller.

Protection against piggybacking and
impersonation is easier if the authorized users keep
a sharp lookout for unauthorized
personnel. Mantraps can be very effective in
keeping physical piggybackers out of the computer
center. Authorized users should not let anyone who
cannot produce identification enter with
them. Another precaution is to have closed-circuit
television cameras scanning the computer
center. Tours of a computer center should not be
given. If there is a visitor to a computer center,
that person should be escorted. To prevent
electronic piggybacking, authorized users should be
sure to log off correctly, and if they suspect that
someone is using their ID numbers and passwords to
get into the system, they should report their
suspicions to the computer manager. When a terminal
is not being used for a long period of time, the user
should log off, and then log on again when
ready. Passwords should be difficult to guess and
changed frequently. Another safeguard is for the
computer to ask for the password several times while
the user is active, especially if he wants sensitive
data. The computer center should be closely
supervised and guarded at all times, even at night.

Concluding section gives general measures for security

General Security. All the examples of crimes
above could have been prevented if the computer

10

managers just took precautions. Other additional
precautions include appointing a computer security
officer to head the security in and around the
computer center (6). This security officer should be
a responsible person who can make fast decisions
without consulting others. Repair men and delivery
men should be checked out to make sure that they are
legitimate. If they have to remove something, the
repair men should have prior approval from the
computer manager. Alarms and locks should be placed
on the outside as well as the inside of computer
centers. If possible, uniformed guards should
patrol the inside and outside of the computer center
during off hours. Prospective employees should be
carefully screened and interviewed. All papers and
computer printouts should be destroyed when not
needed. Employees should be warned when information
is confidential, and expected to keep it
confidential. When an employee leaves for another
job, he should be required not to give out
confidential information. An inventory should be
kept of computer and company equipment, and the
inventory should be checked periodically.

Programs should be thoroughly and carefully
reviewed and tested, not only when first
used. Programs should not be modifiable from
terminals. Another suggestion is to have one or two
trusted persons try to break the security as a test
of the system:

These safeguards may seem troublesome,
time-consuming or expensive, but the loss

Long quote introduced with a colon

11

of confidential company information can
result in loss of contracts, a lawsuit,
losing sales or market, and even financial
ruin (1, p 155).

Computers do not commit crimes, but people
do. In order to have a safe and secure computer
center, there has to be trust and honesty among the
employees. Computer managers should take
precautions now to prevent others from taking
advantage of the computer center even if the center
has not had any previous crime. If precautions are
not taken, then the examples of computer—related
crimes in this review will be small compared to what
could be accomplished by more intelligent and
experienced criminals.

Works Cited

1. Martin, J. D. <u>Security, Accuracy, and Privacy in Computer Systems</u>. Prentice–Hall, Englewood Cliffs, New Jersey, 1973.

2. Tassel, D. V. <u>Computer Security Management</u>. Prentice–Hall, Englewood Cliffs, New Jersey, 1972.

3. Parker, D. B. "Crime and Computer Security." <u>The Encyclopedia of Computer Science and Engineering</u>. Anthony Ralston, ed. Van Nostrand Reinhold, New York, 1983.

4. Parker, D. B. <u>Fighting Computer Crime</u>. Charles Scribner's Sons, New York, 1983.

5. Browne, M. W. "Locking Out the Hackers." <u>Discover</u>. 15 (Sept. 1980) 31–40.

6. Milleen, J. K. "Verifying Security." ACM Computing Surveys (Dec. 1983).

Works cited page uses the number system and documentation style common in computer science and technology. (Note: this form is slightly different from the form used in the model references from the natural and physical sciences.)

CHAPTER 7

Writing a Research Paper in Social Science

■ INTRODUCTION

The social sciences have as their goal the systematic study of human behavior and human societies. For this reason, it is particularly important for social science research to include primary research (for example, interviews, surveys, and questionnaires) in which field research is conducted and reported. You need to know in general how social scientists proceed when gathering information on a particular subject or issue, using both primary and secondary sources.

Necessarily, social science researchers must have knowledge of current research being conducted by others in their field. That is why library work, using secondary sources, is also important. In the social science journals, researchers report their findings for scrutiny and replication by other researchers. As you become familiar with the tools used by social scientists to gain access to current research, several research principles and skills will be important to you. These skills include

1. A familiarity with primary research techniques used by social scientists.
2. A familiarity with library research tools used by social scientists, including bibliographies and indexes.
3. The ability to synthesize and evaluate data and opinions from a variety of primary and secondary sources.
4. The ability to develop a thesis consistent with the evidence found in primary and secondary sources.
5. The ability to organize and write a paper that effectively presents and supports your thesis.
6. The ability to employ the formal conventions of research papers in the social sciences.

■ A GUIDE TO THE SOCIAL SCIENCE RESEARCH PROCESS

First, choose a topic or research problem to investigate. If you are taking a social science course such as psychology or sociology, your textbook is a good place to start looking for research ideas. Remember that the inquiry process generally begins with a felt incongruity, problem, or question. Perhaps something you read in your textbook or in a popular magazine such as *Psychology Today* struck you as problematic, or perhaps a particular issue seemed interesting or intriguing to you. In any case, you need to find a topic that will hold your interest and attention, a topic on which you are willing to spend considerable time and energy. Cheryle Locke, whose research will serve as the model for this chapter, chose the topic of anorexia nervosa, a mental and physical disorder common in young women. She found the seeds of this interest in her own struggles with the pressures and stresses of college life. She discovered that stress can lead to a variety of mental and physical disorders, including anorexia nervosa.

Preparation

You will need to gather the materials for your research, including notecards and a research notebook; then make a time schedule that allows a sufficient period for primary research. Your interest in your particular topic will get you started, but you will still need to think about the problem you have posed for yourself and begin to propose ways to investigate it. For example, Cheryle began with the problem of how stress affects young college women both mentally and physically. She wanted to investigate what "authorities" had to say on the subject, but she also wanted to find out about the particular problems of young women on her own campus. She decided that conducting a small survey of the college women would help her to understand both what she herself was experiencing as a new college student and what other college women were experiencing. The actual questions on her survey evolved as she researched and defined for herself more specifically what she wanted to find out through the survey (see her questionnaire in the sample research paper at the end of this chapter). Knowing that she wanted to conduct such a survey as part of the research project, she budgeted her time so she could finish her library research and still have sufficient time to conduct the primary research.

Developing a Search Strategy

Through her own experience and through her reading, Cheryle had formulated some general impressions about stress and its effects on college women. Now she wanted to explore the current thinking in the social sciences about stress. Her library search proceeded from a look at general sources to a look at more specific works. An outline of her search strategy is presented below (your particular search may differ somewhat from this outline):

Cheryle's Search Strategy
1. Encyclopedias and dictionaries for general background information.
2. Reviews of research already conducted on the topic.
3. Subject indexes and citation indexes for access to listings of specific sources.
4. Abstracts of particular sources.
5. Card catalog for access to particular sources.
6. Primary research data.

As this list makes clear, your library search will probably begin in the reference area of the library. To illustrate the use of a library search strategy in the social sciences, I will lead you through the steps above using Cheryle's research on stress as a model for your own research.

EXERCISE

Outline your own search strategy, beginning with general and working to specific sources. Include any primary research needed for your project. Draw up a research time schedule.

Search 1
Reading general information on your subject will enable you to put it into a context. This will help you focus your search and define a starting question. Reading specialized encyclopedias and dictionaries will help you to define what is considered common knowledge about the subject. Depending upon your particular subject, you may be reading general encyclopedias, such as the *Americana*, and specialized encyclopedias, such as the *Encyclopedia of Human Behavior*. The sources commonly used in the social sciences are listed in Chapter 3. It would be useful for you to review that section of the book now.

Cheryle used the following general sources, which she listed in her notebook as the beginning of her working bibliography:

Dictionary of Psychology, by J. Chaplin. New York: Dell, 1975.

McGraw-Hill Encyclopedia of Science and Technology, 5th ed. New York: McGraw-Hill, 1980.

Encyclopedia of Human Behavior, 1978 ed.

International Encyclopedia of Psychiatry, Psychology, Psychoanalysis, & Neurology. New York: Van Nostrand Reinhold, 1977.

At the end of each general source, such as the encyclopedias mentioned above, you will usually find a list of bibliographic sources. This reference list can be an important place to locate "key sources" and studies written about your topic. List the promising references on your working bibliography; they may lead you to valuable information. It is not necessary for you to look up each entry on your working bibliography at this time. In the specialized encyclopedia, Cheryle found and listed the following references:

Agras, W., Barlow, D. H., Chapin, N., Abel, G., & Leitenberg, H. (1974). Behavior modification of anorexia nervosa. *Archives of General Psychiatry, 30,* 279–286.

Bruch, H. (1973). *Eating disorders: Obesity, anorexia nervosa, and the person within.* New York: Basic Books.

Bruch, H. (1974). Perils of behavior modification in treatment of anorexia nervosa. *Journal of the American Medical Association, 230,* 1419–1422.

Liebman, R., Minuchin, S., & Baker, L. (1974). The role of the family in the treatment of anorexia nervosa. *Journal of Child Psychiatry, 13,* 264–274.

EXERCISE

Find and read background sources relevant to your topic to obtain general information. (See Chapter 3 for a list of general sources and a list of sources commonly used in the social sciences.)

Focusing Your Search

After you have read several general background sources about your subject, you are ready to define a starting question to help you focus your search. The question must be a realistic one that you are able to research given the information and time available to you. This question will be critical to the success of your research paper. Make sure that it is neither trivial nor overly ambitious, but allows you sufficient scope for research. As mentioned earlier, your interest in a topic is the impetus for your choice. Generally, as with most research, the starting question will be motivated by a problematical event or an incongruity you perceive about your topic. As you were reading the encyclopedias and general background sources, you may have noted in your research notebook some important idea or question that could serve as a focus for your research. There is no one right question, nor is there one right way to discover a question, but it should be something that interests and intrigues you, and it should be supportable by evidence in both your primary and secondary sources.

Cheryle, for example, began searching for information on stress. She discovered that one disorder in which stress plays a role is anorexia nervosa. As she looked up and read about this disorder in the specialized encyclopedias, she became intrigued with the question of the causes and effects of anorexia nervosa in young women. These questions—"What causes the disorder?" and "What effects does the disorder have on young women?"—became the starting questions for her research. These were good starting questions because they provided a focus for her search. She was not looking for the history of the disorder; nor was she looking for the major theories concerning the disorder, though these could possibly have been starting questions for another research paper. Information on history and theory would therefore be incidental to her search; she would sort out information in the sources by choosing only material that was relevant to the causes and effects of the disorder. As you can see, the starting question you choose will dictate what information is relevant and what is not. Without such a starting question, your search may ramble aimlessly and get you nowhere. Take care to define carefully what it is you are trying to discover. No amount of diligent effort will substitute for a good starting question.

EXERCISE

Define for yourself a starting question to guide your research. Use this question as a place to start—your research direction may change as you actually begin finding and reading your sources.

Search 2

Reviews of research will be the next step in your library search. Such sources provide extensive materials on a narrower range of topics than those covered in encyclopedias. Also, they typically provide reference lists to help you continue building your working bibliography. Some examples of publications that include reviews of research are

Handbook of Modern Sociology, Faris

Annual Review of Psychology (journal)

Psychological Bulletin (journal)

Cheryle looked up *anorexia nervosa* in several indexes to find articles that reviewed important studies on the topic:

Index to Scientific Reviews

Bibliography of Medical Reviews

Current Contents: Social and Behavioral Sciences

In the *Bibliography of Medical Reviews*, she found the following recent reviews, which she listed on her working bibliography:

> Halmi, K. Anorexia nervosa: Recent investigations. *Annual Review of Medicine*, 1978, *29*, 137–48.
>
> Agras, S., et al. Behavior modification in anorexia nervosa: Research foundations, in Vigersky, R. (Ed.), *Anorexia nervosa*. N.Y.: Raven Press, 1977.

The *Current Contents* journal is particularly useful, because it allows easy and quick access to current articles written on a particular subject. The weekly issues of *Current Contents* contain the tables of contents from the latest journals in a particular discipline. The journals are indexed by key title words and by authors. By looking up *anorexia nervosa* in the subject listing of several volumes of *Current Contents: Social and Behavioral Sciences*, Cheryle discovered the following recent articles:

> Hudson, J., Pope, H., Jones, J., Yurgeluntodd, D. Family history study of anorexia nervosa and bulimia. *British Journal of Psychiatry*, 1983, *142*, 133–140.
>
> Steinhausen, H., & Glenville, K. Follow-up studies of anorexia nervosa: A review of research findings. *Psychological Medicine: Abstracts in English*, 1983, *13*(2), 239–245.

EXERCISE

Locate and read reviews of research available for your topic. (See Chapter 3 for a list of possible sources.)

Search 3

Once you have gathered a substantial amount of information on your subject and have noted several key references, you are in a position to expand your bibliography by gathering the names of additional researchers not listed in the works you have used so far. Providing such information is the principal function of the *subject indexes* and *citation indexes*.

The *subject indexes*, such as *Social Sciences Index*, list articles published in a given year on a particular topic. Start with the most recent volume and work your way back, looking up your subject in several volumes of the index. For example, the *Social Sciences Index*, Cheryle found the following source:

> George, L. K., & Lieberman, S. Paradoxical intention in the treatment of chronic anorexia nervosa. *American Journal of Psychiatry*, 1982, *139*, 650 –653.

The citation index is the second type of index you will need to use in your library search. Citation indexes are relatively comprehensive listings of citations that are typically more efficient sources of available citations than other indexes. The key sources you have found listed in other works are the cited sources in the citation index. Typically, you will know the key sources for your topic after your thorough search of the encyclopedias and reviews of research. Now you follow up by searching each volume of the citation index for citations to those key sources that have appeared since the original publication of the key sources. In this fashion, you will quickly build your working bibliography.

The most important citation index for the social sciences is the *Social Science Citation Index,* 1972–present. Cheryle, for example, knew that H. Bruch was a major researcher on anorexia nervosa because Bruch had written the summary article in one of the specialized encyclopedias and because her name had been listed as the author of several books and studies on anorexia nervosa. For these reasons, Cheryle could assume that Bruch's work would be a key source used by many other researchers. Therefore, Cheryle looked up H. Bruch in the then most recent volume of the *Social Science Citation Index.* She found Hilda Bruch listed as a cited source (meaning that authors had used her work in subsequent research). Under her name were listed all the researchers who had used her works as a basis for their own (that is, the citing sources). Bruch is the cited source in Bruch, H. 73 EATING DISORDERS.

The following are some of the citing sources:

Dietz, W. NUTR RES Vol 3, Pg 43, Yr 83

Garner, D. INT J EAT D Vol 2, Pg 15, Yr 83

Liebman, R. J Am A Chil Vol 22, Pg 128, Yr 83

It may take you some time to become familiar with how the citation indexes work, but it will be well worth the effort. These indexes are a major tool in the social sciences. If you find that the title of the citing source is omitted from the citation index, it will be difficult to know if the article is relevant to your search. Later, however, you can look these sources up in the source index to determine their importance to your topic. Also, in the index, the journal titles of the citing sources are abbreviated. You must look up the abbreviations in the appropriate volume to determine the exact titles of the journals. For example, J AM A CHIL is the abbreviaton for *Journal of American Academy of Child Psychiatry.*

EXERCISE

Use subject and citation indexes to find titles of articles related to your topic. (See Chapter 3 for a list of indexes used in the social sciences.)

Search 4

Next you will need to begin to sort and narrow your list of possible sources on your working bibliography. Not every source you have listed will turn out to be relevant to your starting question. You can use abstracts to narrow down the sources you have listed on your bibliography to those with the greatest relevance for your own research focus. This is one useful function of abstracts. A second function is as initial locating devices. When using abstracts, be prepared for some variation in the indexing procedures and/or some limitations in coverage. The comprehensiveness and accessibility of the information in abstracts vary from field to field. But it is important for you to become familiar with abstracts and to use them in your research. Cheryle found abstracts that offered a condensed version of several of the articles on her working bibliography. In this way, she was able to eliminate articles that were either too technical or completely irrelevant to her question. The important abstracts in the social sciences are

> *Sociological Abstracts.* New York: Sociology Abstracts, 1953–present.
>
> *Psychological Abstracts.* Washington, D.C.: American Psychological Association, 1927–present.

In the 1982 subject listing of *Psychological Abstracts,* Cheryle also found a new source that looked promising:

> daily life experiences, 20 & 23 yr old female anorectics, 8482

Upon looking up reference number 8482 in the 1982 abstracts volume, Cheryle found a discussion of the article and a complete citation:

> Larsen, Reed, and Johnson, Craig. (U. Chicago Committee on Human Development). **Anorexia nervosa in the context of daily experience.** *Journal of Youth and Adolescence,* 1981 (Dec), Vol 10(6), 455–471.

Search 5

At this point in your search you will want to use the card catalog extensively. First, use the card catalog to help you track down the sources you have already listed on your working bibliography. Second, use the card catalog for its cross-referencing function: using the subject headings to locate additional titles on the same or related topics. (For information on the card catalog, see Chapter 3.)

By looking up *anorexia nervosa* in the *Library of Congress Subject Heading* list, Cheryle discovered that *anorexia nervosa* was used as a subject heading in the card catalog. Then, Cheryle looked up *anorexia nervosa* in the card catalog and found the following important books:

> Garfinkle, P., & Garner, D. (1982). *Anorexia nervosa: A multidimensional perspective.* N.Y.: Book Center.

Minuchin, S., Rosman, B., & Baker, L. (1978). *Psychosomatic families: Anorexia nervosa in context.* Mass: Harvard U. Press.

Woodman, M. (1980). *The owl was a baker's daughter: Obesity, anorexia nervosa, and the repressed feminine, a psychological study.* Canada: Inner City Books.

EXERCISE

Use the card catalog's subject listing to find additional books and materials on your topic. Use the *Library of Congress Subject Heading* list to find the heading(s) under which sources on your topic are cataloged.

Evaluation

Once you have located either a book or an article, evaluate it immediately for its relevance and usefulness in your search. It is not unusual for a book or article with a promising title to turn out to be something totally different from what you expected to find. You must continually sort through the sources and discard any that are of no use to you. If, after an initial screening, a book still looks useful, check it out at the circulation desk. In the case of articles, either photocopy them for later use or take notes from them in the library, since they generally are "noncirculating materials" and cannot be checked out. If your library does not carry the source, ask the circulation librarian about the possibility of an interlibrary loan.

EXERCISE

In your research notebook, evaluate each article and book to be used in your research paper. Follow the source evaluation guidelines in Chapter 4.

Taking Notes

As you begin to take notes on the sources, remember to record complete bibliographic information so that you will not need to look up a particular source again. Make a bibliography card for each source on your working bibliography that you locate in the library. On the bibliography card, write the complete library call number in the upper left-hand corner and the control number of the source in the upper right-hand corner. Enter complete bibliographical information on the card: author, title, and publication data (see "Documentation in the Social Sciences," below, for examples of social science citations). If you are using notecards, write the corresponding control number in the upper right-hand corner of the card and title the card. If you are taking notes in your research notebook, identify each source carefully. Put into quotation marks any information taken directly from the source and write down the exact page number on which the note was found at the end of the note itself. Also identify paraphrased or quoted material. Taking care at this stage will be beneficial when you reach the actual writing stage of your research paper.

Search 6

If your research plan calls for some primary research, a good time to start is after you have gathered your library materials. Cheryle wanted to determine whether the conditions and symptoms of anorexia nervosa were in evidence among a small sample of college women on her campus. She designed a questionnaire containing questions about diet and weight control, appetite and exercise, and magazine-reading preferences (see the questionnaire in the sample research paper at the end of this chapter). This questionnaire was administered to fifty college women, twenty-five of whom were members of a college sorority. Cheryle divided the sample up in this way in order to compare the sorority women with the other women on campus. Through the survey, she verified her own hypothesis that the conditions associated with anorexia nervosa, including society's obsession with weight and weight control, were present on her own campus. You will find the results of the survey in the sample research paper at the end of this chapter.

EXERCISE

Conduct any primary research connected to your research project. Analyze that primary research and determine the best method of displaying your results, whether in a graph, table, or discussion.

Illumination

Since you are actively seeking the answer to the starting question you posed at the beginning of your search, continually "talk to yourself" while researching. Try to understand and interpret the source information as you go, synthesizing data from numerous authors and sources, taking what is relevant and discarding what is not. This is where your research notebook can be of particular value to you. Take the time to write down your own thoughts and comments as you go; note for yourself those sources and ideas that you find particularly important or revealing. Think about your topic consciously, but also allow yourself enough time to let your ideas "brew" in your subconscious mind. It is during this stage in your research that you will be seeking the answer to your starting question. Gradually, you will arrive at a tentative answer, a hypothesis or thesis that will satisfactorily explain the question's answer as you see it. Or you may modify or completely change the hypothesis or thesis in light of what you ultimately find in your research.

This is the *illumination* stage of the inquiry process, wherein you begin to "see the light," or the answer to your question. Perhaps your answer will be that there is no definitive answer, and that would be all right too. In such a case, you would provide the most likely hypotheses and argue the relative merits of each. At any rate, you would present your understanding of the subject in a thesis statement that explained the data you gathered. In your thesis, then, state your opinion, articulating what you believe based upon the evidence you have gathered. For example, Cheryle first asked a question; then, through preparation and research, she came to an understanding of her topic, stated in the form of a thesis statement:

1. Starting question: "What are the causes and effects on young women of the mental and physical disorder anorexia nervosa?"

2. Thesis statement: "The internal problems within upper-middle-class and upper-class families, along with tremendous sociocultural pressures, have apparently caused a present rise in the number of anorexia nervosa victims."

EXERCISE

Write a thesis statement that articulates the conclusion you have reached through your research. In your thesis, state your answer to the starting question posed at the beginning of your research.

Verification

Once you have defined a thesis statement for yourself, you will have a guide to use in organizing your actual written presentation of the research. As you write, however, you may find that the thesis statement needs to be revised in some way. The actual writing of the research paper may help you see things in new ways or discover meanings you had not thought of before you began writing. Actually writing down your ideas in a systematic fashion is an important way of verifying the research you have done. As you try to articulate in writing the understanding you have gained of your topic, you may find that there are gaps in your knowledge that you need to fill by further research, or you may find that the thesis you have articulated really does not seem to explain the research findings adequately. In either case, you will need to go back to both your primary and secondary sources for further information. Moreover, you will need to restate your thesis. On the other hand, you may find that your writing has clarified your ideas, thereby verifying them both for you and your potential readers.

■ ORGANIZING AND WRITING THE SOCIAL SCIENCE RESEARCH PAPER

Your thesis statement, if carefully constructed, should suggest an organizational plan to you. Cheryle's thesis statement ("The internal problems within upper-middle-class and upper-class families, along with tremendous sociocultural pressures, have apparently caused the rise in the number of anorexia nervosa victims") implies its own organizational plan. It will be an account of the *causes* of anorexia nervosa, including primarily the family problems and the sociocultural pressures, followed by a discussion of the *effects* of anorexia nervosa on young women and the current rise in the number of victims.

Other possible organizational plans that may have been suggested by your thesis are *chronological* ("Anorexia nervosa has evolved from a little-known, scarcely noted disorder into a widespread disease of near-epidemic proportions"), *comparison and contrast* ("Anorexia nervosa is similar to other stress-related disorders in its effects on its victims"), *process* ("The disease anorexia nervosa progresses from anxiety traits in early childhood to near starvation in young adulthood"), *example* ("Eating disorders are a major health problem among teenage girls. One example of an eating disorder is anorexia nervosa. Another example is bulimia").

These are only examples of the possible organizational plans that you might discern in either your thesis statement or in the materials you have accumulated in your notes and notebook. It is crucial that you pay attention to planning at this stage in your project or the extensive materials you have gathered may seem overwhelming. It is your job to make order out of the chaos.

■ ORGANIZING YOUR MATERIALS

Sort your notecards by related titles—that is, titles on the cards that seem to belong in similar categories. For example, Cheryle had several cards headed *definition of anorexia nervosa;* these she grouped together. Next, read a group of cards and *in your own words* write a brief summary of the material on the cards. Repeat this procedure for each remaining group of cards, writing the summaries in your research notebook. Once you have written summaries for each related group of notes, arrange your summaries in some logical order, using your thesis as an organization guide. Decide how you are going to incorporate your primary data into your term paper. Will you use it to confirm your library information, or what?

Planning and Outlining

Now you are ready to plan and outline your research paper. Your thesis statement and the titles on your cards will provide you with the main headings of your outline. The subpoints on your outline will be the points you have made in your summaries. It is important to write the summaries first and then the outline rather than the other way around, because until you have written the summaries, you will not really know what points you want to make in your research paper.

Do not be overly concerned about formal outline structure. An outline should be a guide to planning and not a constraint that confines and limits your thinking. However, an informal outline is an important organizational device that will help you to construct a logically developed, unified, and coherent research paper. Your own outline will be based on the material you have discovered in your library search and in your primary research. It will describe in an organized way all the material you have gathered.

Many writers go back and forth between their outlines and their actual papers, thus in effect revising and refining their outlines as they write. Others prefer to have fairly comprehensive outlines before beginning to write. Cheryle wrote the following informal outline when she was actually writing the paper. The form of the outline changed several times as she wrote and thought about the paper.

```
                    Informal Outline


    Thesis: The internal problems within upper-middle-class and
    upper-class families, along with tremendous sociocultural
    pressures, have apparently caused a rise in the number of
    anorexia nervosa victims.

    Introduction
     Society's drive for perfection
     Leads to anxiety and frustration
     Can result in physical illness, especially among young women
    Part 1: Description and definition of anorexia nervosa
     Anxiety
          Early personality traits among children
          Meaning of anxiety and its relationship to women
     Physical symptoms of anorexia nervosa
          Brief definition of the disorder
          Hyperactivity
          Distorted self/body image
          Inability to feel normal body functions
          Self-inflicted, harmful weight-control methods
     Emotional characteristics of anorexia nervosa
          Need for control of others
          Loss of control over own life
```

Part 2: Family life of victims

Family characteristics

    Results from Russian, American reports
    Mother's character
    Father's character
    Daughter's feelings toward family

Mother/daughter relationships

    Mother directs and controls daughter's life
    Daughter seeks self-expression through food
    Food is the link between mother and daughter

Characteristics of mothers of victims

    Domineering mother
    Passive mother

Part 3: Society's affects upon the rise of victims

Advertising

Male's frequent exposure to ''ideal'' of beauty

Peer pressure

Fashion

Part 4: Survey of fifty college women

Who was surveyed

Data analysis

Review of magazine choices

Confirmed existence of anorexia nervosa symptoms

Conclusion

EXERCISE

Arrange your source material, decide on an organizational plan, and construct an outline to guide your writing of the first draft of your research paper. Refer to Chapter 5 for help with organization.

Writing the First Draft

After you have completed your informal outline, you are ready to write the first draft of your research paper. Remember, your objective is to present to your readers the answer you have discovered to the starting question. Remind yourself at this time of the question that initially motivated your search. When writing your first draft, use concrete and simple language to explain your thesis and the supporting evidence you gathered in your research as objectively as you can. Your thesis statement and your outline, as well as your section-by-section summaries, will guide the writing of this first draft. You should remain flexible as you write, and be open to any fresh insights you may have along the way.

As you are writing the first draft, it is important to note down which material comes from which sources. Do not be concerned at this point about the formal details of documentation; you can deal with that later. But do mark for yourself in the draft any ideas or words taken from your sources. Place any word or words you copy from a source in quotation marks, and after the quote write down the last name and the date of publication of the source and the page number of the quoted material (in parentheses). For example,

> A woman of twenty, who seemed to be making good progress, admitted, "I really cannot see how thin I am. I look in the mirror and still cannot see it. I know I am thin because when I feel myself I notice that there is nothing but bones" (Bruch, 1973, p. 89).

Similarly, document paraphrases and restatements of ideas taken from a source even though you have recast them in your own words:

> Anxiety is a reaction to frustration and unresolved anger that seems to burn a hole into one's very being (DeRosis, 1979, p. 56).

However, you need not document common knowledge.

When you are not quoting or paraphrasing from a specific page in a source, it is sufficient to include simply the author's name (or names, where there is more than one author) and the publication date:

> Fashion's ideal may indirectly affect adolescents and college women, who eventually believe that weight control is equal to self-control and will lead to beauty and success (Garfinkle, Garner, Schwartz, & Thompson, 1980).

For general information on planning, writing, and revising your social science research paper, refer to Chapter 5. Use the following information on documentation in the social sciences to make your citations. The model paper at the end of this chapter illustrates the writing and documentation styles commonly used in the social sciences.

■ DOCUMENTATION IN SOCIAL SCIENCE: THE NAME-AND-DATE METHOD

In the social sciences, the name-and-date method of documentation is standard. This format is outlined in the *Publications Manual of the Ameri-*

can Psychological Association, 3rd ed., Washington, D.C.: American Psychological Association, 1983. The citations are included in the text and thus help the reader to identify authorities and the dates of the research immediately. This form of documentation is particularly useful when you are citing books and articles but are not quoting or paraphrasing from them.

Internal Citation

At the appropriate place in the text, you will give the author's name, followed by a comma, a space, and the year of publication:

> After the introduction of solid foods to the infant, food and milk become the links between the child's and the mother's bodies (McCarthy, 1980).

As an alternative that prevents monotony and improves readability, you can give the author's name in the text occasionally, supplying only the year in parentheses:

> As McCarthy notes, the refusal to eat is a way of maintaining autonomy and control over the body (1980).

For paraphrases and direct quotations, follow the date with a page number:

> Anxiety is a reaction to frustration and unresolved anger that seems to burn a hole into one's very being (DeRosis, 1979, p. 56).

If you discuss a source extensively in your own text, you need not keep citing that source as long as you do not introduce an intervening source. In such a case, you may want to give the name of the source's author where appropriate to remind the reader that you are continuing to use the same source. Take care, however, to make it clear that you are still discussing source material rather than your own ideas.

If your source has two or more authors, you need to give the authors' last names in the first internal citation; in subsequent citations, you may use the first author's name with "et al." (abbreviation for Latin *et alibi*, "and others"):

> First citation: (Garfinkle, Garner, Schwartz, & Thompson, 1980)
>
> Subsequent citation: (Garfinkle, et al., 1980)

If there is no author's name, use either the title or an abbreviated form of the title:

> (Eating disorders, 1981)

If you have two articles with the same title, list the source as well to distinguish them:

(Anorexia Nervosa, *International Encyclopedia of Psychiatry, Psychology, Psychoanalysis, & Neurology*, 1980)

(Anorexia Nervosa, *Encyclopedia of Human Behavior*, 1980)

If you have two authors with the same last name, use first initials:

(Woodman, M., 1979), (Woodman, J., 1981)

If you have two or more works by the same author published in the same year, identify them on the reference list with lower-case letters in parentheses (a), (b). In the text, use the following format:

(Bruch, 1973a), (Bruch, 1973b)

The Reference List in APA Style

The reference list, at the end of the research paper, contains all the sources actually used in the paper. When you use this documentation style, it is titled "References" or "Works Cited." The purpose of the reference list is to help readers find the materials you used in writing your paper. You must give complete and accurate information so that others may find the works. The following principles are generally accepted in documenting social science works, though many social science journals and fields have their own particular method of documenting. These guidelines have been adopted by the American Psychological Association (APA) in their style manual:

1. Present the author's name first, followed by the date (in parentheses), the title, and the publication information.
2. The publication information required is place and name of publisher and date for books; date, volume and issue number, and page numbers for articles.
3. Place periods after the three main divisions: author, title, and publication information. Within these divisions, use commas to separate information.
4. Use capital letters for the first word only of a book or article title or following a colon in a subtitle.
5. Underline titles of books, journals, magazines, and newspapers. Also underline volume numbers in journal references to indicate italics.

The accompanying model references and the sample term paper that follows both use the APA documentation format as outlined in the 1983 edition of the *Publications Manual of the American Psychological Association*. For additional examples and further information on documentation in the social sciences, consult the *APA Manual*.

MODEL REFERENCES: SOCIAL SCIENCE (APA)

Type of Reference	Example
BOOKS	
1. One author	Bruch, H. (1973). <u>Eating disorders: Obesity, anorexia nervosa, and the person within</u>. New York: Basic Books.
2. Two or more authors	Minuchin, S., Rosman, B., & Baker, L. (1978). <u>Psychosomatic families: Anorexia nervosa in context</u>. Cambridge, MA: Harvard Univ. Press.
3. Two or more books by the same author	Bruch, H. (1973). <u>Eating disorders: Obesity anorexia nervosa, and the person within</u>. New York: Basic Books.
	Bruch, H. (1978). <u>The golden cage: The enigma of anorexia nervosa</u>. Cambridge, MA: Harvard Univ. Press.
	(Note: References are in chronological order.)
4. Book with editor(s)	Hartman, F. (Ed.). (1973). <u>World in crisis: Readings in international relations</u> (4th ed.). New York: Macmillan.
5. Essay, chapter or section of an edited work	Cherns, A. (1982). Social research and its diffusion. In B. Appleby (Ed.), <u>Papers on social science utilisation</u> (pp. 316–326). Loughborough Univ. of Technology: Centre for Utilisation of Social Science Research.

6. Encyclopedia entry (signed)	Bruch, H. Anorexia nervosa. International Encyclopedia of Psychiatry, Psychology, Psychoanalysis & Neurology, 1978 ed.
Encyclopedia entry (unsigned)	Anorexia nervosa. Encyclopedia of Human Behavior, 1978 ed.
7. Corporate author	American Psychiatric Association. (1980). Diagnostic and statistical manual of mental disorders (3rd ed.). Washington, DC: Author. (Note: The word Author here indicates that the author and publisher are the same.)

ARTICLES

1. Journal article (one author)	Holmi, K. (1978). Anorexia nervosa: Recent investigations. Annual Review of Medicine, 29, 137-148.
2. Journal article (two authors)	Steinhausen, H. & Glenville, K. (1983). Follow-up studies of anorexia nervosa: A review of research findings. Psychological Medicine: Abstracts in English, 13(2), 239- 245.
3. Journal article (several authors)	Garfinkle, P., Garner, D., Schwartz, D., & Thompson, M. (1980). Cultural expectations of thinness in women. Psychological Reports, 13, 483-491.
4. Magazine article (noncontinuous pages)	Miller, G. (1969, December). On turning psychology over to the unwashed. Psychology Today, pp. 53-54; 66-74.
5. Magazine article (no known author)	The blood business. (1972, September). Time, pp. 47-48.

6. Newspaper article	Eight APA journals initiate controversial blind reviewing. (1972, June). <u>APA Monitor</u>, pp. 1; 5.

TECHNICAL REPORTS

1. Individual author	Gottfredson, L. S. (1980). <u>How valid are occupational reinforcer pattern scores</u>? (Report No. CSOS–R–292). Baltimore, MD: Johns Hopkins University, Center for Social Organization of Schools (ERIC Document Reproduction Service No. ED 182 465).
2. Corporate author	Life Insurance Marketing and Research Association. (1978). <u>Profit and the AIB in United States ordinary companies</u> (Research Rep. No. 1978–6). Hartford, CT: Author.
	(Note: <u>Author</u> indicates the author and publisher are the same.)

OTHER SOURCES

1. Film or videotape	Maas, J. B. (Producer), & Gluck, D. H. (Director). (1979). <u>Deeper into Hypnosis</u> [Film]. Englewood Cliffs, NJ: Prentice–Hall.
2. Abstracted or unpublished dissertation or thesis (in <u>Dissertation Abstracts</u>)	Foster–Havercamp, M. E. (1982). An analysis of the relationship between preservice teacher training and directed teacher performance (Doctoral Dissertation, University of Chicago, 1981). <u>Dissertation Abstracts International, 42</u>, 4409A.
(Dissertation not in <u>DAI</u>)	Devins, G. M. (1981). <u>Helplessness, depression, and mood in endstage</u>

	<u>renal disease</u>. Unpublished doctoral dissertation, McGill University, Montreal.
3. Unpublished manuscript	Cameron, S. E. (1981). <u>Educational level as a predictor of success</u>. Unpublished manuscript.
	(Note: You can cite university affiliation for such works.)
Unpublished data	Locke, C. (1983). [Survey of college women at Texas Tech University]. Unpublished raw data.
4. Review of book or film	Carmody, T. P. (1982). A new look at medicine from the social perspective [Review of <u>Social contexts of health, illness, and patient care</u>]. <u>Contemporary Psychology</u>, <u>27</u>, 208–209.
5. Interview (published)	Newman, P. (1982, January). [Interview with William Epstein, editor of <u>JEP: Human Perception and Performance</u>]. <u>APA Monitor</u>, pp. 7, 39.
(unpublished)	Hult, C. (1984, March). [Interview with Dr. Lauro Cavazos, President, Texas Tech University].
6. Personal letter	Miller, Henry. (1979, April). [Letter to author].
7. Paper presented at conference	Brewer, J. (1979, October). <u>Energy, information, and the control of heart rate</u>. Paper presented at the Society for Psychophysiological Research, Cincinnati, OH.
8. Television program	<u>Problems of Freedom</u>. (1982, May 21). New York: NBC–TV.

EXERCISES AND RESEARCH PROJECT

Follow the procedures outlined in this chapter to research a limited social science topic and write a social science research paper. Be sure to choose a topic that will require some primary research data. The four exercises below will give you additional practice with skills associated with research projects.

1. For each entry on your research paper bibliography, write a three- or four-sentence annotation describing the contents of that source.

2. Write a "review of the literature" report that summarizes in three to four pages the major ideas found in your sources. Often a literature review, which lists and comments on the works done to date in a particular area, will be a component of a larger social science paper.

3. Write a report that details your primary research project and summarizes your findings. Use tables or graphs where possible to illustrate your results.

4. After you have completed your research paper, write an abstract of about 100 words that succinctly summarizes what your paper is about. An abstract should accurately reflect the scope and organization of your paper. (For information on writing an abstract, see Chapter 5.)

Title page provides title, student & course identification, date

SAMPLE RESEARCH PAPER: SOCIAL SCIENCE FORMAT (APA)
(optional title page)

The Causes and Effects
of
Anorexia Nervosa

by
Cheryle Locke

Psychology 1300–026
Dr. Collins
May 3, 1985

[1 inch]

The Causes and Effects of Anorexia Nervosa

[3 lines]

Over the past thirty years our society has been remodeled by the nation's hunger for perfection and success in all areas of life. Many Americans, as well as those from other countries, strive for perfection in their careers, social standing, and outward appearance. In many instances this striving for excellence is both positive and productive. Yet, in other cases, one's stamina may be pushed beyond its limits when trying to obtain perfection. One group that has faltered amidst the pressure of perfectionism is young women. Through unrealistic demands and expectations concerning academic and social pressures, as well as pressure from ambitious parents and the media, many young women have lost touch with their personal goals and sense of worth. Many young women have no way of coping with these demands and find themselves suffering from mental and physical ailments unexplainable to themselves and their parents. A recent illness suffered by a number of these young women is currently becoming more common. This illness, anorexia nervosa, is both a physical and mental disorder. The internal problems within upper–middle–class and middle–class families, along with the tremendous sociocultural pressures, have apparently caused a rise in the number of anorexia nervosa victims.

General introduction to stress

Narrows to young women and to specific topic of anorexia nervosa

Thesis

2

Description and Definition of Anorexia Nervosa

The "journey" into becoming a victim of
anorexia nervosa begins in early childhood.
According to DeRosis (1979), there are two patterns
of destructive behavior that are commonly found in
children: conduct disorder, wherein behavior is
directed toward the environment (destructiveness,
fighting, temper tantrums), and personality
disorder, wherein behavior is directed toward the
self (fear, anxiety, physical complaints, crying).
Evidence reveals that boys are higher on conduct
disorder, whereas girls are higher on personality
disorder (DeRosis, 1979). Because of the different
personality traits and reactions, women are more
prone to anxiety-related illnesses such as ulcers,
migraine headaches, and anorexia nervosa. As DeRosis
points out, these physical pains often result from
anxiety caused by frustration over personal failure.

To understand a victim's decline into anorexia
nervosa, one must understand the meaning of anxiety.
Anxiety is a word that has become overused in
everyday conversation. In reality, anxiety is a very
serious, harmful emotion. It is a constellation of
physical symptoms, of uncomfortable, troubled
feelings and thoughts that may be either relatively
mild or near panic. Anxiety is a reaction to
frustration and unresolved anger that seems to burn a
hole into one's very being (DeRosis, 1979, p. 56).
This suppressed anger eventually must be ventilated,
and anorexia nervosa is one outlet.

*Name and
date method
of in-text
citation.
See referen-
ces for
complete
citation.*

3

The actual term anorexia nervosa means loss of
appetite. This is a misconception, because although
the victim inflicts starvation upon herself, she
suffers no true loss of appetite. Anorexia nervosa is
a psychosomatic syndrome characterized by both
physical and psychological symptoms. The victim
loses personal identity with her physical and mental
feelings. She is immune to depression, anger, hot and
cold sensations, hunger, fatigue, and menstrual
pains. She has an insatiable desire for vigorous
activity nearing hyperactivity. Many anorexic
patients become obsessed with walking, refusing to
stop until they have burned enough calories.

Anorexics cannot see their own emaciation and
staunchly defend their size as being "just right," as
the protection against the "dreaded fate" of being
fat (Anorexia Nervosa, <u>International Encyclopedia of
Psychiatry, Psychology, Psychoanalysis, Neurology</u>,
1980). At times anorexics even deny their weight
loss. But even after therapy begins and is going
well, they will complain with bewilderment that they
cannot "see" how thin they are. A woman of 20 who
seemed to be making good progress admitted, "I really
cannot see how thin I am. I look in the mirror and
still cannot see it. I know I am thin because when I
feel myself I notice that there is nothing but bones"
(Bruch, 1973, p. 89). Another girl of 19, reports
Bruch, showed her doctor two photographs taken on the
beach, one when she was 15 and of normal weight, one
when she was 17 and weighed only 70 pounds. She asked
him if he could see a difference and admitted that

*To prevent
confusion
with another
source, the
work's name
is listed*

*Includes
page # for
direct quote*

4

she had trouble seeing it, though she knew there was
a difference. This bizarre inability to clearly see
one's own body image is one of the most horrifying
facts of anorexia. If the patient cannot see that
there is a problem, how can she be motivated to help
herself?

Anorexic patients are often extremely
conscientious children of high intelligence with
excellent academic achievements in school and great
persistence at any task. Still, the victim feels a
lack of confidence and, as she continues to lose
weight, she becomes noticeably withdrawn and
isolated. At times the anorexic experiences
uncontrollable eating binges. Terrified by this loss
of control, she will remove the unwanted food by
self-induced vomiting, laxatives, enemas, and
diuretics. Fifteen to twenty percent of anorexia
victims die of direct starvation or starvation-
related illnesses such as heart failure,
malnutrition, and other diseases that their weak,
immuneless bodies cannot combat (Bruch, 1973).

Name of author introduces source so only date is needed

The emotional signs of anorexia are almost as
easy to detect as the physical ones. Marion Woodman,
who conducted extensive interviews with anorexic
patients, established a list of 21 common factors
among the victims (1980). Although there were a
number of common physical attributes, the most
dominant factors were emotional attributes. The most
significant factor was the anorexic's attempt to
gain control over her life through food--eating or
refusing to eat. The victim's refusal to eat is a
pathetic assertion of self against her convictions

5

that she always gives in and will always continue to do so (Bruch, 1973, p. 8). Eventually, her starvation becomes her way of manipulating and controlling others (Anorexia Nervosa, <u>Encyclopedia of Human Behavior</u>, 1980). The disorder itself is horrifying, but in order to grasp what causes it, one must examine the pre-anorexia stages in the victim's life.

<u>Family Life of Anorexia Victims</u>

In most cases, anorexia begins in the home. The parents of an anorexic child drive her to find her own expression of self-frustration and doubt. In desperation, the girl turns to self-starvation as a form of punishment, revenge, or a cry for help. In reports from Finland, Russia, and the United States, parents consistently emphasized the stability and happiness of their homes. Only intensive therapeutic work revealed the distortions and tensions underlying this facade of normality (Bruch, 1973). Most of the anorexics came from prosperous families with highly cultured backgrounds, good living conditions, and quiet family environments. The mothers had often been women of achievement, or career women frustrated in their own personal aspirations. The fathers, despite social and financial success, felt in some sense "second best." The parents were enormously preoccupied with outer appearances, admiring fitness and beauty, and

6

expecting proper behavior and measurable achievements from their children. These feelings are easily conveyed to a daughter, who eventually becomes petrified of succumbing to any type of failure, such as not having a "beautiful" body. Therefore, the child is conditioned to act as the family expects and feels a big responsibility for not embarrassing her family. Her parents do not punish her for so—called social slips, but do admonish her by making her feel guilty. In this atmosphere the child develops a keen sense of intrafamily operations, dependent on parental assessment and highly loyal to family values (Minuchin, Rosman, & Baker, 1978).

From the time of the anorexic's early childhood, her activity and bodily functions are kept under close scrutiny by family members. The child is unable to rebuke her family because they defend the rules as their way of expressing their concern for her. They subtly manipulate their daughter's life by masking control with unselfish concern. "I want this because it is good for you," the common defense of parents, becomes their way of forcing the child to go along with their wishes without ever helping the child learn to make her own decisions. Not eating, though it seems insignificant at first, gives the overprotected and controlled child a sense of being her own person. The anorexic who drives herself toward starvation does not really know why food has become her target for rebellion. Yet, there are very strong reasons pushing her toward her refusal to eat.

Multiple authors—all listed the first time. Subsequently, use (Minuchin, et al., 1978)

7

After the introduction of solid foods to the infant, food and milk become the links between the child and mother (McCarthy, 1980). As the child grows, feeding may be her way of rejecting her mother and maintaining autonomy and control over her body. As McCarthy observes, the body is identified with the mother's and starvation becomes the anorexic's sole means for controlling this process. Although there are not set personality traits for the anorexic's mother, two characteristics are common: they are either domineering or nagging.

The domineering mother controls both her husband and her children. She feels cheated by life and is determined to see her dreams fulfilled through her daughter. She controls everything from her daughter's social activities and friends to her daughter's choice of food and clothing. The daughter feels she is her mother's puppet and is obligated to perform and please. Refusing to eat becomes her only means of quiet, elusive self-expression. The nagging mother is less aggressive and determined. She is a peacemaker who will do anything to keep friction and conflict out of the family, making compromises to smooth things over. She pours her time and attention into her children, hovering over them, whining at them "eat more, drink more, sleep more, study harder." The daughter looks for an escape and finds it in her refusal to eat. The causes of anorexia are many, but numerous psychologists and doctors believe that it first stems from such conflicts between mother and daughter.

8

<u>Society's Effect upon the Rise of Anorexia Victims</u>

A second direct cause of anorexia is the expectation society has regarding beauty. Over the years, society's ideal of a beautiful body has changed. Thirty years ago a rounded, voluptuous, curved body was idealized. The current look is angular and lean. Starved, emaciated models portray this image in the media, and it is promoted through diet pills, drinks, foods, weight-loss centers, and bulge-hiding clothes (Garfinkle, Garner, Schwartz, & Thompson, 1980). Adolescents, vulnerable to peer pressure, see these norms and strive to conform. The male is exposed to ideal beauty also, through such models as Miss America or <u>Playboy</u> centerfolds appearing on television and in magazines. These models tend to exaggerate parts of the body (DeRosis, 1979). A number of researchers have linked these sociocultural pressures to the apparent increase of anorexia victims. Dieting is a "sociocultural epidemic" and fashion's ideal may indirectly affect adolescent women who eventually believe that weight control is equal to self-control and will surely lead to beauty and success (Garfinkle, et al., 1980).

<u>Survey</u>

In order to discover whether or not the family and cultural pressures that lead to anorexia in young

First reference uses all authors

Second reference uses et al.

Student's primary data used to reinforce Conclusions

9

women were evident on my college campus, I conducted a survey dealing with anorexia, its symptoms, and the various attitudes on weight control that can lead to the disorder. Fifty women on the Texas Tech University campus, between the ages of 18 and 21, were surveyed. Half the women were members of the sorority system and the other half were not. This division enabled me to compare the sorority women with the nonsorority women. My hypothesis was that since the women who pledge a sorority are obligated to pay expensive initiation fees and dues they would come from more financially successful families. Second, the goals of each sorority include high scholastic achievement, heavy involvement in extracurricular activities, and a commitment to social standing. Many women who become involved in sorority life do so for social status and to please their parents. These are all factors that can lead to anorexia nervosa.

Describes method

In my survey, I discovered that the women in both groups actually came from families with similar financial backgrounds, yet the sorority women were more preoccupied with weight control. Of the 50 women surveyed, 34 said they were unhappy with their present weight. The number of sorority women unhappy with their weight was 10% greater than the number of nonsorority women. Fourteen of the women surveyed admitted to self-inflicted vomiting after overeating (10 of the 14 were sorority women). Eleven of the women surveyed said they used laxatives and diuretics to control their weight (9 of the 11 were sorority women). Out of the 50 women, 32 felt that

Presents findings

10

they had succeeded in completing a major task when they lost weight. Six of the women had actually stopped their menstrual cycles because of severe weight loss. Twenty of the sorority women stated that weight gain or loss was a strong determining factor in their moods, compared to 14 of the nonsorority women. One-third of the women surveyed felt that becoming thinner would help them to fit in better with their peers and solve their dating problems. One-third of the women also revealed that they felt very guilty and angry with themselves if they went on eating binges. An important point is that among the 50 women surveyed, only 7% were clinically overweight, yet 32% were unhappy with their present weight.

Another portion of the survey asked the women to list the three magazines they read most frequently. The top two magazines were Glamour and Mademoiselle, both fashion magazines for young women. Only six women did not list at least one of these magazines. In the November 1983 issue of Mademoiselle, there were four diet-related articles. In the February 1983 issue of the same magazine, there were eight diet-related articles. In the December 1982 issue of Glamour, there were five diet-related articles, including one six-page article entitled "Fat: 28 Tips, Tricks, and Foods to Fight Back." The March 1983 issue contained eight diet-related articles, one entitled "Pound-Hiding Party Clothes." The effect of these magazines on their readers cannot be underestimated.

The results of the survey show a surprising and frightening fact: the symptoms and conditions of

11

anorexia nervosa are in existence among women on our college campuses today. This is not a disease that only strikes odd, imbalanced young girls. It is a sickness that will only continue to become more common as society's obsession with weight persists.

Conclusion

Our culture's relentless insistence that only the slim are beautiful and that thinness is a visible sign of virtue places a doubly heavy burden on the unhappy minority in our society whose inner conflicts lead to weight disorders. Society persists in measuring the success or failure of individuals by the number of pounds gained or lost rather than by the health and happiness of the "person within." Through family awareness and family counseling, many young women may be able to escape the horror of self-inflicted starvation. As Bruch points out (1973), the media, society, and parents must come to a decision on the standards for weight control. Health must come before any personal standard of "beauty."

QUESTIONNAIRE

1. Are you a member of a college
   sorority?   yes no
2. Are you happy with your present
   weight?   yes no
3. Is weight gain or loss a strong
   determining factor in your
   moods?   yes no

12

4. Do you feel you have succeeded in completing a major task when you lose weight?   yes no

5. Have you ever used laxatives or diuretics to control your weight?   yes no

6. Have you ever used self-induced vomiting to control your weight?   yes no

7. Have you ever stopped your menstrual cycle from weight loss?   yes no

8. If you were thinner, would it help you fit in with peers?   yes no

9. If you were thinner, would it solve your dating problems?   yes no

10. Do you feel guilty or angry after overeating or binge eating?   yes no

11. Are you happy with your present weight?   yes no

12. Do you wish you weighed more or less than you do right now?   more less

13. Please indicate your present height and weight.   height weight

    _____

14. Please list the three magazines you most frequently read.   1.
                                                                  2.
                                                                  3.

15. Please indicate your parents' income level (per year). $0–10,000
                                                                $10–20,000
                                                                $20–50,000
                                                                over $50,000

References

Anorexia nervosa. <u>Encyclopedia of Human Behavior</u>,
    1978 ed.

Bruch, H. Anorexia nervosa. <u>International
    Encyclopedia of Psychiatry, Psychology,
    Psychoanalysis, Neurology</u>, 1978 ed.

Bruch, H. (1978). <u>Eating disorders: Obesity,
    anorexia nervosa, and the person within.</u> New
    York: Basic Books.

DeRosis, H. (1979). <u>Women and anxiety</u>. New York:
    Delacorte.

Feldman—Toledano, Z., & Groen, J. (1966). Educative
    treatment of patients and parents in anorexia
    nervosa. <u>British Journal of Psychiatry</u>, <u>27</u>,
    671–681.

Garfinkle, P., Garner, D., Schwartz, D., & Thompson,
    M. (1980). Cultural expectations of thinness in
    women. <u>Psychological Reports</u>, <u>13</u>, 483–491.

Holmi, K. (1978). Anorexia nervosa: Recent
    investigations. <u>Annual Review of Medicine</u>, <u>29</u>,
    137–148.

McCarthy, J. (1980). <u>Death anxiety</u>. New York:
    Halsted Press.

Minuchin, S., Rosman, B., & Baker, L. (1978).
    <u>Psychosomatic families: Anorexia nervosa in
    context</u>. Cambridge, MA: Harvard Univ. Press.

Woodman, M. (1980). <u>The owl was a baker's daughter:
    Obesity, anorexia nervosa, and the repressed
    feminine, a psychological study</u>. Montreal,
    Canada: Inner City Books.

*References
follow
APA style:
Note position
of date in
citation*

CHAPTER 8

Writing a Research Paper in the Humanities

■ INTRODUCTION

In many research projects in the humanities, the researcher must read a primary text carefully and interpret it. Such a research task, performed frequently by working scholars in the humanities, requires a thorough reading of the text, a systematic search for information written about the text, extensive preparation time, and a knowledge of formal conventions in the field. The same principles and skills you have learned in the earlier chapters apply when you use a primary text. These skills include

1. The ability to read the primary text carefully and critically.
2. A familiarity with bibliographic indexes and other library resources relating to humanities.
3. The ability to synthesize and evaluate data and opinions from a variety of secondary sources.
4. The ability to develop a thesis consistent with the evidence found in both the primary and secondary sources.
5. The ability to organize and write a paper that effectively presents and supports your thesis.
6. The ability to employ the formal conventions of research papers in the humanities.

■ REPORTS AND RESEARCH PAPERS

Some of the writing you will be expected to do in the humanities is report writing, in which you report on the current consensus within the field on a particular topic or issue. In report writing, you research only in the sense of finding out what others have said on a topic. Usually, reports are written on noncontroversial subjects in which the writer can discover the facts easily and present them without the need to interpret their significance. For example, in a history class, you might be asked to write a report on early colonial life in Plymouth, Massachusetts. As a reporter, you would look up relevant, authoritative history resources written about colonial New England and write down what those sources say about life in Plymouth.

In contrast, a research paper does more than report the facts or widely held beliefs on a particular topic. A research paper is necessarily more evaluative than a report, because it interprets the available evidence. Often, a research paper will be written about a subject or topic that has sparked controversy in the field. A controversial issue will be evident when scholars in the field do not agree on interpretations, or when the range of know facts is great enough to allow differing opinions. A question such as "Were colonists at Plymouth significantly helped or hindered by local American Indian tribes?" would allow the researcher to locate and interpret a wide range of known facts. The researcher would investigate a question that other scholars in the field had grappled with. For example, current mythology has the colonists of Plymouth sitting down to Thanksgiving dinner with benevolent Indians. The researcher would ask, "Is this picture based on facts? Or were the colonists really constantly on guard against Indian attack?" Some writers today portray the colonial settlers as the aggressors, indiscriminately killing Indians to satisfy their own need for land and food. Which is the true picture? What facts do we actually have? What is a reasonable interpretation of the relationship between colonial settlers and Indian tribes based on those known facts?

The questions posed above are typical of the kinds of problems often researched in the humanities. There is room for differences of opinion provided those opinions are supported by, and consistent with, the known facts on the subject. The researcher will arrive at a thesis through lengthy preparation and investigation. Then, the researcher will verify that thesis by constructing a persuasive argument woven from and supported by the known facts. Such a thesis will be a reasonable answer to the question, an answer that "fits" the known facts and helps to explain them.

In your work for this chapter, you will be expected to write a *research paper*, not a report paper. In other words, you need to go beyond reporting the known facts to interpretation of those facts, to formulate your own interpretation, your own thesis. The examples in this chapter are taken from a research project in an English class in which the students were asked to interpret a literary text critically. Such a research project assumes more than reporting; the student must read the primary text carefully and formulate his or her own impressions of its "meaning." The research itself will mainly involve comparing those impressions to other interpretations made by scholars in the field.

■ A GUIDE TO THE HUMANITIES RESEARCH PROCESS

First, choose a literary text (novel, play, short story, or poem) that seems to you to be significant in some way. Often in your college classes these texts will be assigned reading, since your instructor will already be aware of which literary texts are considered significant by others in the field. Sally Batten, whose research will serve as the model for this chapter, chose John Steinbeck's novel *East of Eden*.

Before beginning your research, obtain notecards and a notebook. You will use the notecards in recording all notes you take while reading the primary text and while reading the secondary sources in which the primary text is critiqued or interpreted. You will use a second set of notecards for your bibliography: the listing of all the publication information from each source you use in your research. The notebook will be your "research notebook." In it, you will record your library search strategy and the working bibliography that results from your library search. Also in your research notebook, you will record your own impressions and comments on both the primary text and the secondary sources. It is crucial that, as you read, you not only report what the sources say, but you *understand* what they say. Putting that understanding into your own words in your research notebook will prove invaluable to you when you actually sit down to write the research paper. You may also write drafts of your research paper in your research notebook. How can you hope to explain to someone else the complexities of the subject if you have not adequately explained them to yourself? Keeping the notes from the sources and your own interpretations separate will prevent your confusing later on what you read in a source with what occurred to you on your own. If it is recorded on a notecard, it is someone else's idea; if it is in your notebook, it is your idea.

Preparation

You will need to read the primary text carefully, taking notes from the text on your notecards. Your notes should record important comments by the author about the characters and incidents in the text. Notice and record as much as you can. The notecards should contain either direct quotes or paraphrases from the text. List each idea on a separate card to allow for easy sorting later. Label the idea with a key word or phrase so that you will be able to identify it easily: "Cathy as a child," or "Cathy's evil behavior as an adult." Each card should also be identified as to its source, the primary text, which for convenience you should label (1). Each card containing notes from the primary text, then, will be identified with a (1) in the upper right-hand corner. Additionally, a second number will indicate the sequence in which you took the notes: the first note will be (1.1), the second note will be (1.2), and so on. Once you have labeled and numbered a card, enter the note, using quotation marks to indicate the author's exact words. Mark down at the end of the card the page number or numbers on which you found the note.

You need to make a bibliography card for your primary text. On this card you will record all the pertinent bibliographic information for the text: the author, title, and publication data. Your bibliography card on the primary text will be numbered to correspond with the notecards from the primary text (1). Also, be sure to write down the library call number in the upper left-hand corner of the bibliography card in case you need to find the book later.

In addition to the notes from the primary text that you take on note-cards, write your own comments in your research notebook. Jot down possible questions that occur to you as you read, particularly any that seem interesting or problematic: "What makes Cathy in *East of Eden* tick?" "Is she psychologically disturbed?" "Is there some medical disorder or mental disease that controls or would help explain her behavior?" and so on.

RESEARCH NOTEBOOK

My Comments

I'm glad I picked this book. I think it's interesting to see how people think from the inside. I started out wondering what ''disease'' Cathy had. But I don't think she really had a mental problem. I just believe that Steinbeck wanted to show the reader how he would be as an individual if he let the bad within rule him. She was totally consumed by her evilness and there was no turning back.

EXERCISE

Carefully read and take notes from your primary text. Make evaluative comments in your research notebook.

Developing a Search Strategy

You have now completed reading the primary text and taking notes on it. You should have formed some general impressions about the text and what it means. In our example, Sally shows that she is beginning to understand what Steinbeck was trying to say about Cathy, the most important character in *East of Eden*. Do not be concerned if you do not yet have a "topic" to write about. It may still be too early to have come up with either a starting question or a thesis that you can support in your research paper. These will come as you begin your library search. Remember, in the inquiry process in general, the writer always needs a lot of time to prepare for an understanding of the subject before writing about it. Make a time schedule for your research, allowing enough time for ideas to "incubate." Do not leave everything until the week before the project is due. To be effective, a research project must alternate times of conscious and subconscious activity.

Your library search will probably proceed from a look at general information about your primary text to specific works written about it. An outline of a search strategy is presented below. (Your particular search may differ somewhat from this outline):

Sally's Search Strategy

1. Encyclopedias, dictionaries, biographies for general background information.
2. Critical reviews and commentary on *East of Eden*.
3. Subject indexes for access to listings of specific secondary sources.
4. Abstracts of particular secondary sources found in subject indexes.
5. Card catalog for location of sources and access to new material.

As you can see in this outline, your library search will probably begin in the reference area in the library. To illustrate the use of a library search strategy, I will lead you through the steps above using Sally's research on *East of Eden* as a model for your own research.

EXERCISE

Outline your own research strategy, beginning with general and working to specific sources. Draw up a time schedule for your research.

Search 1

By reading general information on your primary text you will help put the work in a context. Reading specialized encyclopedias, dictionaries, and bibliographies will indicate what is considered common knowledge about the work and the author. Depending upon your particular text, you will be reading general encyclopedias, such as *Academic American*, specialized encyclopedias, such as *Cassell's Encyclopedia of World Literature*, and biographies, such as *Twentieth Century Authors*. General sources commonly used in the humanities are listed in Chapter 3. Sally used the following sources, which she listed in her research notebook, as the beginning of her working bibliography:

The World Book Encyclopedia, 1979 ed.

Cassells Encyclopedia of World Literature. J. Buchanan-Brown, ed. New York: Morrow, 1973.

American Writers, IV. Leonard Unger, ed. New York: Charles Scribner's, 1974.

Twentieth Century Authors. Stanley Kunitz and Howard Haycraft, eds. New York: Wilson, 1942.

Sally used the references listed at the end of each general source to continue to build her working bibliography. Using the references listed is often an important way to locate "key sources" written about your primary text or author. For example, the major critical work by Peter Lisca, *The Wide World of John Steinbeck,* was listed in the bibliography of the Steinbeck article in *American Writers.* It is not necessary for you to look up each entry on your working bibliography at this time. Rather, it is sufficient for you to continue to list on your working bibliography any promising references you run across.

EXERCISE

Find and read background sources relevant to your topic to obtain general information (see Chapter 3 for a list of sources commonly used in the humanities).

Focusing Your Search

After you have read several general background sources about your primary text and author, you are ready to define a starting question that will help you to focus your search. The question must be a realistic one that you are able to research given the information and time available to you. This question will be critical to the success of your research paper. Take care that it is neither trivial nor overly ambitious, but that it allows you sufficient scope for research. As you can imagine, with any primary text there are any number of questions that you could ask to guide your search. Generally, as with all research, the question is motivated by a problematic event or an incongruity you perceive in your text. As you were reading the primary text, you should have noted in your research notebook some of these important events. If you did not, return to the primary text at this time with an eye to discovering such a question. Your starting question should be something that interests and intrigues you, and it should be supportable by evidence in the text and in secondary sources.

Good Questions (supportable by evidence in the text):
1. Are Cathy's immoral actions in *East of Eden* the result of a psychotic personality?
2. Did Steinbeck portray Cathy as a human or a demon?
3. Is Steinbeck's portrayal of Cathy believable and/or realistic?
4. Is Cathy's affect on those around her in the novel the result of her own nature or defects in the other characters?
5. How is this work related to others by Steinbeck?

Poor Questions:
1. What happens in the novel *East of Eden*? (too broad)
2. How was the novel critically received and how have others interpreted it? (reporting rather than researching)
3. What poison did Cathy use to kill herself at the end of the novel? (too trivial)
4. What is Steinbeck trying to say about human nature in general in the novel? (too broad)

Once you have defined a starting question for yourself, it will be easier to decide which sources are relevant to your own particular search. Not every source will contain pertinent information. If you do not have a starting question, it is easy to wander aimlessly from one source to another, taking copious notes but getting nowhere. The question serves as a *focus* for your search and keeps you on a carefully delineated path.

EXERCISE

Define a starting question for yourself to guide your research. Make sure that it is not too trivial or too broad.

Search 2
Since you are working with a primary text that has been generally received as an important work of literature, you will probably find that numerous book reviews have been written about it. These can be useful to you in your search. The two most commonly used tools for finding book reviews are

Book Review Digest, 1905–present

Book Review Index, 1965–present

Sally looked up Steinbeck's *East of Eden* in the *Book Review Digest* of 1952, the year the novel was published, to find listings of reviews. She added these references to her working bibliography. The following is an example of a review she found in the *Digest*:

STEINBECK, JOHN. East of Eden. 602p $4.50 Viking "At the outset Steinbeck has a firm command of his materials, but the novel degenerates as it goes along. The improbabilities grow more flagrant, the sentimentality thicker, the intellectual naivete more exasperating." Charles Rolo Atlantic 190:94 0 '52 350w

---

EXERCISE

Locate and read reviews of your primary text (see Chapter 3 for a list of sources).

Search 3

There are other important indexes that will give you access to scholarly articles written about your primary text and author. These indexes are bibliographical listings of secondary sources. The indexes may differ slightly in their organization, so it is important for you to get acquainted with the indexing system of a particular index. When using an index for the first time, read the preface for instructions or consult the reference librarian for help. The following index was used by Sally in her search:

MLA International Bibliography of Books and Articles on Modern Language and Literature. New York: Modern Language Association of America, 1921 to present.

Sally began by looking up Steinbeck in the then most recent edition of the MLA bibliography. She found a listing of books and articles written on Steinbeck in 1981 and discovered that a journal, the *Steinbeck Quarterly*, was devoted entirely to studies of Steinbeck's work. Again, she noted promising sources found in the index on her working bibliography so she could look them up later:

McCarthy, Paul. *John Steinbeck.* New York: Ungar, 1980 (Mod. Lit. Monog.).

Cox, Martha Heasley. "Steinbeck's Family Portraits: The Hamiltons." StQ. 1981; 14: 23–32.

McDaniel, Barbara. "Alienation in *East of Eden*: The 'Chart of the Soul.' " StQ. 1981; 14: 32–39. (Sources in Bible)

EXERCISE

Use indexes to find titles of articles related to your primary text and topic (see Chapter 3 for a list of bibliographies and indexes).

Search 4

Next, begin to sort and narrow your list of possible sources on your working bibliography. Not every source you have listed will turn out to be relevant to your starting question. The books and articles are generally indexed by their titles, and these can be misleading. Sometimes you can use abstracts, short descriptive summaries of books and articles, as a method of initially sorting the relevant sources from the irrelevant sources. Sally used the abstracts listed below to eliminate some of the sources she had noted on her working bibliography and to add new sources she had not come upon before:

Abstracts of English Studies. Urbana, Ill.: National Council of Teachers of English, 1958 to date.

Bryer, Jackson, ed. *Sixteen Modern American Authors: A Survey of Research and Criticism.* New York: Norton, 1973.

Pownall, David E. *Articles on Twentieth Century Literature: An Annotated Bibliography, 1954 to 1970.* New York: Kraus-Thomson, 1978.

As you can see, the process of searching in the library involves evaluating, eliminating, and adding sources as you refine your working bibliography to include only those actually relevant to your own starting question. As you evaluate the sources you have listed on your working bibliography, some useful tools can help you judge the relative merits of the sources—for example, Katz's *Magazine for Libraries* and Farber's *Classified List of Periodicals for the College Library.* You can look up journals and magazines on your working bibliography to find out if they are respected, reputable sources. Sally looked up the *Steinbeck Quarterly* in Katz's guide and discovered the following information:

> *Steinbeck Quarterly,* 1968. Tetsumaro Hayashi, ed. "Many essays on any aspect of Steinbeck, reviews, and bibliographies comprise this small journal. Subscribers also receive the annual Steinbeck monograph series."

According to Katz, the *Steinbeck Quarterly* is a useful journal for articles, reviews, and bibliographies on Steinbeck.

Search 5

The last step of your search usually involves actually locating the sources listed in your working bibliography. Often the titles of the journals and magazines are listed in the indexes with abbreviations or initials. For example, if you have noted an article from the *PMLA*, you need to know that this abbreviation stands for *Publications of the Modern Language Association.* Look up the journal abbreviations in the front of the index and, if you have not already done so, write down the complete name of the journal on your working bibliography.

You can locate the books and articles listed on your working bibliography by looking them up in the card catalog and/or your library's serials listing. You may also want to use the subject index cards in the card catalog: by looking up *Steinbeck* in the subject index, you can locate all the books on Steinbeck in your library. These will include critical, biographical, and bibliographical works. Sally found several important books in this way, including the following:

Hayashi, Tetsumaro. *John Steinbeck: A Concise Bibliography.* Metuchen: Scarecrow Press, 1967.

Hayashi, Tetsumaro. *John Steinbeck: A Dictionary of His Fictional Characters.* Metuchen: Scarecrow Press, 1976.

Lisca, Peter. *John Steinbeck: Nature and Myth.* New York: Crowell, 1978.

EXERCISE

Use the card catalog's subject listing to locate sources and to find additional books and materials about your primary text. Use the *Library of Congress Subject Heading (LCSH)* list to find any other headings under which your topic might be listed in addition to the book's title and author.

Evaluation

Once you have found either a book or an article, evaluate it for its relevance or usefulness to your search. You must continually evaluate your sources and discard any that are not immediately applicable to your search. If, after an initial screening, a book looks as though it could be useful, check it out at the circulation desk. Since articles are usually non-circulating and therefore cannot be checked out, you can either photocopy ones that interest you for later use or take notes from them while you are in the library. If a source is not available, check with the librarians about the possibility of an interlibrary loan.

EXERCISE

In your research notebook, evaluate each article and book to be used in your research paper. Follow the source evaluation guide in Chapter 4.

Taking Notes

As you begin to take notes on the secondary sources, remember to keep two sets of cards, the bibliography cards and the notecards, for each source you read. Be sure to keep complete information on both cards so you will not have to look up that particular book or article again. Taking care at this stage will benefit you when you actually begin to write your research paper. (For more information on notecards and bibliography cards, see Chapter 3.)

Illumination

Since you are actively seeking the answer to the starting question you posed at the beginning of your search, you must continually "talk to yourself" while researching. Try to understand and interpret the source of information as you go, synthesizing data from numerous authors and sources, taking what is relevant and discarding what is not. This is where your research notebook can be of particular value. Take the time to write down your thoughts and comments as you go; note for yourself those sources and ideas that you find particularly important or revealing. Gradually, you will arrive at a tentative answer to the question you posed, a thesis that will satisfactorily explain the answer to the question as you see it.

It is during this *illumination* stage of the inquiry process that you begin to "see the light" or the answer to your question. Perhaps your answer will be that there is no definitive answer; that would be perfectly acceptable. At any rate, present your understanding of your primary text, arrived at through your extensive preparation and research, in your thesis statement.

You will state your thesis, the proposition that explains your opinion of the primary text, as an opinion statement about what you believe based upon the evidence you have gathered. For example, Sally first asked a question; then, through preparation and research, she came to a thesis that would guide the actual written presentation of the research:

1. Starting Question: "Are Cathy's immoral actions the result of a psychotic personality?"
2. Thesis Statement: "The character of Cathy in *East of Eden*, as seen in her behavior in childhood, young adult years, and adult life, reveals her totally evil nature and its effect on others."

EXERCISE

Write a thesis statement that articulates your understanding of the primary text. Your thesis statement should be an opinion statement based on your own judgment as well as on the secondary criticism you have read.

Verification

Once you have defined your thesis statement, you will have a guide to use in organizing your actual written presentation of the research. As you write, however, you may find that the thesis statement needs to be revised in some way. The actual writing of the research findings will sometimes help you see things in new ways or discover new meanings. Actually writing down your ideas in a systematic fashion is an important way to verify the research you have done. As you try to articulate in writing your understanding of the topic, you may find that there are gaps in your knowledge that need further research, or you may find that your thesis really does not seem to explain the facts adequately. In the latter case, you will need to go back to both your primary and secondary sources for further information so you can restate your thesis. However, you may find that your writing has clarified your ideas, thereby "verifying" them for you and your potential readers.

■ ORGANIZING AND WRITING THE RESEARCH PAPER

Your thesis statement, if carefully constructed, should suggest an organizational plan to you. Sally's thesis sentence ("The character of Cathy in *East of Eden*, as seen in her behavior in childhood, young adult years, and adult life, reveals her totally evil nature and its effect on others") implies its own organizational plan. In this case, the paper will be a *chronological* account of Cathy's behaviors in her childhood, youth, and adult life showing how her evil nature affects others in the novel.

Other theses might suggest other organizational plans—for example, *cause and effect* ("Cathy's evil nature caused catastrophes in the lives of those around her"), *comparison and contrast* ("Cathy is the most evil of Steinbeck's characters"), *process* ("The evil in Cathy's nature progressed from mild pranks to murder through the course of her life"), and *example* ("Steinbeck's preoccupation with the evil in human nature is evident in his novel *East of Eden*").

Sort your notecards by their titles and set aside any notecards that do not seem to fit in with your thesis statement. Do not hesitate to set aside material that doesn't fit. When you have sorted the cards by related titles, read all the information on a group of cards and write a brief summary, *in your own words*, of the material on the cards. Repeat this procedure for each remaining group of cards, writing the summaries in your notebook. Once you have written summaries for each related group of notes, arrange your summaries in some logical order. Again, use your thesis statement as an organizational guide.

Outlining

Now you are ready to outline your research paper. Your thesis statement and the titles on your cards will provide you with the main headings on your outline. The subpoints on your outline will be the points you have made in your summaries. Do not be overly concerned about formal outline structure. An outline should be a guide to planning, not a constraint that confines and limits your thinking. Many writers move back and forth between a sketchy outline and their written draft, changing both as they go along. Use your outline to help you plan, but be open to the discoveries to be made about your topic while you are actually writing. Follow your teacher's instructions on your final outline form, since some teachers may prefer a formal sentence outline to a phrase outline. Sally constructed the following outline:

Sentence Outline

Thesis: The character of Cathy in *East of Eden*, as seen in her behavior in childhood, young adult years, and adult life, reveals her totally evil nature and its effect on others.

I. Cathy Ames is an evil child.
   A. Cathy is described as having the appearance of an angel and the mind of a devil.
      1. Cathy Ames is a beautiful, yet demonlike child.
      2. Despite Cathy's childlike appearance, her emotional mentality is that of a much older, vindictive person.
   B. Cathy's parents are unable to determine whether she is a normal child or whether there is something evil about her.
      1. Her father has contact with normal children and finds her somehow different and sinister.
      2. Cathy manipulates and finally murders her parents.

II. When Cathy becomes a young adult, she does not end her evil ways.
   A. Cathy's experiences with Mr. Edwards in Boston change her into a worldly woman who is suspicious of everyone.
   B. Cathy becomes increasingly more suspicious.
   C. She manipulates men, particularly the Trasks, who take her in after a severe beating that nearly kills her.
   D. Cathy's babies become the victims of her vicious and wicked schemes.

III. As an adult, Cathy spreads her evil influence to other people and finally causes her own death.
   A. As Cathy matures, her ability to overpower others becomes stronger, as in the case of Faye.
   B. Kate, as she calls herself, seems to reach a peak of destruction, and her evil force causes her own deterioration.
   C. It appears that Cathy's corruption has been transmitted to her son, Cal, even though she was not directly involved in his life.
   D. Cathy becomes physically and mentally old before her time and in her increasing bitterness, finally takes her own life.

EXERCISE

Arrange your source material and notes, decide on an organizational plan, and construct an outline to guide your writing. Refer to Chapter 5 for help with organization.

Writing the First Draft

After you have completed your outline, you are ready to write the first draft of your research paper. Remember, you are writing to present to your readers the answer that you have discovered to the starting question. Remind yourself of your starting question at this time. If you have prepared sufficiently, the actual writing of the paper will be an important way for you to verify the truth of your thesis. However, remain flexible as you write your first draft, and be open to any fresh insights you may have along the way.

As you are writing the first draft, it is important to note which material comes from which source. Do not be overly concerned at this point about the formal details of documentation, which you can deal with later, but do mark for yourself in the draft any ideas or words taken from your sources. Place any words you copy from a source, either the primary or secondary sources, in quotation marks, and follow them with the author's last name and the page number of the source in parentheses:

> *East of Eden* is "a symbolic story about the need for brotherhood" (Riddel 46).

Similarly, identify paraphrases and restatements of ideas taken from a source even though you have recast them in your own words:

> Cathy's parents are unable to determine whether she is a normal child, or if there is something evil about her. They really do not trust her, but are never sure why (Cooperman 80).

For general information on planning, writing, and revising your humanities research paper, refer to Chapter 5. Use the following information on documentation in the humanities to create your citations. The research paper at the end of this chapter illustrates the proper format and documentation used in the humanities.

■ DOCUMENTATION IN THE HUMANITIES

The MLA (Modern Language Association, 1984) documentation style, which uses in-text citation similar to that used in the social sciences, has been generally adopted by writers of research papers in language and literature. Other disciplines in the humanities and fine arts may use the footnote/bibliography system. I will first discuss the MLA style (as detailed in the *MLA Handbook for Writers of Research Papers*, 2nd ed., Joseph Gibaldi and Walter S. Achtert, eds., New York: Modern Language Association, 1984) and then describe the footnote and bibliography styles commonly used in the humanities other than language and literature.

■ 1984 MLA STYLE

The MLA documentation style consists of parenthetical in-text citations and a list of works cited at the end of the paper. In the humanities, specific sources and page numbers are more important than the recency of the work. Thus, in-text citations show the author's name and the page number of the source rather than the name and date, as in the sciences and social sciences.

Internal Citation

Both the author cited and the page number of the source are important for the internal citation. Observe the following principles in your internal citations.

1. Generally, introduce any paraphrase or direct quote with the name of the author. Then, indicate the page number of the source in parentheses at the end of the material:

French observes that one night Cal becomes angry with Aaron and takes him to visit "Kate's circus" (146).

2. When you do not use the author's name to introduce the paraphrased or quoted material, place the author's name along with the specific page number in parentheses at the end of the material:

However, unlike his mother, Cal has "recognized the evil in himself, and is ready to act for good" (Cooperman 88). [Note: Do not separate author and page with a comma.]

3. Indicate every instance of borrowed material for the reader. You can indicate a paragraph taken from a single source by mentioning the author's name at the beginning of the paragraph and giving the parenthetical citation at the end:

Judging from Steinbeck's description, Cathy Ames is a beautiful, yet demon-like child. She has an innocent heart-shaped face, golden hair, wide-set hazel eyes, a delicate and thin nose and high, wide cheekbones. She has a child's figure—narrow hips, straight legs, delicate arms and tiny hands. Her voice is "soft and husky—so sweet as to become irresistible, fascinating, and horrible" (Steinbeck 73).

4. When you have two works by the same author, identify them by the author, abbreviated title, and page number of the source:

According to Lisca, Samuel, who has been working in the field all day, "associates the buried meteorite (falling star, hence Lucifer), which wrecks his well drill with Cathy . . ." *(Wide World* 269). After her children's birth, Cathy is once again compared with a serpent. Lisca comments that "Cathy gives birth to the twins as easily as a snake lays eggs" *(Nature and Myth* 168).

5. When it is apparent that your citations refer to the same work, you need not repeat the author's name. The page number will suffice:

Steinbeck says it is "easy to say she was bad, but there is little meaning unless we know why" (184). The question of Cathy's wicked and sinful existence "goes forever unanswered—just as the 'reason' for the presence of evil itself goes unanswered" (184).

6. For a primary source requiring frequent in-text citation, you can add a content footnote:

(in-text) "irresistible, fascinating, and horrible."[1]

[Footnote] [1] All citations to Steinbeck's novel are to the Viking Press, 1952, edition.

[Note: Subsequent in-text references need only the page number.]

7. Other content footnotes may be included for the following:
A. Blanket Citations

[2] For further information on this point, see Lisca (168), French (56), and Hayashi (29).

B. Related Matters (Not Included in Your Paper)

[3] Though outside the scope of this paper, major themes in the novel are discussed by Hayashi and French.

C. Suggested Sources (and Related Topics)

[4] For an additional study of Steinbeck's fictional characters, see Hayashi's *Dictionary of Fictional Characters.*

D. Comparisons with Another Source

[5] On this point, see also the article by Stanley Cooperman, in which he discusses symbolism in other Steinbeck novels.

[Note: If you have several content notes, you may type them on a separate endnote page, which will immediately follow your text and be titled "Notes" or "Endnotes." Be sure any references listed in your footnotes or endnotes are also listed on your works-cited page.]

The Reference List

The reference list, at the end of the paper, contains all the sources actually cited in the paper (titled "Works Cited") or all the sources you used in writing your paper (titled "Bibliography"). The purpose of the reference list is to help readers find the materials you used in writing your paper, so you must provide complete, accurate information. These principles should be followed for your reference list:

1. Sources should be listed alphabetically by the last name of the author or (when there is no author given) by the first word of the title (excluding *a, an, the*). Type the first word of the entry at the left margin. Indent subsequent lines of the same entry five spaces. You should double space the entire reference page both between and within entries.

2. When you have more than one work by the same author, give the name for the first entry only. For subsequent works by the same author, subsititute three hyphens and a period for the author's name and arrange the titles alphabetically:

Hayashi, Tetsumaro. *John Steinbeck: A Concise Bibliography*. Metuchen: Scarecrow Press, 1967.

- - - . *A Dictionary of His Fictional Characters*. Metuchen: Scarecrow Press, 1976.

3. For books and monographs, give the author's name in full form as it appears on the title page, listed by the surname first followed by a comma, the given name, initial(s), and a period:

Steinbeck, John.

4. After the author's name, give the complete title of the work, underlined and followed by a period. Important words in the title should be capitalized:

Steinbeck, John. *Journal of a Novel: The East of Eden Letters*.

[Note: Do not underline a title within a title.]

5. Include the editor or translator, edition of the book, series, or number of volumes (if appropriate).

6. Indicate the city of publication (followed by a colon), publisher (followed by a comma), and date of publication (followed by a period):

Steinbeck, John. *Journal of a Novel: The* East of Eden *Letters.* New York: Viking, 1969.

7. For articles, follow a similar order: Author. Title of the article. Publication data. The title of the article is in quotation marks; the title of the journal is underlined. If a volume number is provided, it goes after the title, followed by the date in parentheses. A colon follows the parentheses. Then, inclusive page numbers are provided for the entire article. For magazines that are published weekly, give only the date (not in parentheses) in order of day/month/year. A comma precedes and follows the date. Then, inclusive page numbers are provided for the whole article:

McDaniel, Barbara. "Alienation in *East of Eden:* The 'Chart of the Soul.'" *Steinbeck Quarterly* 14 (1981): 32–39.

Greenfield, Meg. "Accepting the Unacceptable." *Newsweek,* 1 July 1985, 64–65.

The model references that follow are based on the MLA documentation style as described in the 1984 *MLA Handbook* (see the citation above). The sample paper at the end of this chapter also uses MLA documentation.

MODEL REFERENCES: LANGUAGE AND LITERATURE (MLA)

Type of Reference	Example
BOOKS	
1. One author	Frohock, William Merrill. <u>The Novel of Violence in America</u>. Dallas: Southern Methodist UP, 1958. (Note: UP is the abbreviation for University Press.)
2. Two or more authors	Halliday, M. A. K., and Raquaia Hasan. <u>Cohesion in English</u>. London: Longmans, 1976.
3. Book with editor(s)	Kunitz, Stanley J., and Howard Haycraft, eds. <u>Twentieth Century Authors</u>. New York: Wilson, 1942.

4. Book with editor and author	Twain, Mark. <u>Letters from the Earth</u>. Ed. Bernard Devoton. New York: Harper & Row, 1962.
5. Essay, chapter or section in edited work	Gray, James. "John Steinbeck." <u>American Writers, IV</u>. Ed. Leonard Unger. New York: Scribner's, 1974. 47–65.
6. Encyclopedia entry (signed)	Riddel, Joseph N. "John Steinbeck." <u>The World Book Encyclopedia</u>, 1983 ed.
(unsigned)	"John Steinbeck." <u>Encyclopedia Americana</u>, 1976 ed.

ARTICLES

1. Journal article (one author)	Cox, Martha Heasley. "Steinbeck's Family Portraits: The Hamiltons." <u>Steinbeck Quarterly</u> 14 (1981): 23–32.
2. Journal article (two or more authors)	Flower, Linda, and John R. Hayes. "The Cognition of Discovery: Defining a Rhetorical Problem." <u>College Composition and Communication</u> 31 (February 1980): 21–32.
3. Magazine article (signed)	Will, George F. "Machiavelli from Minnesota?" <u>Newsweek</u>, 16 July 1984, 88.
(unsigned)	"It Started in a Garden." <u>Time</u>, 22 Sept. 1952, 110–111. (Note: For a monthly magazine, give only month and year.)
4. Newspapers	Engle, Paul. "A Review of John Steinbeck's <u>East of Eden</u>." <u>Chicago Sunday Tribune</u>. 21 Sept. 1952: A3. (Note: <u>A3</u> stands for section A, page 3.)

OTHER SOURCES

1. Film or movie	<u>Indiana Jones and the Temple of Doom</u>. Dir. Steven Speilberg. Paramount Pictures, 1984.
2. Dissertation, unpublished	Balkema, Sandra. "A Study of Revision Using Word Processing." Diss. U of Michigan, 1984.
3. Interview	Johnson, James, President, A–1 Mobile Homes, Inc. Personal Interview. 12 March 1984.
4. Personal letter	Reagan, Ronald. Letter to author. 8 Sept. 1983.
5. Unpublished paper or manuscript	Welter, William. "Word Processing in Freshman English: Does It Compute?" Unpublished essay, 1985.
6. Television program	"The Great Apes." <u>National Geographic Special</u>. New York: PBS. WGBH, Boston. 12 July 1984.

■ FOOTNOTE AND BIBLIOGRAPHY STYLE

In the humanities and fine arts other than language and literature, a two-part documentation system is common. This system uses footnotes (or endnotes) plus a bibliography. The footnotes appear at the bottom of the page on which the source is cited; the endnotes are typed in consecutive order on a separate page at the end of the paper. The bibliography, like the bibliography in the MLA style, is a typed list of sources arranged alphabetically. Since the bibliography style is generally the same, I will discuss here only the footnote (and endnote) form. Please refer to the section on the reference list above for the style of the bibliography page. Principles to follow for notes are:

1. In the text, a note is indicated by a superscript number typed immediately after the source paraphrase or quotation:

The *New York Times* called his work "a vital, sensitive, timely contribution which sheds light on mankind's spiritual heritage."[1]

2. For footnotes:
  A. Type single spaced at the bottom of the page on which they occur.
  B. Double space between notes if there is more than one note per page.
  C. Indent the note five spaces; use a superscript number followed by a space and the note itself.
  D. Number notes consecutively throughout the text.
  E. Separate footnotes from the text by typing a twelve-space bar line from the left margin.

3. For endnotes:
  A. Type endnotes on a separate page at the end of your paper, titled "Notes" or "Endnotes."
  B. List the notes as they occur in the text and number them consecutively using a superscript number followed by a space.
  C. Double space the entire endnote page.

4. The format of both footnotes and endnotes is as follows:
  A. Indent the first line of the note five spaces, type the superscript note number, skip a space, and begin the note.
  B. The second line and each subsequent line of the same note should return to the left margin.
  C. Begin notes with the author's name (given name first) followed by a comma:

[7] Thomas Merton,

  D. Then provide the title of the book or article (underlined in quotation marks):

BOOK[7] Thomas Merton, *Mystics and Zen Masters*

ARTICLE[9] Steven Brachlow, "John Robinson and the Lure of Separatism in Pre-Revolutionary England,"

  E. Provide the publication information after the title. Include the place of publication, the publisher, the date of publication, and the page number of the source. The form differs slightly for books and articles:

BOOK[7] Thomas Merton, *Mystics and Zen Masters* (New York: Dell, 1967), p. 315.

ARTICLE[9] Steven Brachlow, "John Robinson and the Lure of Separatism in Pre-Revolutionary England," *Church History* 50 (1983), 288–301.

5. In subsequent references to the same text, you need not repeat all the information of the first note; use only author's last name and a page number:

⁹ Brachlow, p. 289.

6. Where there are two or more works by the same author, you must include a shortened version of the work's title:

¹² Merton, *Mystics*, p. 268.

¹⁵ Merton, *Buddhism*, p. 15.

MODEL NOTES: HUMANITIES

Type of Reference	Example

BOOKS

1. One author
^{13} Francis A. Schaeffer, <u>How Should We Then Live? The Rise and Decline of Western Thought and Culture</u> (Old Tappan, N.J.: Revell, 1976), p. 39.

2. Two or more authors
^{20} William Ebenstein, C. Herman Pritchett, Henry A. Turner, and Dean Mann, <u>American Democracy in World Perspective</u> (New York: Harper & Row, 1967), p. 365.

3. Book with editor(s)
^{21} Louis Schneider, ed., <u>Religion, Culture, and Society</u> (New York: Wiley, 1964), p. 127.

4. Book with editor and author
^{15} Albert Schweitzer, <u>An Anthology</u>, ed. Charles R. Joy (New York: Harper & Row, 1947), p. 107.

5. Essay, chapter, section in an edited work
^{34} Morris R. Cohn, "Baseball as a National Religion," in <u>Religion, Culture, and Society</u>, ed. Louis Schneider (New York: Wiley, 1964), p. 74.

6. Encyclopedia entry (signed)
^{15} Frank E. Reynolds. "Buddhism," <u>The World Book Encyclopedia</u>, 1983 ed.

(unsigned)	[16] "Buddhism," <u>Encyclopedia Americana</u>, 1976 ed. (Note: No page numbers are necessary in alphabetically arranged works.)

ARTICLES

1. Magazines and journals (signed)	[33] Edward Voutiras, "Dedication of the Hebdomaiston to the Pythian Apollo," <u>American Journal of Archaeology</u> 86 (April 1982), p. 229.
(unsigned)	[34] "An Unmellowed Woman," <u>Newsweek</u>, 9 July 1984, p. 73.
2. Newspapers	[45] P. Ray Baker, "The Diagonal Walk," <u>Ann Arbor News</u>, 16 June 1928, sec. A, p. 2, col. 1.

EXERCISES AND RESEARCH PROJECT

Follow the procedures outlined in this chapter to research a primary literary text and write a humanities research paper. The exercises below will give you additional practice with skills related to research projects.

1. Write an extended description of one major character in the primary text you have chosen to research. Describe the person's physical appearance, mental state, actions, and the like, so that your reader will be able to "picture" that person. Use direct evidence from the text to illustrate and support your description.
2. Discuss one major theme from your primary text. Trace the development of that theme through the text, using evidence to support your idea of how the author develops the theme.
3. For each entry on your bibliography, write a three- or four-sentence annotation describing the contents of that source.
4. Write a three to four-page "review of the literature" report, summarizing the major ideas in your sources. Often a literature review, which lists and comments on the sources, will be a component of a larger research project.

SAMPLE RESEARCH PAPER: HUMANITIES FORMAT (MLA)
(optional title page)

Cathy, the "Eve" of Eden

by

Sally Batten

English 1302-011
Dr. Harvey
April 2, 1983

Title page includes title, student and course identification, date

[1 inch]

Cathy, the "Eve" of Eden

[3 lines]

John Steinbeck, one of America's favorite authors, wrote the novel <u>East of Eden</u> in 1952. The story takes place in Salinas, California, where Steinbeck was born and raised. His mother's family name, Hamilton, is one of the names used in his novel (Kunitz and Haycraft 1338). According to Riddel, <u>East of Eden</u> is "a symbolic story about the need for brotherhood." Joseph Fontenrose, one of Steinbeck's critics, states,

Long quote set off from text — MLA style

> The design and magnitude of <u>East of Eden</u>, and Steinbeck's own remarks about it, indicate that it was meant to be a climactic work, his greatest achievement, for which every earlier book was practice. . . . The majority [of readers] may see it as a second peak in his career, but not nearly so high as the first (126).

when the author's name introduces the quote, only the page # is needed

Warren French notes that <u>East of Eden's</u> "most conspicuous and provocative figure" (54) is Cathy Ames Trask. She is, he says,

Brackets indicate words & phrases changed from the original

> The wayward wife and successful brothelkeeper single-mindedly bent on exercising [her] will, ready to destroy anything that stands in [her] way, and will scruple nothing to achieve [her] end. [She is] also clever enough to manipulate other people in order to achieve [her] purpose, and is responsible for [her] own destruction (56).

In-Text citations, 1984 MLA style.

2

The character of Cathy, as seen in her behavior in childhood, young adult years, and adult life, reveals her totally evil nature and its effect on others.

Judging from Steinbeck's description, Cathy Ames is a beautiful, yet demonlike child. She has an innocent heart-shaped face, golden hair, wide-set hazel eyes, a delicate and thin nose and high wide cheekbones. She has a child's figure--narrow hips, straight legs, delicate arms and tiny hands. Her voice is "soft and husky--so sweet as to become irresistible, fascinating, and horrible."[1] According to Lisca, her beauty seems angelic in this sense, but "Cathy is often described in the terms of a serpent" (<u>Wide World</u> 268). She "has a preference for dark dens and the colors of a rattlesnake (rust and yellow)" (<u>Nature and Myth</u> 168). Her angelic looks are very deceiving. She is not an angel. She is a devil.

Despite Cathy's childlike physical appearance, her emotional mentality is that of a much older, vindictive person. Many of Steinbeck's critics go so far as to compare her mental state to that of a monster. Steinbeck himself says,

> And just as there are physical monsters,
> can there not be mental or psychic
> monsters born? The face and body may be

---

[1]All citations to Steinbeck's novel are to the Viking Press, 1952, edition. Subsequent references to this work occur in the text.

Thesis

Content note

Use title when two works have the same author

3

> perfect, but if a twisted gene or a
> malformed egg can produce physical
> monsters, may not the same process produce
> a malformed soul? (<u>Eden</u> 72).

Cathy is "not like other people, never was from
birth" (<u>Eden</u> 72). She seems to have no love or
conscience. Hayashi observes that she is "a
consummate liar and learns to use selfishness, lust,
and fear to manipulate people" (<u>Dictionary</u> 28).
However, she never feels as though she is different,
even though she wants to be:

> Cathy had some quality that made people
> look at her, then look away, then look back
> at her, troubled at something foreign.
> Something looked out of her eyes, and was
> never there when one looked again. She
> moved quickly and talked little, but she
> could enter no room without causing
> everyone to turn toward her (<u>Eden</u> 73).

But even though she makes people uneasy, they
want to stay by her and find out the cause of this
"disturbance she gives out" (<u>Eden</u> 73). Cathy uses
this power to get the things she wants. Steinbeck
says she has this power "because she has simplified
[people's] weaknesses and has no feeling about their
strengths and goodnesses" (<u>Journal</u> 44). This might
be explained by the fact that "to a monster, everyone
else is a monster. . . . Once you know Cathy is a
monster then nothing she does can be unusual"
(<u>Journal</u> 44). Because of her power, "Cathy is going
to worry a lot of children, and a lot of parents about

4

their children" (<u>Journal</u> 46). She tells so many lies
that "you can believe her lies, but when she tells
the truth, it is not credible" (<u>Journal</u> 60).
Steinbeck explains that Cathy's life is "one of
revenge on other people because of a vague feeling of
her own lack" (<u>Journal</u> 124). He also justifies her
monstrous actions by the fact that Cathy feels
rejected. Steinbeck puts it this way:

> The greatest terror a child can have is
> that he is not loved and rejection is the
> hell he fears. I think everyone in the
> world to a large or small extent has felt
> rejection. And with rejection comes anger,
> and with anger some kind of crime in
> revenge for the rejection, and with the
> crime, guilt (<u>Journal</u> 57).

Maybe Cathy has a valid reason for her
vindictive acts, but perhaps she truly is a psychic
monster.

Cathy's parents are unable to determine whether
she is a normal child, or if there is something evil
about her. They really do not trust her, but they are
never sure why (Cooperman 80). They are unaware of
her many lies. Cathy's lies are "never innocent.
Their purpose [is] to escape punishment, or
responsibility, and they [are] used for profit (<u>Eden</u>
74). She never forgets any of them, so she is never
caught telling a contradicting story. Mrs. Ames, her
mother, does not believe Cathy is abnormal:

> Since Cathy was an only child, her mother
> had no close contrast in the family. She

Student uses a variety of introductions to incorporate quotes into the text

5

thought all children were like her own.
And since all parents are worriers she was
convinced that all her friends had the
same problems (<u>Eden</u> 74).

Mr. Ames, however, is "not so sure. [He comes] in
contact with other children away from home, and he
[feels] that Cathy is not like other children" (<u>Eden</u>
75). But he cannot put his finger on what makes her
seem different, sinister. When Cathy discovers she
is not fully trusted, she learns to manipulate her
parents. She gains their full trust, and in their
eyes, she can do no wrong. But her parents are
getting in the way of what Cathy wants. She must rid
herself of them. So she sets a fire at three in the
morning, locks the door from the inside, takes the
key and leaves town. Her parents are now out of the
way and the entire community believes that she, too,
is dead. Possibly, Cathy's parents are the only
people who might have discovered her hidden
identity. Maybe Cathy knew this, and it was the
reason for their sudden deaths.

Cathy's experiences with Mr. Edwards, her pimp
in Boston, will change Cathy from a naive child who
believes she can handle anything, to a worldly young
woman who will become suspicious of everyone. She
begins as a prostitute and does an excellent job of
bringing in money. Mr. Edwards becomes fascinated by
her charms, and she is able to camouflage her true
self. Cathy is now "more than a shadowy 'Eve' figure,
more than Woman who not only succumbs to the Serpent,
but becomes the serpent itself. . . . Cathy triumphs

Student uses secondary sources to reinforce her judgment

6

over her victims——and consumes her own substance"
(Cooperman 77). Cathy steals Mr. Edwards's money,
keeps men on the side, and uses every possible
situation to get her way. However, her charade is
over the day she drinks a little wine with Mr.
Edwards. Although Cathy tries to disguise "her
innate evil nature, it reveals itself at the
slightest loss of control, such as from a little
alcohol" (Gray 57). For the first time, Cathy shows a
weakness. The warm alcohol loosens her tongue and
lowers her defense, turning her into an irate animal
who begins to reveal to Mr. Edwards everything. When
he finds out that she has burned the house, killed
her parents, stolen his money and used him, he begins
to beat her mercilessly. He hits her on the forehead
with a rock, and leaves her dead, or so he thinks.
Steinbeck reveals that the scar left on her forehead
becomes a symbol of evil——like Cain in the Bible when
he was sent away by God because of his wickedness
(<u>Journal</u> 63). Cathy is alone once more. But this
time, she has learned an important lesson, one that
she must never forget. She will now be very careful
about the people she becomes personally involved
with, and will never try to be vulnerable to a man, as
she was to Mr. Edwards.

Cathy's new knowledge of men becomes evident
when she appears on the front steps of Adam and
Charles Trask's house. She uses her experience with
Mr. Edwards as a lesson in manipulating the two
unwitting brothers. She is close to death at this
point; Adam, being the caring and trusting nurse,
brings her back to her health. Charles never trusts

her, maybe because they are the same in many ways. He also bears the evil scar upon his forehead. He tries to warn Adam that there is something sinister about Cathy, but Adam has already fallen in love. He is "bedazzled into marrying Cathy, an embodiment of evil . . ." (French 144). Steinbeck writes:

Colon often used to introduce a long quote

> Why Adam Trask should have fallen in love
> with her is anybody's guess but I think it
> was because he himself was trained to
> operate best under a harsh master and
> simply transferred that to a tough
> mistress (<u>Journal</u> 39).

Cathy's feelings for Adam seem almost genuine at first. However, there is never any real love in Cathy. She "really couldn't understand Adam's love for her; but when he proposed, she accepted because she knew she could control him" (Cooperman 80). Cathy does not plan to stay married long. However, complications begin to arise. On the night of their wedding, Cathy tells Adam that she is not well enough to consummate the marriage. She gives him her sleeping medicine and climbs into bed with her drunken brother-in-law, Charles. That night, she conceives Charles's child and begins the first stages of destroying her faithful husband, Adam.

Cathy's babies also become the victims of her wicked and vicious schemes. She is very unhappy being pregnant. She even tries once to abort the babies, but is unsuccessful. Steinbeck describes Cathy at this time "sitting quietly waiting for her pregnancy to be over, living on a farm she did not like, with a

8

man she did not love" (<u>Eden</u> 184). She tells Adam all
along that she wants to leave and that she will after
she gives birth; but he thinks that she is just
nervous about becoming a mother. Adam's good friend,
Samuel Hamilton, helps Cathy through labor. He
thinks she is very strange because she demands total
darkness and becomes like an animal with pain. She
bites Samuel (who has fever for three days afterward)
and refuses to look at the twins after they are born.
According to Lisca, Samuel, who has been working in
the field all day,

> associates the buried meteorite
> (falling star, hence Lucifer) which wrecks
> his well drill with Cathy, who bites his
> hand while he is helping her give birth to
> her twin sons, on the same day he discovers
> the meteorite (<u>Wide World</u> 269).

At her children's birth, Cathy is once again
compared to a serpent. Lisca comments that Cathy
"gives birth to the twins as easily as a snake lays
eggs" (<u>Nature and Myth</u> 168). As soon as Cathy
recovers from giving birth, she once again tells Adam
that she is leaving him:

> Why doesn't Adam listen when Cathy says
> she will be going away. . . . Men don't
> listen to what they don't want to hear. . .
> . Adam has a picture of his life, and he
> will continue to maintain his picture
> against every influence until his world
> comes down (<u>Journal</u> 76).

9

Adam's only way of keeping Cathy at home is locking her in. But she is able to convince him that she has changed her mind, and promises to stay. When he opens the door, she shoots him with a .44 Colt in the leg. Adam is so upset that he goes into a state of emotional shock. He has thought of Cathy as the perfect wife and he cannot accept the fact that she is anything less. He does not even name the twins for almost a year. Once again, Cathy has managed to destroy a part of someone's life, and once again she spreads her evil upon her closest acquaintances.

As Cathy matures, her ability to overpower others becomes stronger, as in the case of Faye, Cathy's new madam. She learns of Faye's brothel and goes there to work. She changes her name to Kate and dyes her hair black, but this conversion will never cover up her evil. Steinbeck says, "They [the readers] will forget I said she [Kate] was bad. And they will hate her because while she is a monster, she is a little piece of the monster in all of us" (Journal 97). Once again Kate is going to use the people she associates with to accomplish what she wants. Warren French reminds the reader that "Kate is a witch whose spell must be exorcised if her activities are not to continue to destroy innocent people" (57). Kate even manages to get Faye to leave the entire estate to her when Faye dies. Of course, it is in Kate's plan, not Faye's, that the death happen soon. Kate slowly poisons Faye. No one suspects the act—everyone believes that Faye has an illness that is making her weaker and pushing her closer to death. In the meantime, Kate is learning to be an expert prostitute:

10

[She] knows the power of the sexual
impulse, and that is her most profound
weapon against the people she destroys.
She knew, too, about the guilts that
accompany sexual indulgence, and she
turned these into a fine profit by
catering to the masochistic wishes of the
men of Salinas. Whips and matches were
tools of her whorehouse trade, and the
need for them was developed by her
deliberately, making her house essential
in the community (Cooperman 87).

Finally, Faye dies. Now Kate is in charge. Kate
has once again eliminated the one who was getting to
know her too well and was in the way of her success.

Kate seems to have reached her peak in
destruction, but then, her evil begins to
deteriorate. The origin of this suicidal process
occurs when Adam comes to the brothelhouse to
confront Kate. Only when he

confronts the reality of Cathy (Adam never
refers to her as Kate), only when he sees
the essential blasphemy of his attempt to
create an Eden morality itself, can he
redeem his own manhood (Cooperman 77).

He discovers when he sees her again that she
means nothing to him. Cathy hates him for being freed
from her evil grasp. Later, one of her partners, Joe,
begins to take monetary advantage of her—at first
without her knowledge. Kate realizes that she is
losing her ability to overpower others. Even her

*Frequent
examples
from
primary text
used for
support*

beloved pictures of the senators, congressmen, and
other important government officials that had
visited her business, no longer seem important to
her. She has been saving them for years as blackmail
if they do not continue to come to her "house":

> [Kate] commits suicide when she supposes
> that, even if she can outwit Joe, she will
> eventually be outwitted by someone else of
> her own ilk. . . . Her death is not a
> catastrophe, but an unmixed blessing to
> the community. . . . Paranoia will destroy
> itself without disrupting society (French
> 155).

Lisca observes that toward the end of the book,
"the reader learns . . . that the monster, Cathy, has
become a religious penitent (Episcopal) and has
committed suicide because of moral loneliness" (<u>Wide
World</u> 267). As Kate slowly poisons herself, as she
had Faye, alone in the dark, Steinbeck seems almost
sympathetic; but he was "just putting it down as it
might have happened" (<u>Journal</u> 169). Lisca notes that
"Cathy is too much like Satan to be a credible human-
being, and too much like a weak, pitiful human-being
to be properly Satanic" (<u>Wide World</u> 273). Cathy is
only thirty, but, as Hayashi observes "her cheeks
(have) become chubby, her stomach and shoulders
plump, and her legs and feet thick and bulging. Her
hands are crippled with arthritis" (<u>Dictionary</u> 28).
Even though Kate is physically gone, her malevolence
lives on in those she has emotionally destroyed.

It appears that Cathy's corruption has been
transmitted to her son, Cal, even though she is not

involved with him in any way. Steinbeck explains it
as follows:

> If she [Cathy] were simply a monster, that
> would not bring her in [the story]. But
> since she had the most powerful impact on
> Adam and transmitted her blood to her sons
> and influenced the generations--she
> certainly belongs in this book (Journal
> 42).

Cal has dark moods like his natural father,
Charles. He is lonely because the people who are
afraid of him ignore him. He is also jealous of his
brother, Aaron. However, unlike his mother, Cal has
"recognized the evil in himself, [and] is ready to
act for good" (Cooperman 88). When Cal finds out who
his mother is, he is convinced that he is evil like
her. But Lee, the Chinese housekeeper, points out
that "all men have evil in their ancestry, but the
final choice of good or evil is solely the
individual's" (Cooperman 83). Before Cathy commits
suicide, Cal visits her. He does not tell his brother
Aaron, who is studying to be a priest, that his
mother is still alive, because Cal always protects
him. But one night he becomes angry with Aaron and
takes him to "Kate's circus" (French 146). Aaron is
so upset that he runs away and joins the army, where
he is killed in action. When Adam learns that his
beloved Aaron has died, he has a stroke. The family
also learns at this point that Cathy has committed
suicide. Cal takes full blame for everything that has
gone wrong. However, with Lee's help, Adam forgives
Cal and Cal is released from his guilt. Cal now

realizes that he does not have Cathy's evil in him
and that if he is evil, it's the evil within his own
nature, an evil that he can control (French 146).
Finally, Cathy's evil has ended. Even though she has
almost killed Adam and destroyed Cal's emotional
state, her monstrous effects have been snuffed out.
Adam and Cal are free.

Cathy Ames Trask's continuous evil effect on
her family and acquaintances is shown in Steinbeck's
novel, East of Eden. Frohock states that it may be
easy to believe women like Cathy exist:

> [And] that they burn home and parents,
> commit adultery with their brothers—in—
> law, and retire from family life to resume
> the oldest of professions; but it is
> extremely difficult to make a woman like
> Cathy take on the kind of actual existence
> which could make her believable as a
> central character in a novel——especially
> when, as in the case of East of Eden, such a
> woman is seen entirely from the outside
> and the reader has no clear notion of the
> reason for her behaving as she does
> (Frohock 141).

But Steinbeck's character, Cathy, is still a
mystery. The readers can never know if she is really
a monster, because they do not know what she wanted
out of life or if she got it. It is "easy to say she
was bad, but there is little meaning unless we know
why" (Eden 184). Steinbeck says, the question of
Cathy's wicked and sinful "existence goes forever

Conclusion returns to original question

14

unanswered--just as the 'reason' for the presence of
evil itself goes unanswered" (<u>Eden</u> 184).

Bibliography

Cooperman, Stanley. <u>The Major Works of John
    Steinbeck: Notes</u>. New York: Monarch, 1964.

Cox, Martha Heasley. "Steinbeck's Family Portraits:
    The Hamiltons." <u>Steinbeck Quarterly</u> 14 (1981):
    23-32.

Fontenrose, Joseph. <u>John Steinbeck: An Introduction
    and Interpretation</u>. New York: Holt, Rinehart &
    Winston, 1963.

French, Warren. <u>John Steinbeck</u>. Boston: Twayne,
    1975.

Frohock, Wilbur Merrill. <u>The Novel of Violence in
    America</u>. Dallas: Southern Methodist UP, 1958.

Gray, James. "John Steinbeck." <u>American Writers, IV</u>.
    Ed. Leonard Unger. New York: Scribner's, 1974.
    47-65.

Hayashi, Tetsumaro. <u>John Steinbeck: A Concise
    Bibliography</u>. Metuchen: Scarecrow Press, 1967.

---. <u>John Steinbeck: A Dictionary of His Fictional
    Characters</u>. Metuchen: Scarecrow Press, 1976.

Kunitz, Stanley J., and Howard Haycraft, eds.
    <u>Twentieth Century Authors</u>. New York: Wilson,
    1942.

Lisca, Peter. <u>The Wide World of John Steinbeck</u>. New
    Brunswick: Rutgers UP, 1958.

---. <u>John Steinbeck: Nature and Myth</u>. New York:
    Crowell, 1978.

Second work by same author

Alphabetical listing follows 1984 MLA style

McCarthy, Paul. <u>John Steinbeck</u>. New York: Ungar,
    1980.

McDaniel, Barbara. "Alienation in <u>East of Eden</u>: The
    'Chart of the Soul.'" <u>Steinbeck Quarterly</u> 14
    (1981): 32–39.

Riddel, Joseph N. "John Steinbeck." <u>The World Book
    Encyclopedia</u>. 1983 ed.

Steinbeck, John. <u>East of Eden</u>. New York: Viking,
    1952.

---. <u>Journal of a Novel</u>: <u>The</u> East of Eden <u>Letters</u>.
    New York: Viking, 1969.

Do not underline a title within a title

CHAPTER 9

Writing a Research Report in Business

■ INTRODUCTION

In business, writers often produce research reports in which they seek to become "experts" on particular topics in order to communicate that expertise to other concerned individuals. The businessman or woman must have knowledge of the business world in general and should be familiar with library tools used by those in business to gain access to current information in their field.

In the business report, your task is to summarize for your readers the present situation in a particular field or market. Your contribution, then, will be to organize the information you find, thus making it easily accessible to your reader. Generally, in the business report, you are not interpreting data or arguing for a particular position (as you often are in the social sciences and humanities). Rather, through paraphrase and summary, you are presenting the information you discovered in your research as objectively as you can. The research report in business resembles most closely the scientific review paper discussed in Chapter 6.

Some business research reports use primary research, such as marketing reviews, technical studies, or computer data. For many business research projects, some library research is also involved. Several library research principles and skills will be important for you as you investigate your chosen topic. These skills include the following:

1. Familiarity with library resources, including bibliographies and indexes used in business.
2. The ability to understand and evaluate data from a variety of sources.
3. The ability to paraphrase and summarize information in your own words.

4. The ability to synthesize the information gathered into an organized presentation of the data.
5. The ability to employ the formal conventions of business reports.

■ A GUIDE TO THE BUSINESS RESEARCH PROCESS

To begin your report, first determine a topic and narrow it to a manageable, researchable size. If you are taking a business course now, look in your textbook for research ideas, checking the table of contents in your textbook as well as any references that may be listed. Another source of ideas is current business journals. Penny Cogdell, whose research will serve as a model for this chapter, became interested in the subject of sexual harassment in the business world, since she was concerned about her role as a woman in business. She conducted her research as an assignment in a business course called Managerial Communications. You should select a topic that will hold your interest and attention, preferably one that you already know something about, so that you will be an informed and objective reporter.

Preparation

You will need to gather the materials you need for your research project, including notecards and a research notebook; then make a schedule that will give you enough time to conduct your library research and to write a draft and final copy of your report. If your research project involves any primary research, be sure to allow yourself enough time to gather and analyze the data. Careful planning at the outset of such a major project will ensure that you have time to carry out the research necessary to write an informed report.

Developing a Search Strategy

Penny had formulated some general impressions about sexual harassment at work through her own reading. She wanted to find out the current thinking in the business world about what constituted sexual harassment and how the various kinds of harassment could be prevented. She began her library search, then, with a look at general background sources in an effort to define what constitutes sexual harassment. Next, she looked more closely at articles specifically about sexual harassment. An outline of her search strategy is presented below (your particular search may differ somewhat from this outline):

Penny's Search Strategy

1. Encyclopedias and dictionaries (general and specialized), for background information

2. Reviews of research and biographies (may be omitted depending on topic)
3. Indexes and abstracts, for access to source articles
4. Card catalog, for access to books and other sources
5. Primary research, such as marketing reviews, computer data, or technical studies (if appropriate)

When you are writing a business report, you are often looking for very recent information. You will find recent information primarily in serials related to the specific field. Your library search will probably begin in your library's reference area, since the reference area contains the tools that give you access to serial articles. To illustrate the use of a library search strategy in business, I will lead you through the steps above, using Penny's research on sexual harassment as a model.

EXERCISE

Outline your own search strategy, beginning with general and working to specific sources. Include any primary research needed for your project. Draw up a time schedule to guide your research.

Search 1

To begin your research, read general information about your topic to put it into a context and to help you focus by narrowing your topic to a manageable size. Also, reading general and specialized encyclopedias and dictionaries will help you define what is considered common knowledge on the topic. Depending on your particular topic, you will be reading general encyclopedias, such as the *World Book,* and specialized encyclopedias, such as the *Encyclopedia of Management.* The sources commonly used in business are listed in Chapter 3. Penny used the following background sources, which she listed in her notebook as the beginning of her working bibliography:

> *Encyclopedia of Business Information Sources.* Detroit: Gale, 1976.
>
> *Encyclopedia of Management,* 3rd ed., C. Heyel, ed. New York: Van Nostrand Reinhold, 1982.

At the end of each general source, such as the encyclopedias mentioned above, you will usually find a list of references that may lead you to other related sources on your topic. List any promising references on your working bibliography, but do not necessarily look up each entry at this time.

EXERCISE

Find and read background sources relevant to your topic to obtain general information (see Chapter 3 for a list of sources often used in business).

Focusing Your Search

After reading several background sources about your topic, you are ready to narrow the focus of your report. Penny, for example, decided to report on what sexual harassment is, how it affects companies and individuals, and how it can be prevented. Without such a focus, she could have wandered aimlessly through the material with no clear idea of what she was looking for. Take care to define carefully for yourself just what topic you are trying to research for your report.

EXERCISE

Define clearly for yourself what topic you wish to report on. Narrow the focus of that topic to a manageable size.

Search 2

For many business topics, reviews and reports may be important. For a current topic such as the one chosen by Penny, reviews and reports were not relevant. For that reason, I will not discuss them here. Please refer to Chapter 6, Search 2, for a discussion of reviews and reports.

Search 3

The main resources for anyone investigating a current topic in business will be the indexes and abstracts. The indexes, such as *Business Periodicals Index* and *Business Index*, list articles published in a given year by subject and/or author. By using these indexes, you can search for titles of journal articles written on your topic. Unless you are doing an historical study, you should start with the most recent volume of the index and work your way back, looking up your topic in several volumes of the index. For example, in the *Business Periodicals Index*, Penny looked up *sexual harassment* and was referred by a cross-reference to the heading *sex in business*, where she found the following sources listed:

Sexual harassment at work: why it happens, what to do about it. J. C. Renick. *Pers J* 59:658–62 Ag '80

Sexual harassment: confronting the issue of definition. G. N. Powell. *Bus Horiz* 26:24–8 Jl–Ag '83

What behavior constitutes sexual harassment. P. Linenberger. *Labor Law J* 34:-238–47 Ap '83

The second type of reference tool you may use is the abstract. An abstract provides a brief summary of the important works in a field. For example, the *Economic Titles/Abstracts* provides access to books, reports, and journal articles in economics. Depending on your topic, you may find such a source useful.

EXERCISE

Use indexes and/or abstracts to find titles of articles related to your topic (see Chapter 3 for a list of indexes used in business).

Search 4

At this point in your search, you may wish to use the card catalog. One function of the card catalog is to help you track down citations listed on your working bibliography. A second function of the card catalog is its cross-referencing function: using the subject listing to locate additional book titles on the same or related topics. Since Penny was most interested in discovering what recent journals said about sexual harassment, she did not use the subject listing in the card catalog to find books. (For information on using the card catalog, see Chapter 4.)

EXERCISE

Use the card catalog to locate sources and to find additional source material on your topic. Use the *Library of Congress Subject Heading (LCSH)* list to find the heading(s) under which materials on your topic are cataloged.

Evaluation

Once you have located either a book or an article, evaluate it for its relevance or usefulness in your search. If, after an initial screening, a book looks as though it can be useful to you, check it out at the circulation desk. In the case of articles, either photocopy them for later use or take notes from them in the library, since they are generally "noncirculating materials," and cannot be checked out.

EXERCISE

In your research notebook, evaluate each article and book to be used in your research. Follow the source evaluation guidelines in Chapter 4.

Taking Notes

As you begin to take notes from your sources, remember to keep two cards, the bibliography card and the notecard, for each source you read. Keep complete information on both cards so you will not have to look up a particular source again. Be certain to put into quotation marks any information you take directly from the source, and to mark down the exact page number on which you found the note at the end of the note itself. Also specify whether you paraphrased the author's words or quoted directly. Taking care at this stage will benefit you when you get to the actual writing stage of your report.

Search 5

If your business report project includes any primary research, such as marketing reviews, computer data, or technical studies, you will need to design and conduct that research and analyze your data.

EXERCISE

Conduct any primary research connected to your project. Analyze your data and determine the best way to display your results, whether in a graph, table, or discussion.

■ ORGANIZING AND WRITING THE BUSINESS REPORT

A major task in writing a business report is organizing the material you have gathered. It is your job to make sense of the information you have found and to present it logically for the reader in an objective, comprehensive manner. When Penny narrowed her topic, she decided to report on the causes, effects, and prevention of sexual harassment. After gathering her information, she decided to first define sexual harassment, then present its causes and effects on individuals and businesses, and finally indicate ways in which sexual harassment could be prevented. She outlined an organizational plan that would include major sections as follows:

```
Definition and Recognition of Sexual Harassment

Causes of Sexual Harassment

Effects of Sexual Harassment
        Effects on Women
        Effects on the Organization

Prevention of Sexual Harassment

Conclusion
```

Once she had decided on the organizational plan, she sorted her notecards by their titles to fit the subtopics of the plan. She set aside any information that did not seem to fit in the paper. To have a unified, coherent presentation of your research, you must also discard any information that is irrelevant to your particular focus.

Planning and Outlining

Your preliminary plan will give you the skeleton for an outline of your paper, which will guide you when you write but not constrain or limit your thinking. Your outline may change several times as you make new discoveries while writing:

```
Informal Outline

Title: Sexual Harassment in the Business World

Definition and recognition of sexual harassment
        EEOC standards as guidelines
        Survey to determine nature and scope

Causes of sexual harassment
        Women's social status
        Men's ''macho'' image

Effects of sexual harassment
        Effects on women—physical and psychological
        Effects on organizations—absenteeism, loss of morale

Prevention of sexual harassment
        Employer awareness and strong action
        Employee training and guidance

Conclusion
        Sexual harassment: Growing problem needing correction
```

EXERCISE

Organize your source material, decide on an organizational plan, and construct an outline to guide your writing of the first draft of your research report. Refer to Chapter 5 for help with organization.

Writing the First Draft

After you have completed your outline, you are ready to write the first draft of your report. Remember, you are writing to report to your readers the current status of a particular issue or topic. Remind yourself at this time of your general understanding of your topic. When writing your first draft, use concrete and simple language to explain as objectively as you can your understanding of the topic. Your outline will guide the writing of this first draft.

As you write the first draft, it is important to note down which material comes from which sources. Do not be overly concerned at this point about the formal details of documentation, which can be dealt with later, but do mark for yourself in the draft any ideas or words you take from your sources. You should place any word or sentence you copy from a source in quotation marks, followed by the last name, the date of publication, and the page number of the source (in parentheses):

> "Harassment cannot be eliminated, but it can be reduced in frequency, intensity and duration" (Renick, 1980, p. 662).

Similarly, document paraphrases and restatements of ideas taken from a source even though you have recast them in your own words:

> Employers are beginning to recognize the problems caused by sexual harassment: low morale, lost time, and decreased productivity (Saunders, 1984, p. 43).

When referring generally to a source, it is not necessary to provide a page reference:

> Powell (1983) reports on a survey conducted to determine what women considered sexual harassment to be.

For general information on planning, writing, and revising your business report, refer to Chapter 5. Use the following information on documentation in business and economics for the correct form for citations. The sample research report at the end of this chapter can serve as a model for a business report.

■ DOCUMENTATION IN BUSINESS AND ECONOMICS

In business and economics, it is common to use the same general author and year system used in the sciences and social sciences. This system includes (1) in-text citations giving the author's name and the publication year of the source, and (2) an alphabetized list of references at the end of the paper.

Internal Citations

For a description of the author and year system of in-text citation, see Chapter 6.

The Reference List

The reference list in business and economics (similar to that used in the social sciences) is an alphabetized list of all the sources actually cited in the paper. It is titled "References." The actual format of the entries differs somewhat from that in the sciences or social sciences. The following principles are generally accepted in business and economics journals:

1. Authors are listed by complete name (when known) or by surname and initials.

2. Capital letters are used for all important words in the title of an article and the title is enclosed by quotation marks.

3. Names of books and journals are underlined. Names of journals are not abbreviated.

4. For books, the title is followed by the place of publication, the publisher, and the date:

Melman, Seymour. *Our Depleted Society.* New York: Del Publishers, 1965.

5. For articles, the date, volume number (underlined or in italics) and the inclusive page numbers follow the name of the journal:

Powell, Gary N. "Sexual Harassment: Confronting the Issue of Definition." *Business Horizons,* July–August, 1983, 9, 24–28.

[Alternate style: Powell, Gary N. "Sexual Harrassment: Confronting the Issue of Definition." *Business Horizons* 9 (July–August 1983): 24–28.]

6. The first word of the entry is typed at the left margin. Subsequent lines of the same entry are indented five spaces. The entire reference page is double spaced.

If you are writing a research paper for a class in business or economics, it is important for you to consult your instructor for the documentation form he or she prefers. A style manual frequently used in business and industry is *The Chicago Manual of Style,* 13th ed., published by the University of Chicago Press (1982). You may wish to refer to this manual for your papers in business courses. The model references below use the style outlined in the *Chicago Manual.* The sample business report at the end of this chapter uses the documentation style most commonly found in business and economics journals, which is slightly different from that described in the *Chicago Manual.*

MODEL REFERENCES: BUSINESS AND ECONOMICS

Type of Reference	Example
BOOKS	
1. One author	Cole, Robert H. <u>Consumer and Commercial Credit Management</u>, 5th ed. Homewood, Ill.: Irwin, 1976.
2. Two or more authors	Weston, J. Fred, and Eugene F. Brighman. <u>Managerial Finance</u>, 5th ed. New York: The Dryden Press, 1975.

3. Book with editor	Rathe, Alex W., ed. <u>Gantt on Management</u>. New York: American Management Association, 1961.
4. Essay, chapter or section or edited work	Ogilvy, David. "The Creative Chef." In <u>The Creative Organization</u>, edited by Gary A. Steiner, 199–213. Chicago: University of Chicago Press, 1965.
5. Corporate author	International Monetary Fund. <u>Survey of African Economies</u>. Vol. 7, <u>Algeria, Mali, Morocco, and Tunisia</u>. Washington, D.C., 1977.
6. Encyclopedia entry	"Sexual Harassment." <u>Encyclopedia of Management</u>, 3rd ed., edited by Carl Heyel. New York: Van Nostrand Reinhold, 1982.

ARTICLES

1. Journal article (one author)	Boyer, Ernest. "The Recovery Is Shaping the Economy." <u>Fortune</u> 108 (Oct. 1983): 60–65.
2. Journal article (two or more authors)	Lear, Ronald, and C. Groneman. "The Corporate PhD.—Humanities Scholars Bring New Perspective to Business Problems." <u>Management Review</u> 72 (September 1983): 32–33.
3. Journal or magazine (no known author)	"The Applications Still Flood in, but Slight Rise in Vacancies Cheers Graduate Recruiters." <u>Personnel Management</u> 15 (August 1983): 12–13.
4. Newspaper article	Schickel, Richard. "Far Beyond Reality: The New Technology of Hollywood's Special Effects." <u>New York Times</u>, 18 May 1980.

OTHER SOURCES

1. Dissertation or thesis	King, Andrew J. "Law and Land Use in Chicago: A Pre–History of Modern Zoning." Ph.D. diss., University of Wisconsin, 1976.
2. Paper presented at conference	Saunders, Robert. "Today's Manager." Paper presented at the annual meeting of the American Institute of Industrial Engineers, New York, 1983.
3. Personal communication (letters, interviews)	Ewing, Nancy. Letter to author. 24 January 1985. Hughes, Howard. Interview with author. Las Vegas, Nevada, 15 July 1970.
4. Public documents	U.S. Department of Justice Law Enforcement Assistance Administration, 1970. <u>Criminal Justice Agencies in Pennsylvania</u>. Washington, D.C.: Government Printing Office.

EXERCISES AND RESEARCH PROJECT

Complete the exercises in this chapter as you research and report on a carefully defined business topic. The exercises below will provide additional practice with skills associated with business reports.

1. For each entry on your bibliography, write a three- or four-sentence annotation describing the contents of that source.

2. Write a "review of the literature" report that summarizes in three to four pages the major ideas found in your sources. Often, a literature review, which lists and comments on the works done to date in a particular area, will be a component of a larger paper. The review of the literature will proceed in chronological order based on the publication date of the source, and thus will differ from the report itself, which may be organized around concepts or other categories.

3. When you have finished writing your report, write a synopsis 50–100 words in length in which you summarize the main points of your

paper. A synopsis is a brief, general condensation of the report. See the sample synopsis included with the model paper in this chapter; also see the discussion of abstracts in Chapter 5.

4. When you have finished writing your report, write a table of contents for your report. See the table for the model paper in this chapter.

SAMPLE RESEARCH REPORT: BUSINESS AND ECONOMICS FORMAT
(optional title page)

Sexual Harassment in the Business World

Presented to:
Professor Grant Savage
Management 3373

Presented by:
Penny Cogdell
29 March 1984

SYNOPSIS

Sexual harassment is an increasing problem in
business, and one that needs to be addressed. Sexual
harassment is caused by the unequal social status of
women to men and also by the tough image men feel they
have to live up to. Sexual harassment affects both
the individual and the organization. The individual
may suffer psychological problems because of sexual
harassment, and the organization's productivity and
efficiency may decrease. To prevent sexual
harassment from occurring, the Equal Employment
Opportunities Commission has issued guidelines.
Employers wishing to prevent sexual harassment in
their own business can provide training programs for
their employees and can take strict disciplinary
action against proven harassers.

In business reports, a synopsis is common. Like an abstract, it summarizes the main points of the report

<u>TABLE OF CONTENTS</u>

[1 inch]

Sexual Harassment in the Business World

[3 lines]

Sexual harassment in the business world
continues to be a problem. <u>Redbook</u> surveyed 9000
women on the issue of sexual harassment and found
that 92 percent of the women who responded had
experienced some form of harassment (Somers, 1980).
When sexual harassment does occur, it has negative
effects on both the individual and the working
environment. In 1980, the Equal Employment
Opportunities Commission (EEOC) issued guidelines
concerning sexual harassment (Powell, 1983).
Companies are expected to adhere to these rules and
to apply them to sexual harassment cases.

*Uses author/
year method
of in-text
citation*

[4 lines]

<u>Defining and Recognizing Sexual Harassment</u>

[3 lines]

Sexual harassment is a difficult term to define
due to the differences in people's perceptions.
Sexual harassment has occurred in the business world
for years; however, Powell (1983) reports that it has
only been recognized as a serious problem in the last
five years. As cited by several authors
(Linenberger, 1983; Powell, 1983; Saunders, 1984),
the EEOC has set the following standards as
guidelines:

*Subheads,
set apart
from the
text by
blank lines,
provide
easy access
for the
reader*

[3 lines]

Unwelcome sexual advances, requests for
sexual favors and other verbal and
physical conduct of a sexual nature

*Multiple
source
citation,
colon
introduces
long quote*

Long quotes are set off from the text

constitute sexual harassment when (1)
submission to such conduct is made either
explicitly or implicity a term or
condition of an individual's employment,
(2) submission to or rejection of such
conduct by an individual is used as the
basis for employment decisions affecting
such an individual, or (3) such conduct
has the purpose or effect of unreasonably
interfering with an individual's work
performance or creating an intimidating,
hostile, or offensive working environment
(EEOC Guidelines).

[3 lines]

No quotation marks needed when quote is indented

Powell (1983) reports on a survey conducted to
determine what women considered sexual harassment to
be. The results included the following: sexual
propositions, touching, grabbing, brushing, sexual
remarks, suggestive gestures, and sexual relations.
However, Powell concludes that perceptions of sexual
harassment may vary from one individual to the next.

The definition of sexual harassment by the EEOC
will most likely be relied on in the future. The
problem with this definition is that it is very broad
and leaves the management of each organization with
the responsibility of recognizing sexual harassment
and handling it in a positive way. Another setback is
that women often do not report harassment for fear of
losing their jobs or being ignored, and, as a result,
employers have no way of knowing that it is
happening.

2

The Causes of Sexual Harassment

The causes of sexual harassment in the business world stem from women's unequal social status and men's need to dominate (Renick, 1980). One of the main causes is that women's social status is still unequal to men's. Renick says that women are stereotyped as not being career oriented and as belonging in the home. In addition, Renick believes that the macho image that some men attempt to live up to is a cause of sexual harassment. He thinks men feel they have to be strong, tough, and aggressive to meet the standards set for being a man, while women are supposed to be gentle and receptive to male dominance. In short, the motivation behind sexual harassment is not sex; it is power (Saunders, 1984).

The Effects of Sexual Harassment

Sexual harassment affects both individuals and organizations. All of the results of sexual harassment create long-range problems that should be corrected when discovered.

The Effects on Women

Sexual harassment has many detrimental effects on women. These range from physical and psychological illnesses to family disruptions to alcoholism and excessive drug use (Renick, 1980). Renick also notes that sexually harassed women have many of the same feelings as women who have been raped: humiliation, cheapness, embarrassment, and anger. In addition, he found that victims of sexual harassment often fear that their complaints will go unheard, that they will be blamed for what happened, or that they will be considered "unprofessional."

The Effects on the Organization

Sexual harassment not only effects the individual but also has a tremendous effect on the organization in which it occurs. Where harassment goes on without anything being done, there will be a lack of trust between the employees and the employer. Sexual harassment also creates a lot of stress and pressure (Somers, 1980), which can lead to absenteeism or even termination because of negative work attitudes. Employers are beginning to recognize the problems caused by sexual harassment: low morale, lost time, and decreased productivity (Saunders, 1984, p. 42).

The Prevention of Sexual Harassment

Because sexual harassment can be so harmful to a person's health and career, steps should be taken to help prevent it. Though the EEOC has set down guidelines, these alone do not solve the problem. Preventive measures must be taken by employers.

The first step is for employers to realize that sexual harassment is a potential problem in all business organizations (Somers, 1980). Then, employers need to state specifically that sexual

4

harassment will not be tolerated in their
organizations. Employers should also provide
training so that all the employees will understand
the organization's stand on sexual harassment.
Consulting firms such as the Working Women's
Institute in New York (Saunders, 1984) provide
trainers to teach corporate employees self—help and
ways of ending sexual harassment. "Harassment cannot
be eliminated, but it can be reduced in frequency,
intensity and duration" (Renick, 1980, p. 661).

Conclusion

Sexual harassment is a potential problem in all
business organizations. It can have detrimental
effects for the organization if not corrected.
Organizations must realize how serious the problem
can be and take steps to prevent it from happening.
According to Renick, "with the changing economic
conditions and the decreasing emphasis on sex roles,
women not only deserve but expect to be treated as
equals in the work place" (1980, p. 662).

References

[3 lines]

Goldman, Martin, and Marian Goldman. "Don't Call Me Honey," <u>Working Woman</u>, December 1983, <u>9</u>, 162–171.

Linenberger, Patricia. "What Behavior Constitutes Sexual Harassment," <u>Labor Law Journal</u>, April 1983, <u>34</u>, 238–247.

Powell, Gary N. "Sexual Harassment: Confronting the Issue of Definition," <u>Business Horizons</u>, July–August 1983, <u>26</u>, 24–28.

Renick, James. "Sexual Harassment at Work: Why It Happens, What to Do About It," <u>Personnel Journal</u>, August 1980, <u>59</u>, 658–662.

Saunders, Jolene. "Sexual Harassment," <u>Working Woman</u>, February 1984, <u>11</u>, 42–43.

Somers, Patricia. "Sexual Harassment in the Office," <u>Management World</u>, November 1980, <u>9</u>, 10–11, 44.

Author and year in-text documentation plus reference list using the style common to business and economics journals. Note: this style differs slightly from that of the Chicago Manual used for the model references earlier in the chapter.

Index